TOWARDS SUSTAINABLE TRANSPORT PLANNING

For my parents

Towards Sustainable Transport Planning

A Comparison between Britain and the Netherlands

GARY HAQ
Department of Geography, University of Lancaster

Avebury

Aldershot • Brookfield USA • Hong Kong • Singapore • Sydney

Published by
Avebury
Ashgate Publishing Limited
Gower House
Croft Road
Aldershot
Hants GU11 3HR
England

Ashgate Publishing Company
Old Post Road
Brookfield
Vermont 05036
USA

British Library Cataloguing in Publication Data
Haq, Gary
    Towards sustainable transport planning : a comparison
    between Britain and the Netherlands
    1.Transportation and state - Great Britain 2.Transportation
    and state - Netherlands 3.Transportation - Great Britain -
    Planning 4.Transportation - Netherlands - Planning
    I.Title
    388

Library of Congress Catalog Card Number: 96-79118

ISBN 1 85972 382 9

Printed in Great Britain by the Ipswich Book Company, Suffolk

Contents

List of figures and tables

Preface

The study on which this book is based was undertaken between 1991-1995 at Lancaster University and depicts the state of transport policy and practice in Europe, Britain and the Netherlands during this period. At the beginning of the study there was a sharp contrast in the differences between British and Dutch transport policy. However, the past four years have seen a large number of policy developments taking place within the transport sector. The British government is now slowly awakening to the need to deal with the problem of transport and it is hoped that this new *enlightenment* in government thinking on transport will continue until Britain has an integrated transport policy; with clear objectives and with explicit targets to implement sustainability in practice.

This book examines how the concept of sustainability has been interpreted in transport and environmental policy at the European, national and local level. The approaches of Britain and the Netherlands to transport and environmental policy are compared. With the use of case studies of transport corridors it illustrates how different policy approaches affect choices and decisions taken at the project level. It demonstrates the advantages of a strategic planning approach which is objective-led and which sets out specific targets for sustainability. The book concludes by outlining an environment-based approach for transport planning.

This book will be of interest to planners, transport professionals, policy makers, geographers and environmentalists who are interested in how the rhetoric of policy is translated into practice and how a more sustainable transport planning approach can be developed.

Acknowledgements

A great number of people have assisted me in the completion of this study and I am indebted to them all for their help and encouragement. I would like to especially thank Monique Bense and Marc Raessen for their willingness to help me with Dutch translations. Also, Machiel Bolhuis, Ministry of Transport, Public Works and Water Management for keeping me up-to-date on the policy developments taking place in the Netherlands.

A special acknowledgement goes to the following individuals and organisations who were willing to provide me with information and answer my queries:

Drs J Dekker, Rijkswaterstaat, Utrecht
Dutch Railways, Utrecht
EIA Centre, University of Manchester
Environmental Resources Unit, University of Salford
Mr Mike Hayward, Department of Transport (Northwestern Region), Manchester
Drs Mahiel Odijk, EIA Commission, Utrecht
Peak District National Park.

I am grateful to Professor John Whitelegg for his guidance, enthusiasm and encouragement in undertaking this study. Thanks also to Nicky Higgitt for preparing the diagrams and to Marion Porter and Sheila Hargreaves for their critical comments and helpful suggestions.

List of abbreviations

AADT	Annual Average Daily Traffic
ACTRA	Advisory Committee on Trunk Road Assessment
ARC	Amsterdam-Rhine Canal
AUC	Amsterdam-Utrecht Corridor
BEA	Best Environmental Alternative
BMP	Bicycle Master Plan
CBA	Cost Benefit Analysis
CBI	Confederation of British Industry
CEC	Commission of the European Communities
CFC	Chlorofluorohydrocarbons
CEST	Centre for the Exploitation of Science and Technology
COBA	Economic evaluation computer programme of the Department of Transport
CPRE	Council for the Protection of Rural England
CTP	Common Transport Policy
DOE	Department of the Environment
DOT	Department of Transport
EA	Environmental Assessment
EEC	European Economic Community
EIA	Environmental Impact Assessment
EIS	Environmental Impact Statement
EMU	Economic and Monetary Union
EPA	Environmental Protection Agency
ERM	European Exchange Rate Mechanism
EMS	European Monetary System
EU	European Union
FoE	Friends of the Earth

GLC	Greater London Council
GNP	Gross National Product
HC	Hydrocarbon
HGV	Heavy Goods Vehicle
HMSO	Her Majesty's Stationery Office
IHT	Institution of Highways and Transportation
IPCC	Inter-governmental Panel on Climatic Change
IPPR	Institute for Public Policy Research
IUCN	International Union for the Conservation of Nature
LTT	Local Transport Today
MAPAC	Manchester Area Pollution Advisory Council
MEA	Manual for Environmental Appraisal
MER	Milieu Effectrapportage (Environmental Impact Assessment)
MVW	Ministerie van Verkeer en Waterstaat (Ministry of Transport, Public Works and Water Management)
NBP	Nationaal Natuurbeleidsplan (National Nature Policy Plan)
NC	Northern Trans-Pennine
NEPA	National Environmental Protection Act
NGO	Non-governmental Organisation
NMP	National Milieubeleidsplan (National Environmental Policy Plan)
NMP+	National Milieubeleidsplan Plus (National Environmental Policy Plan Plus)
NMP2	National Milieubeleidsplan 2 (National Environmental Policy Plan 2)
NO_x	Nitrogen oxides
NPAH	Nitro-polycyclic aromatic hydrocarbons
NPV	Net Present Value
NRTF	National Road Traffic Forecasts
4NRO	Vierda Nota Ruimtelijke Ordening (Fourth Report on Physical Planning)
NS	Nederlandse Spoorwegen (Dutch Railways)
NT	North Trans-Pennine
OECD	Organisation for Economic Co-operation and Development
PAH	Polyaromatic-hydrocarbons
PPG12	Planning Policy Guidance 12

PPG13	Planning Policy Guidance 13
PPPs	Policies, Plans and Programmes
PTA	Passenger Transport Authority
QUADRO	Queues Delays and Road works
RCEP	Royal Commission on Environmental Pollution
RIVM	Rijksinstituut voor Volkgezondheid en Milieuhygiëne (National Institute of Public Health and Environmental Protection)
RVVPs	Regionaal Verkeer en Vervoersplannen (Regional Transport Plans)
SACTRA	Standing Advisory Committee on Trunk Road Assessment
SCA	Supplementary Credit Approval
SCB	Social Cost Benefit
SEA	Strategic Environmental Assessment
SEM	Single European Market
SSSI	Site of Special Scientific Interest
ST	South Trans-Pennine
SVV2	Tweede Structuurschema Verkeer en Vervoer (Second Transport Structure Plan)
TCPA	Town and County Planning Act
T&E	European Federation for Transport and Environment
TPP	Transport Policies and Programmes
TSG	Transport Supplementary Grant
UK	United Kingdom
UN	United Nations
UNCED	United Nations Conference on Environment and Development
UNECE	United Nations Economic Commission for Europe
UNEP	United Nations Environment Programme
VOCs	Volatile Organic Compounds
VROM	Ministerie van Volkshuisvesting, Ruimtelijke Ordening en Milieuhygiëne (Ministry of Housing, Physical Planning and Environment)
WABM	Wet Algemene Bepalingen Milieuhygiëne (General Environmental Provisions Act)
WCED	World Commission of Environment and Development
WCS	World Conservation Strategy
WWF	Worldwide Fund for Nature
WHO	World Health Organisation
WRI	World Resources Institute

1 Introduction

Transport, whether it is by road, rail, air, sea or inland waterway, offers many benefits to society, transporting goods and people over distances. It gives the individual freedom and independence to travel and facilitates trade, taking on an important role in modern developed economies. Increasing prosperity has been coupled with rising car ownership and an increased demand for travel over longer distances, with a greater dependence on the transport of freight by road to the detriment of other less polluting modes of transport. The global number of motor vehicles has increased rapidly in the post-war period. In 1950 about 53 million cars were on the world's roads. Four decades later, this number had risen to over 400 million, with an average growth of 9 million motor vehicles per year (MacKenzie & Walsh, 1990, p.11).

Transport has a wide range of direct and indirect environmental impacts. It consumes large amounts of finite resources in the form of fuels and materials for construction. It produces carbon dioxide, which contributes to climatic change, and other air pollutants which are deleterious to human health and well-being. Large amounts of land are consumed by the transport sector in the construction of infrastructure and consequent secondary developments such as car parking and service stations. High rates of growth in car and lorry traffic, regionally and globally, are indicative of a non-sustainable trend. In order to move towards environmentally sustainable development, the issue of transport will need to be addressed.

Transportation can be categorised between intra-urban or inter-urban. Intra-urban transportation relates to the movement of people and goods within cities and is important in order to achieve more human-centred and sustainable cities which give greater priority to the individual pedestrian, cyclist and collective transport than to the motor vehicle.

Inter-urban transport plays a significant role in the movement of goods and people between major centres of economic activity. The development of the Single European Market and Eastern European countries means that the role of inter-urban transport will become more important in the transportation of goods between different European centres of trade. The growth in traffic may place pressure on specific strategic transport corridors, leading to congestion, pollution and an exacerbation of global and regional environmental problems.

With the need to move towards a more sustainable development, it is necessary to devise a transport system which is both economically and environmentally efficient. This poses a number of difficulties if policy is biased towards road transport. In response to the need for a change in traditional transport planning, a more multi-modal approach is increasingly gaining acceptance. Strategic transport planning approaches based on explicit objectives and targets are now being considered by some countries. The Netherlands is widely acknowledged as a country which has been in the vanguard with its approach to transport and the environment. The Dutch have published a number of strategic policy plans, such as the National Environmental Policy Plan and the Second Transport Structure Plan. In contrast, Britain has, as yet, no equivalent strategic policy plan for transport.

The concept of sustainable development has now been widely accepted by national governments and international agencies as a legitimate planning goal. The main challenge faced by such organisations is how to operationalise this general concept into practice. It is important that sustainability is considered early in the planning process in the formulation of policies, plans and programmes. The implementation of sustainability in the transport sector will depend on the nature of policy and whether or not national transport policies have explicit objectives which are inherently sustainable.

International comparisons play an important role in providing an assessment of the range and effectiveness of transport planning approaches available in different countries and the dissemination of information regarding best practice. The aim of this book is to provide an assessment of the different approaches taken to transport and the environment within the context of the European Union, and to determine the effectiveness of each approach in implementing sustainability within the transport planning process. Britain and the Netherlands were chosen as countries which provide contrasting approaches to transport, the British approach being more road-based while the Dutch approach is considered to be more multi-modal. The importance of the European Union within the field of transport and the environment continues to grow, with its environmental policy providing tighter regulatory constraints, while its economic policy encourages greater mobility and transport over longer distances.

This book first examines the concept of sustainability and its application within the transport sector. It reviews how this general concept has been interpreted into transport and environmental policy at the European, national and local level. It examines the different policy approaches of the European Commission, Britain and the Netherlands to deal with transport problems. A case study of a transport corridor in each country is used in order to discover the extent to which national policy influences and directs transport planning in practice. An assessment is made of the main advantages and disadvantages of different transport planning approaches and the efforts being made towards a style of transport planning founded on sustainable development principles. The contribution which differing approaches can make towards implementing sustainability in the transport sector and at the project level is discussed.

This book consists of nine chapters. Chapter 2 examines the background and emergence of the concept of sustainable development as a new environmental philosophy, and discusses the impacts associated with the transport sector.

Chapter 3 addresses the issue of the European Union and discusses the development of European transport and environmental policy and the contradictions which presently exist. Within the context of the European Union, two examples of Member States are taken to examine the differing national approaches to transport.

Chapter 4 examines post-war transport and environmental policy in Britain and the principal changes which have taken place in the last few years. It discusses the main contradictions which still lie in policy and the need to develop a more strategic form of transport planning to be implemented in practice.

In contrast to British policy, Chapter 5 examines the Dutch approach with their transport, environmental and physical planning policy plans which set objectives and targets. The development of Dutch policy plans is examined and whether the rhetoric of Dutch policy actually achieves what it sets out to do is discussed. An analysis of the progress being made towards meeting set targets for transport and environment is undertaken.

Chapter 6 examines the 1985 Directive on Environmental Impact Assessment (EIA). EIA enables the impacts associated with transport to be taken into consideration in the decision-making process, with the objectives of policy determining and justifying projects to be implemented in practice. EIA has come under criticism for a number of reasons:

1. It comes too late in the planning process.
2. It does not always evaluate all possible alternatives.
3. It examines impacts in isolation from one another.

In response to these criticisms a more strategic form of EIA is increasingly being adopted with some form of policy appraisal being implemented by a number of countries. The benefits of Strategic Environmental Assessment (SEA) are examined and the possible advantages of applying SEA to the transport sector are discussed.

Sustainable development will ultimately be judged on what is achieved in practice at the grass roots level. Chapters 7 and 8 examine how the differing approaches taken to transport in Britain and the Netherlands influence decisions in transport planning for important strategic transport corridors. In Britain the Trans-Pennine corridor is taken as a case study while the Amsterdam-Utrecht corridor is used as a case study in the Netherlands. The differing transport planning approaches are examined and the benefits and drawbacks are discussed. Chapter 9 concludes with a discussion of what can be learnt from the differing transport planning approaches. It outlines an environment-based approach to transport planning.

2 Sustainability and transport

The impact of mankind on the environment is not a new phenomenon, for human societies have had an effect on the environment since time immemorial. The rate and scale of the trends in environmental degradation, however, have been rising significantly with greater industrialisation. Growing environmental awareness has led to the belief that infinite growth within a finite system is untenable and that natural limits or ecological carrying capacities should be respected. Environmental degradation, whether it be loss of tropical rain forests, ozone depletion or the spread of desertification, can no longer continue unabated. Development which is within the ecological carrying capacity of the planet is now considered necessary for the sake of human survival. The concept of sustainable development has offered a new approach to halt the trends in environmental degradation, to ensure that the impact of human activity on the environment is minimised, so that future generations can enjoy the benefits of natural capital.

Since the 1960s, there has been growing concern over the human impact on the environment. The 1972 United Nations conference on the Human Environment (*Only One Earth*) was attended by 113 nations and was the culmination of the first main wave of environmentalism which had developed in the 1960s. This movement was triggered off by a number of dramatic events such as the wreck of the oil tanker *Torrey Canyon* off the coast of Cornwall in 1966, followed a year later by the explosion of an oil well off the coast of Santa Barbara in the United States. Influential publications which were produced at the time included *Silent Spring* (Carson, 1962), *A Blueprint for Survival* (Goldsmith et al. 1972) and *The Limits to Growth* (Meadows et al., 1972).

A number of environmental issues have gained increased attention since the 1960s, such as global warming, acid rain, depletion of the ozone layer, population growth, protection of tropical rain forests and biological diversity. The 1980s saw an interest in the environment gaining momentum once again, after a period of decline due to economic recession. Green consumerism, ethical investment and increased activity of Non-governmental Organisations (NGOs) characterised this second wave of environmentalism. In 1987 the World Commission on Environment and Development (WCED) report, *Our Common Future,* developed the concept of 'Sustainable Development' which has now become a main feature of environmental discourse. This second wave culminated in the 1992 United Nations Conference on Environment and Development (UNCED) in Brazil, which was intended to build upon the 1972 Stockholm conference. The agreements made in Brazil firmly established the concept of sustainable development on the political agenda of the world's governments.

Sustainable development has come to embody a way of living without causing a deterioration in environmental quality. Sustainability covers every sector of society, including the transport sector. Now that there has been wide acceptance of the concept, the main task faced by international organisations and agencies at different levels is how to operationalise the concept in practice into specific goals and criteria at the international, national, regional, local and project level. This is a considerable task since the concept is general in nature and definitions of what actually constitutes sustainability have varied widely. It has come to mean whatever suits the particular advocacy of the individual concerned (Pearce, 1991). The aim of this chapter is to examine the background to and definition of the concept of sustainable development and the importance of transport for a sustainable society.

Sustainable development

The term 'sustainable development' was first mooted by the World Conservation Strategy (WCS) in 1980, although the need for a more sustainable society was discussed in the early 1970s. *A Blueprint for Survival* (Goldsmith et al., 1972) outlined proposals to create what it termed a 'sustainable society'. It noted four principal conditions: firstly, minimum disruption of ecological processes; secondly, maximum conservation of materials and energy; thirdly, a stable population where growth equals loss; and, fourthly, a social system in which the individual can enjoy rather than feel restricted by the first three conditions above. Since *A Blueprint for Survival* a number of studies have been undertaken to define further sustainability and its implications for different sectors (WCED, 1987, Pearce et al., 1989, Pearce, 1991, IUCN et al., 1991, Pearce, 1993).

6

The World Conservation Strategy stressed the interdependence of conservation and development and emphasised that humanity is a part of nature and has no future unless nature and natural resources are conserved. It stated that conservation cannot be achieved without development to alleviate the poverty and misery of hundreds of millions of people. Emphasis was placed on maintaining ecological processes and life support systems, preservation of genetic diversity and sustainable use of species or ecosystems. The WCS acknowledged the importance of sustainable development, although the World Commission on Environment and Development emphasised the concept further by placing it on the political agenda. WCED was created by the United Nations (UN) as a result of a General Assembly resolution in Autumn 1985. It was to be the third of three initiatives taken by the UN. The first was the Brandt Commission Programme for Survival and Common Crisis; the second the Palmes Commission work on Security and Disarmament. The Brundtland Report (so called after the Chairperson, Gro Harlem Brundtland) asserted that humanity has the ability to make development sustainable, to ensure that it meets the needs of the present without compromising the ability of future generations to meet their own needs (WCED, 1987, p.8). The report recognised that, although interpretations of sustainability would vary, it must show certain general features and must flow from a consensus on the basic concept of sustainable development (WCED, 1987, p.45). A main objective of development is the satisfaction of humans needs and aspirations. The Commission saw sustainable development as meeting the basic needs of all and extending to all the opportunity to satisfy their aspirations for a better life (WCED, 1987, p.44). The report established that, where living standards go beyond the basic minimum, they can only be defined as sustainable if consumption has regard for long-term sustainability. It states:

At a minimum sustainable development must not endanger the natural systems that support life on earth: the atmosphere, the waters, the soils and the living beings.

The report goes on:

In essence, sustainable development is a process of change in which exploitation of resources, the direction of investments, the assumptions of technological development, and institutional change are all in harmony and balance and enhance both current and future potential to meet human needs and aspirations (WCED, 1987).

The Brundtland Report was followed by *Blueprint for a Green Economy* (Pearce et al., 1989) which investigated the economic implications of sustainable development in Britain.

Blueprint for a Green Economy saw sustainable development as involving a social and economic system which ensured that these goals are sustained, i.e. that real income rises, that educational standards increase, that the health of the nation improves and the general quality of life is advanced. In 1991 *Caring for the Earth: A Strategy for Sustainable Living* was produced by IUCN, UNEP and WWF. The strategy defined sustainable development as:

> ... improving the quality of human life while living within the carrying capacity of supporting ecosystems.

As Blueprint for a Green Economy examined the economic implications of sustainable development, the Caring for the Earth Strategy outlined a broad strategy for a sustainable society. The Strategy included nine main principles for a sustainable society:

1. respect and care for the community of life;
2. improve the quality of human life;
3. conserve the earth's vitality and diversity;
4. minimise the depletion of non-renewable resources;
5. keep within the earth's carrying capacity;
6. change personal attitudes and practices;
7. enable communities to care for their own environments;
8. provide a national framework for integrating development and conservation; and
9. create a global alliance.

United Nations Conference on Environment and Development

The 1992 United Nations Conference on Environment and Development (UNCED) which was held in Rio de Janeiro, Brazil ensured that sustainable development was acknowledged by the world's nations. The result of UNCED were agreements on a Climatic Change Convention, a Biodiversity Treaty, Forest Principles, the Rio Declaration and Agenda 21.

The objective of the Climatic Change Convention is to stabilise greenhouse gas concentrations at a level which would prevent dangerous anthropogenic interference with the climate system. Stabilisation should be achieved within a time frame sufficient to allow the ecosystem to adapt naturally, to ensure that food production is not threatened and to enable economic development to proceed in a sustainable manner (Holmberg et al., 1993, p.25). The Biodiversity Treaty sets out to conserve the world's biodiversity via sustainable use of its components and fairer and equitable sharing of benefits from the use

8

of genetic resources. Forest Principles are non legally binding principles which aim to contribute to the management, conservation and sustainable development of forests and to provide for their multiple and complementary functions and uses (Holmberg et al., 1993, p.28).

As a global environmental statement, the Rio Declaration on Environment and Development set out 27 non legally binding principles on which sustainable development should be based (UNCED, 1992). Principle 1 of the Declaration claims that:

> Human beings are the centre of concerns for Sustainable Development. They are entitled to a healthy and productive life in harmony with nature.

To achieve sustainable development and a higher quality of life for all people, Principle 8 states that action should be taken to:

> ... reduce and eliminate unsustainable patterns of production and consumption and promote appropriate demographic policies.

A programme for the implementation of the principles enunciated in the Rio Declaration was contained within Agenda 21. The main theme of Agenda 21 is the application of sustainability to a wide range of areas in accordance with the principles in the Rio Declaration.

Agenda 21

Chapter 7 of Agenda 21 concerns the promotion of sustainable human settlement and development. Within this Chapter, Section 6 covers the promotion of sustainable energy and transport systems in human settlements, with the objectives to:

> ... extend the provision of more energy-efficient technical and alternative/renewable energy for human settlements and to reduce the negative impacts of energy production and use on human health and the environment.

Activities needed to provide a comprehensive approach to human settlement should include the promotion of sustainable energy development in all countries. This includes the promotion of an efficient and environmentally sound urban transport system. A comprehensive approach to urban transport planning and management should be adopted in every country. Thus, all countries should adopt urban transport which encourages a high occupancy public transport.

Non-motorised forms of transport should be encouraged, with the provision of safe cycleways and footways in urban and suburban centres. Land use and transportation planning should be encouraged to reduce the demand for travel. Attention should also be given to the management of traffic and the efficient operation of public transport and maintenance of transport infrastructure.

Section 2(B) of Agenda 21, on Conservation and Management of Resources for Development, is further devoted to transportation. The basis of action is outlined below:

> The transport sector has an essential and positive role to play in economic and social development, and transportation needs will undoubtedly increase. However, since the transport sector is also a source of atmosphere emissions, there is a need for a review of existing transportation systems and the most effective design and management of traffic and transportation systems.

The objective of the programme on transportation is to develop and promote cost-effective policies which limit, reduce and control harmful emissions and other adverse environmental effects of the transport sector. Six activities were outlined which governments should undertake in co-operation with intergovernmental and non-governmental agencies. Activities needed to implement Agenda 21 in the transport sector are:

1. The development and promotion of cost-effective, more efficient and less polluting and safer transport systems, particularly integrated urban and rural mass transit, as well as an environmentally sound road network taking into consideration the needs of sustainable economic and social development.
2. Facilitate access to and transfer of safe, efficient, resource efficient less polluting transport technologies at the international, national, regional and subregional levels. This is of particular importance for developing countries with appropriate training programmes.
3. Action should be taken to strengthen efforts at collecting, analysing and exchanging relevant information on the relation between transport and environment, with emphasis on the systematic observations of emissions and the development of a transport database.
4. Cost-effective policies and programmes should be promoted, including administrative, social and economic measures, in order to encourage the use of transportation modes that minimise adverse impacts on the atmosphere in accordance with national socio-economic development and environmental priorities.

5. Mechanisms should be developed and enhanced to integrate transport planning strategies and urban and regional settlement planning strategies with a view to reducing the environmental impact of transport.
6. Within the framework of the United Nations and its regional economic commissions, the feasibility of convening regional conferences on transport and environment should be studied.

A question of definition

Definitions of sustainable development have been wide-ranging, but all have been variations on a theme. The main features consistent throughout the various definitions include the following: the notion of intergenerational equity and a long time horizon, which concerns providing a quality environment for the future generations. This includes an adequate stock of non-renewable and renewable resources. Development and growth should be maintained within the ecological boundaries and should not overshoot the carrying capacity of the natural environment. A lifestyle should be maintained which does not mean irreparable damage to the environment.

The concept of sustainable development should be viewed as a continuum with varying degrees of sustainability and unsustainability. The spectrum of sustainability definitions which exist illustrates this view. Sustainability has been further distinguished between 'weak' and 'strong' sustainability.

English Nature (1992) defined weak sustainable development as one which requires environmental considerations to be taken into account in policy making, but which allows 'trade-offs' to occur to achieve other goals or to develop a more socially desirable solution. Strong sustainable development is one which constrains the achievement of other social goals, although development is allowed if it is subject to particular conditions, which are often known as sustainability constraints or environmental limits. Pearce (1993) considers weak sustainability as one where no special place is given for the environment, where all forms of capital are completely interchangeable and the environment is seen as another form of capital. In contrast, strong sustainability requires that the overall stock of natural capital (e.g. air, water, fossil fuels) should be maintained.

Transport and the environment

A wide range of transport modes exist; and all differ in the extent to which they have an impact on the environment. Transport modes include motor vehicles, rail, air, water and cycling.

Transport plays an important role in the economy and in the transportation and distribution of goods and services nationally and internationally. For some countries, such as the Netherlands, transport contributes a significant amount to the national product. Motorised transport has become the main mode of transporting goods and people, with the motor car being the most popular form of personal transport. The motor car has come to symbolise freedom and status of mobility. The popularity of the car is a sign of a modern society; it has been encouraged in media images and has influenced land use planning, with an increasing amount of money being devoted to the construction of infrastructure for vehicle use. A large proportion of goods are now being distributed by road and the development of the Single European Market is expected to increase economic development and the number of vehicle kilometres travelled.

Transport growth

Transport tends to be a means to an end rather than an end in itself, with the demand for transport considered to be 'derived demand' which has been linked to economic growth. The rate of the world's motor vehicle growth is projected to outpace both the total and urban population. As developing countries begin to increase their economic activity, the growth in transport will increase to levels already seen in the developed world. Car ownership in developing countries is expected to be responsible for a greater share of the growth in the global motor vehicle fleet. Today, some developing countries are already experiencing the consequences of traffic in major urban conurbations. Transport is increasingly becoming a problem, with the growth of urbanisation leading to a greater dependence on motorised transport. Investment in most developing countries has begun to concentrate on motor vehicles, with hostility or indifference shown towards informal, non-motorised transportation modes such as bicycles, tricycles, carts, little boats and locally produced carrying devices, despite the importance they play in the life and mobility of the poorer sectors of society (Replogle, 1988).

Due to the importance given to transport in society, the direct and indirect environmental impacts caused by transport have often been ignored in both economic and development planning.

Yet transport has a significant impact on the environment; it is responsible for 22% of global energy consumption and 25% of fossil fuel burning. Transport also demands a great number of resources, and causes air pollution which affects human health. A large number of accidents and injuries result from the use of transport.

The environmental impact of transport has now become a global issue for transport affects the availability of non-renewable resources and the sustainability of renewable resources, human health, safety and the quality of life. The environmental impact of transport activities and their importance depends on the mode (road, rail, air, sea or inland waterway), the construction of infrastructure, the production of vehicles, and the intensity of use. Transport also generates waste, especially from road vehicles, which need to be scrapped once they have become obsolete.

Environmental impact of transport

The transport sector uses a wide variety of the earth's resources. The mobilisation of resources via extraction, refining and manufacture has an impact on the different components of the environment (air, water, and soil). Transport is mainly oil-based, with the motor vehicle being the biggest consumer of energy compared with all other transport modes. The motor vehicle is as reliable as its fuel source and has been influenced in the past by fluctuations in oil prices and the disruption of world oil reserves. On a global scale, motor vehicles powered solely by oil account for one third of world oil consumption (MacKenzie & Walsh, 1990). Energy consumed by transport is closely related to air pollution, with the production of pollutants having significant atmospheric effects. Fossil fuel use produces carbon dioxide (CO_2), carbon monoxide (CO), chlorofluorocarbons (CFCs), nitrogen oxides (NO_x), and volatile organic compounds (VOCs), which are precursors to tropospheric ozone and acid rain, as well as contributing directly or indirectly to global warming.

The energy efficiency of different transport modes varies considerably, with a more than six-fold difference in energy intensity between the most efficient (walking and cycling) and the least efficient motorised passenger transport mode (UNEP, 1993a). Road transport is the most common form of transport used in the movement of both passengers and freight. The motor vehicle has become a convenient mode of transport which has bestowed a new form of freedom and independence on a great section of society, at the same time restricting the freedom of children, pedestrians and cyclists.

Transport consumes a considerable amount of energy, from the extraction of raw materials to the production of vehicles and infrastructure. Energy is used in the operation of vehicles, in the manufacture of vehicle components (e.g. tyres and engine components) and in the construction and maintenance of infrastructure such as road and railways. The demand for the manufacture of vehicles also requires the disposal of old and used vehicles.

Despite a significant increase in the volume of vehicles sold from 1970-1990 in the OECD, developing countries tripled their sale volumes and achieved a higher growth rate than the OECD area, increasing their relative share of total vehicle sales. In the future there will be an increasing demand for fuel from these developing countries (Birol & Guerer, 1993). For every gallon of oil consumed by a motor vehicle about 19 pounds of CO_2 (containing 5.3 pounds of carbon) are emitted directly into the atmosphere (MacKenzie & Walsh, 1990). The main contribution to nitrogen oxide emissions from human activities has been from the transport sector. NO_x are emitted at the source of fossil fuel combustion during the process of internal combustion in the motor vehicle. Between one third to one half of national emissions of NO_x are due to the transport sector (Tolba et al., 1992).

Global warming

The global average concentration of carbon dioxide has been increasing from its pre-industrial levels of about 270 parts per million by volume (ppmv) to 335 ppmv in 1991 (UNEP, 1993b). Only recently has carbon dioxide been classed as a 'pollutant' and identified as being responsible for 50% of global warming due to the greenhouse effect (Transnet, 1990). The Earth's atmosphere absorbs most of the solar radiation which passes through it. However, some of this radiation is reflected back by the earth and is trapped by a number of greenhouse gases in the atmosphere. The heat trapped from this radiation warms the surface and lower atmosphere of the earth causing the phenomenon known as the 'greenhouse effect'. The main source of CO_2 is from fossil fuels which in combustion are oxidised to form carbon dioxide. Carbon dioxide is only one of the many main greenhouse gases with CH4, CFC-11, CFC-12 and HCF22 being the other principal sources. Other pollutants emitted from transport such as NO_x directly contribute to global warming or form secondary pollutants. Although the level of CO_2 emissions are increasing, CO_2 is not as potent as CFC-11 and CFC-12, which have a higher global warming potential.

The relative contribution of motor vehicles to global carbon dioxide emissions has gradually increased. In 1971 motor vehicles accounted for only 12% of total global CO_2 emissions due to the combustion of fossil fuels; by 1985 this had risen to 14%. Regional differences in the emission of carbon dioxide can also be distinguished, with signs of stabilisation in the more developed regions such as North America and Western Europe. Emissions from less developed regions of South America, the Far East, Central Asia and Africa have, however, continued to increase (UNEP, 1993b). In developing countries, emissions of carbon dioxide from motor vehicles have risen by 3.5% per year and account for 45% of the global emissions from motor vehicles (MacKenzie & Walsh, 1990). However, the more developed regions of the USA, Canada, Japan, Europe, the former USSR, Australia and New Zealand still account for a high percentage of the global total of carbon dioxide emissions.

The Inter-governmental Panel on Climatic Change (IPCC) has estimated that the global mean temperature has risen by 0.3°C to 0.6°C over the last thirty years. Global warming will involve an increase in global mean temperature of 1.8°C above the present level by the year 2030 and an increase of 3°C before the end of the twenty-first century (Tolba et al., 1992, p.74). Global warming will have a number of effects and may result in a change in climate, especially rainfall patterns, which would increase the likelihood of more intense tropical storms and will have significant consequences for agriculture belts. In addition sea levels will rise due to thermal expansion of the ocean and melting of glaciers, which will pose a threat to wetlands, thus, accelerating coastal erosion, exacerbating flooding and increasing the salinity of estuaries and aquifers (CEST, 1993). To stabilise the concentration of CO_2 in the atmosphere, the IPCC recommends a reduction of 60% in the annual rate of CO_2 emissions at 1990 levels by 2005.

Transboundary environmental impacts

The long-range movement of air pollutants and the atmospheric deposition of SO_2 and NO_x has caused widespread acidification of terrestrial and aquatic ecosystems. Pollutants from transport have been implicated, especially in the development of regional acidification problems in North America and Europe. In Sweden, out of the 85,000 lakes greater than one hectare in area, it has been estimated that acidification 'affects' 14,000 as a result of air pollution, with about 4,000 classed as 'seriously affected' (where pH has fallen by more than 0.6 since pre-industrial times). The Swedish Environmental Protection Agency estimates that if acidification continues unabated, with no reduction in deposition, nearly 34,000 lakes will be acidified within a few decades. Only if deposition is reduced by 75% can a long-term improvement be expected (Alcomo et al., 1987; Swedish EPA, 1992).

The transboundary movement of air pollutants was recognised as early as 1968, when Odèn noted the potential of acid deposition to degrade ecosystems, due to the long-range movement of air pollutants across national

15

boundaries. Since then, there has been increased concern about the impacts caused by acidification to lakes, forests, soils, peat lands and historic buildings up to 1,000 kilometres from the source of pollution (Gorham, 1989). Acidification results from the combustion of fossil fuels and agricultural practices that have been manifest in heavily industrialised areas of Europe and North America. In many respects, acidification is more of a regional problem rather than a global problem, which is not the case for carbon dioxide emissions and global warming.

Natural emissions of sulphur are equally divided between the North and South. However, it is estimated that over 90% of emissions from anthropogenic sources originate in the Northern hemisphere (UNEP, 1993b). The sulphur deposition in Europe and North America is more than ten times higher than it would be if it occurred naturally. Global emissions of sulphur oxides have been estimated to have increased by 18% between 1970 and 1986 from 57 million tonnes of sulphur to 67 million tonnes (Hameed & Dignon, 1992). Emissions of sulphur in North America and Europe are expected to decline, with nitrogen oxide emissions remaining constant (Rodhe, 1989).

In the European Union, road transport is responsible for 2.3% of total sulphur dioxide emissions, 54% of nitrogen oxide emissions and 27% of volatile organic compounds. Both SO_2 and NO_x have been the principal causes of acid deposition and urban smog (CEC, 1992a). Over the past 20 years in Europe there has been a reduction in these emissions. Any gains, however, have been offset by traffic growth. A further decline in emissions of SO_2, VOCs, and CO from motor vehicles is expected, although the European Commission predicts an increase in CO_2 and NO_x emissions.

The transboundary movement of air pollutants from transport, such as oxides of sulphur and nitrogen and volatile organic compounds including hydrocarbons and ammonia, has resulted in the formation of acid deposition. Some of these pollutants (NO_x, HCs, VOCs) react through photo-oxidation to produce ozone (O_3) which damages crops and vegetation and affects human health. There is a global trend towards an increase in NO_x arising from motor vehicles, to which must be added emissions from the increasing number of aircraft. These have been estimated to be about 3 million tonnes each year, which is equivalent to about 15% of NO_x emissions from automobiles (Tolba et al., 1992). Acid deposition has caused damage to broad-leaved trees and conifers in Europe. In 1991, 18.5% of broadleaves and 24.4% of conifers were moderately or severely defoliated, where 'moderate' defoliation is defined as a 25-60% loss in leaves, and 'severe' is where over 60% loss occurs (WRI, 1994).

Impact on the urban environment

The effects of greater industrialisation and urbanisation in both the developed and the developing world have resulted in the concentration of people in large urban conurbations. More than 100 million urban residents worldwide are exposed to outside air pollution levels higher than those recommended by World Health Organisation (WHO). The growth of motorised transportation has resulted in greater levels of congestion, energy consumption and air pollution. The rate of urbanisation has resulted in a number of environmental problems unique to the city. Increased motorisation has been one of the effects which has been enhanced by rapid urbanisation. This has caused greater levels of air and noise pollution, and more accidents and injuries from motor vehicles. In some developing countries there has been a rural-urban exodus with migration of the rural poor on a large scale. In 1970, 62.9% of the world's population lived in rural areas, by 1990 this had declined to 57.4%. A further decline of 40% is expected by the year 2025 (UNEP, 1993b). Migration of the population to urban areas has been facilitated by a number of factors, including the improvement of the road network which has allowed greater accessibility to cities.

In many major cities of the world air pollution has resulted in WHO guidelines being exceeded on a regular basis. Urbanisation and increasing motorisation have led to a deterioration in ambient urban air quality. In 1992 the World Health Organisation Commission on Health and Environment undertook a study on urban air pollution and health and concluded that urban air pollution is a major environmental health problem which deserves high priority, especially if one considers the United Nations estimates which suggest that by the year 2010 56% of the global population could be living in urban areas (WHO, 1992).

Urban air pollution

Motor vehicles are responsible for a number of primary pollutants which are emitted into the atmosphere in urban areas. Exhaust emissions from petrol and diesel engines contain carbon monoxide, nitrogen oxides, sulphur oxides, hydrocarbons and particulate. Secondary pollutants are also produced from the creation of new compounds which result from the chemical reaction of primary pollutants in the atmosphere. Some of these pollutants affect human health at the local level in urban conurbations.

An examination of urban air pollution in twenty megacities (those cities which currently have or are projected to have 10 million inhabitants by the year 2000), by UNEP/WHO (1992) showed that the motor vehicle was a major source of air pollution. Each of the megacities examined had one major pollutant which exceeded WHO health guidelines, with 14 cities having two pollutants which exceeded the guidelines and 7 cities having three or more. In nearly half of the 20 cities, transport was considered the single most important cause of urban air pollution, with Bangkok, Jakarta, Manila, Mexico City, São Paulo and Seoul having significant traffic related air pollution and high emissions of CO, HC, NO_x and lead. In those cities where a greater proportion of the vehicles were powered by diesel, such as Bangkok, Manila and Seoul, there was a higher concentration of suspended particulate matter, SO_2 and NO_x (UNEP/WHO, 1992).

Motor vehicles in developing countries tend to be in poor condition and badly maintained with poor quality fuels. This, together with poor traffic management, inefficient public transport systems and a high concentration of motor vehicles, has resulted in a greater level of congestion. These factors have influenced the level of air pollution, with a high proportion of the population being exposed to airborne pollutants, as well as a high incidence of road traffic accidents (Dimitriou, 1990; Serageldin, 1993).

Noise

Noise pollution is another impact which results from road and air transport and the growth of motorisation. Noise is socially intrusive (from whatever source) and interferes with human activity, such as speech, communication and sleep. The OECD (1988) defines noise as any acoustical phenomenon producing a sensation perceived by an individual or a group as disagreeable or disturbing. Noise can have a number of effects on health. By interfering with sleep it can influence mood and reduce the performance of the cardio-vascular system, as well as affecting intellectual and mechanical tasks. Long-term exposure to noise can cause deafness and lower auditory acuity, with noise annoyance resulting in stress and psychological and physiological effects.

Road traffic has been identified as a major contributor to environmental noise in England and Wales. In 1986 the Department of the Environment recorded 11,422 offences relating to noise from motor vehicles, 90% of which involved faulty silencers (Godlee, 1992). In OECD countries over 130 million people are exposed to noise levels of more than 65 dB(A) from road, rail or air traffic (Tolba et al., 1992). Despite current regulations on noise abatement, forecasts in some countries suggest that the impact from noise will increase unless greater determination is shown by policy makers to develop policies to reduce the impact of noise (OECD, 1988).

Land use

Transport consumes large areas of land for the construction of roads, railways, airports and ports, excluding them from other uses. Transport has two effects on land, which can be divided into primary and secondary land use. Primary land use relates directly to the construction of transport infrastructure such as road, rail and airports. Secondary land use is developments which are derived from the construction of infrastructure, for example, the construction of motorway service stations and retail development near motorway junctions, as well as land taken up for parking places and the extraction of raw materials used in the construction of transport infrastructure.

In Britain, roads occupy 2,553-4,400 km^2 of land, with secondary land taken for car parking and aggregate extraction amounting to 634.1 km^2 (CPRE, 1995). In EU countries, roads occupy about 1.3% of total land area of the region, while railways demand forty times less land than road (Tolba et al., 1992). The amount of land required per transport mode also varies. Teufel (1991) showed that a lorry requires 0.007 m^2 of space per tonne kilometre, in comparison with rail which needs 0.0025 m^2. The lorry therefore requires three times as much space for the transportation of freight as rail.

Land use planning has important implications for energy consumption and sustainability. Travel and transport developments have interacted to allow significant land use changes. The result has been the development of more energy-intensive land use and activity patterns, which are interrelated and influence the demand for travel, with new transport projects generating land use developments and vice versa. The development of out-of-town retail developments such as the Metro Centre in Gateshead near Newcastle-upon-Tyne, means greater distances to be travelled to undertake leisure and shopping activities and large amounts of land allocated for car parking. The average provision of car parking in town centres is estimated to be 3.6 spaces per 1000 square feet (gross) compared with 7.4 spaces per 1000 square feet (gross) in out-of-town centres (CPRE, 1995).

Inter-urban transport

The problem of transport has tended to be dominated by the urban issue in towns and cities and by the growth in the number of private motor vehicles, congestion, and poor provision of public transport facilities. A wide range of initiatives are being taken to deal with the problem of urban transportation around the world, such as the introduction of road pricing, greater investment in public transport and the banning of motor vehicles and non-essential traffic from city centres.

The urban transport problem deserves greater attention, especially with increasing urbanisation and the development of megacities. However, inter-urban transportation should not be neglected in the quest to achieve sustainable cities. A large proportion of transport is inter-urban, which consists of the movement of both passengers and freight along road, rail and waterway links between major urban conurbations. Inter-urban transport is defined as transport which involves roads, railways, waterways and airways connecting areas classified as urban, which are mainly dominated by principal cities (Turton, 1992).

The growth in domestic and international traffic will not be equally distributed throughout the whole transport network. Those inter-urban corridors which play an important role in the economy of urban centres are expected to take the largest share of traffic. International transport patterns have come to reflect the consumption and production of goods and services. This process has been influenced by an increasing division of labour, which has affected the transport of goods, and the growing affluence of industrialised nations.

Main transport routes or corridors act as important passageways which can be of local, regional, national and international importance connecting separate developments and urban centres. The length and extent of the corridors can vary according to importance, with local corridors being of less than 5 kilometres. The UNECE (1992) define transport corridors as a distinct area where traffic flows mainly in one direction. This is in contrast to a transport network where traffic flows in different directions, although corridors may in themselves consist of a diverse network with only one main direction of traffic.

The demand for transport can be related to population density, for large conurbations which contribute to economic growth require high standard links between other conurbations and beyond. Transport corridors can be mono-modal, with road being the main mode, or multi-modal, with road, rail and canal being in close alignment. Strategic transport corridors will play an important role in the Single European Market and the development of Eastern Europe and of East-West traffic. The UNECE (1992) undertook an assessment of transport axes for international traffic flow, which will be of major importance in the future for infrastructure investment. It concluded that road infrastructure in Eastern Europe is of poor quality, if compared with the rest of Europe, and thus a need exists for upgrading the Eastern European road network. Although a dense train network exists, it is also in need of modernisation. The developments taking place within the transport sector in mainland Europe and in Eastern Europe will have important implications for the development and increasing use of transport corridors.

Table 2.1 shows the growth in vehicle kilometres on different types of roads in Britain. The type of roads which carry the most traffic are all minor roads,

20

followed by principal roads in built-up areas, motorways and trunk roads in non-built up areas on inter-urban routes. It is not surprising that minor roads carry the most traffic as these are the roads which are most commonly used in built-up and non-built up areas and cater for trips of less than 5 kilometres, followed by principal routes in built-up areas. Motorways and trunk roads in non-built up areas carry a high proportion of traffic because they act as inter-urban corridors connecting urban centres together.

Table 2.1
Growth of traffic on different road types, 1982-1992
(billion vehicles kilometres)

	1982	1984	1986	1988	1990	1992
Motorways	30.2	36.3	40.8	54.5	61.7	61.0
Built-up roads:						
Trunk	9.1	9.2	10.5	10.1	10.1	9.6
Principal	55.7	56.9	58.0	64.5	68.2	68.7
Non built up roads:						
Trunk	36.9	41.9	45.2	52.3	59.0	59.7
Principal	37.8	43.4	44.9	51.0	55.9	59.1
All	74.6	85.3	90.1	103.3	114.9	118.8
Minor roads	114.8	115.4	125.9	143.3	156.1	150.7
All roads	284.5	303.1	325.3	375.5	410.8	408.8

Source: DOT, 1993a

The growth in traffic from 1982-1992 (Table 2.2) has been highest on motorways where it has increased by 102% in vehicle kilometres followed by a 62% growth on trunk roads in non-built up areas. Strategic inter-urban transport corridors play an important role in the transport and distribution of goods and services. These corridors are expected to have the greatest growth in traffic volumes both in passenger and freight vehicles.

Table 2.2
Percentage growth in traffic on different road types, 1982-1992

Road type	Growth (%)
Motorways	102
Built-up major roads:	
Trunk	5.0
Principal	23.34
Non built-up major roads:	
Trunk	62.0
Principal	56.34
Minor roads	31.3

Source: DOT, 1993a

The effect of the Single European Market and the removal of barriers to the free movement of goods and people are predicted to result in an increase in freight transportation. The growth in road haulage is expected to affect environmental conditions along the main transport corridors within the European Union, for example, air quality, noise levels and the fabric of cities, towns and villages resulting in community severance (CEC, 1990a).

In the Netherlands, the Amsterdam-Utrecht-Arnhem route has been identified as an important strategic link to Germany, while in Britain a North-South corridor can be distinguished running from Scotland to the North-West, the Midlands and London. This corridor continues in France from Lille-Paris-Lyon to Marseilles. The North-South corridor in Britain is represented by primary routes such as the A74, M6, M1, M25, M20 and the Channel Tunnel to mainland Europe. Rail includes the West Coast main line and the proposed rail link through Kent to the Channel Tunnel and beyond (Callery, 1991). A North-South corridor has been a dominant feature in Britain and transport investment has been directed to improving communications along this axis.

Each country within the EU has developed its own national transport policy, which include measures to deal with the increase in the growth of road traffic. The approach taken to deal with the traffic growth on strategic transport corridors will be indicative of national transport and environmental policy and the priority given to a particular mode of transport. The study of transport corridors can reveal how national transport and environmental policy is actually implemented in practice. By examining the approaches taken by national government to congestion on strategic corridors, an assessment can be undertaken of the extent to which progress is being made towards developing a more sustainable transport system. Transport corridors can be seen as a microcosm of the main issues which exist in the debate on transport and environment. These include the need to provide accessible links for the economic activity of urban centres and the possibility of providing alternatives to road transport, while at the same time ensuring the protection of the environment and no deterioration in environmental quality.

Due to the growth in freight and passenger traffic, there is now an increasing need to take a multi-modal approach to deal with congestion problems in European transport corridors. The approach taken in the future to solve the transport problem will have important implications for sustainable development.

Sustaining transport

The full life cycle of transport has an impact on the environment at every stage, from production to use and disposal. These effects vary with each transport mode, with the motor vehicle considered to have the greatest environmental impact. The transport sector has been implicated in either causing or contributing to a number of social and environmental problems, such as use of public space, freedom of children and pedestrians, and air and noise pollution. The disparate impacts caused by each transport mode affect the global, regional and local environment and pose a threat to the quality of life. Present growth in vehicle ownership and use is unsustainable both in the developed and developing countries. Measures need to be taken at a number of levels (e.g. national, regional and local) to mitigate the effects of transport and reduce the need and demand for travel. A return to more sustainable modes of transport such as walking and cycling is necessary together with investment in public transport. The extent to which policy succeeds in reducing the effects of transport depends on the level of co-ordination and integration of transport, environmental, planning and economic policies. A more multi-modal approach to transport planning is required to deal with transport problems generally, especially for strategic inter-urban transport corridors in order to limit the environmental effects of increasing passenger and freight traffic between major urban conurbations.

The following Chapter will examine transport and environmental policy within the European Union. An example of two Members States (Britain and the Netherlands) is taken to illustrate the contrasting approach to transport and the environment. How these differences in national policy affect the planning approach adopted to deal with congestion on inter-urban transport corridors is examined with the use of case studies.

3 The European dilemma

The 1957 Treaty of Rome, which established the European Economic Community, outlined the need for a Common Transport Policy within Europe to reduce economic inefficiencies. The European Commission has attempted over the past thirty years to achieve this objective but with little success. Now that greater importance is being given to the environment and sustainable development, both in Europe and internationally, the European Union is faced with a dilemma. The EU will need to take action to deal with the environmental impact of transport and to find a balance between the conflicting interests of mobility and environmental protection.

The development of the Single European Market (SEM), which has removed the obstacles to the free movement of goods and people, will have important implications for the transport sector. The SEM is expected to encourage greater mobility, which is predicted to result in an increase in the number of passenger and freight kilometres travelled.

This Chapter will examine the approach taken by the European Union to resolve the problem of transport and the environment in Europe. It will review the development of a Common European Transport Policy and Environmental Action Programmes. The main contradictions and conflicts which presently exist in European policy on transport and the environment are discussed.

Transport and the environment in Europe

Since the 1970s the growth of transport has been increasing in Europe. The demand for passenger and goods transport has been related to economic growth, which has averaged 2.6% per year over the period 1970-1990. During this period, the average growth for transport services was 3.1% for passengers and 2.3% for goods (CEC, 1992b, p.7). The International Road Federation (1990) predicts a 35% increase in passenger kilometres in Western Europe from 1988 to the year 2000. On major European routes road transport is expected almost to double over the next 20 years for both passenger and freight. Freight transport could continue to grow by 90% by the year 2010, while international traffic could increase by up to 156% during this period (CEC, 1992b, p.23).

Table 3.1 shows the growth in freight transport over the period 1970-1990. Freight transport during this period has increased by 53%. The greatest share of EU freight transport has been by road, which accounted for 50.6% of freight in 1970, followed by rail (27.8%) and inland waterways (13.6%) (see Table 3.2). The share of freight transported by road has increased and in 1990 accounted for 69.9%, while the movement of freight by rail decreased by 12.4% (from 27.8% to 15.4%). Passenger transport in the EU has increased by 92.4% during the period 1970-1990 (see Table 3.3)

Table 3.1
EU freight transport, 1970-1990
(thousand million tonne kilometres)

Mode	1970	1980	1985	1990
Road	337(1)	581(2)	634(3)	797(4)
Rail	207	194	181	176
Inland waterway	101	104	95	105
Pipeline	60	80	61	63
Total	745	959	971	1141

(1) without Portugal, Ireland
(2) without Greece
(3) without Portugal
(4) without Portugal, Greece, Ireland

Source: CEC, 1992b, p.9

Table 3.2
Percentage modal share of EU freight transport, 1970-1990

Mode	1970	1980	1985	1990
Road	50.6%	60.6%	65.3%	69.9%
Rail	27.8%	20.2%	18.6%	15.4%
Inland waterway	13.6%	10.8%	9.8%	9.2%
Pipelines	8.0%	8.4%	6.3%	5.5%

Source: CEC, 1992b, p.9

Table 3.3
EU passenger transport, 1970-1990
(thousand million passenger kilometres)

Mode	1970	1980	1985	1990
Private car	1390(2)	2033(2)	2200(2)	2776(3)
Rail	182	209	218	231
Buses & coaches	214(2)	278(2)	284(2)	313(4)
Air (1)	41	92	138	196
Total	1827	2612	2840	3516

(1) estimates; traffic departing and landing inside EC only
(2) without Luxembourg, Ireland
(3) without Luxembourg, Greece, Ireland
(4) without Belgium, Greece, Ireland, Luxembourg

Source: CEC, 1992b, p.10

The percentage modal share of EU passenger transport is outlined in Table 3.4. In 1970 the private car was responsible for 76.1% of passenger transport, followed by buses and coaches (11.7%), rail (10%) and air (2.2%). In 1990 the share of the private car had increased by 2.9% and air by 3.4%, while the share of buses and coaches had fallen by 2.8% and rail by 3.4%.

Table 3.4
Percentage modal share of EU passenger transport, 1970-1990

Mode	1970	1980	1985	1990
Private car	76.1%	77.8%	77.5%	79.0%
Rail	10.0%	8.0%	7.7%	6.6%
Buses & coaches	11.7%	10.6%	10.0%	8.9%
Air	2.2%	3.5%	4.9%	5.6%

Source: CEC, 1992b, p.10

The growth in transport is attributable to a number of varying factors. These have included: the dispersal of economic activities due to changes in the manufacturing industry, causing firms to locate on new industrial sites as opposed to existing urban areas. Changes in production methods have resulted in a more flexible, diverse and tailored transport with reductions in shipment size and increases in the frequency of shipment. The increased share of the service industry has resulted in multi-site businesses nationally and on a European scale. This has influenced the mobility of professionals over short, medium and long distances. Probably one of the most significant factors has been the increase in net disposable income, which, together with demographic changes, has led to an increase in car ownership, leisure time and holidays abroad (CEC, 1992b, p.7).

The transport sector has had a considerable impact on the environment with economic and technological developments exacerbating the areas of conflict between transport and the environment. Emissions of CO_2 from the transport sector increased by 76% between 1971 and 1989, which is an average annual increase of 4.2%. Emissions of NO_x, HCs and particulates have increased by 68%, 41% and 106% respectively over this period (CEC, 1992b, p.13). Table 3.5 shows the percentage share of CO_2 emissions from the transport sector, with road transport being responsible for the greatest share of CO_2 emissions followed by aviation.

Table 3.5
Share of total carbon dioxide emissions in the transport sector

Means of transport	Share
Total road transport	79.9%
Private car	55.4%
Goods vehicles	22.7%
Buses & coaches	1.6%
Total railway transport	3.9%
Passengers	2.8%
Goods	1.1%
Aviation	10.9%
Inland waterways	0.7%
Other transport	4.3%

Source: CEC, 1992b, p.13

The incidence of congestion has risen due to the increase in the volume of traffic, which has doubled over the period 1970-1989 for both private and freight vehicles. One of the main contributory factors considered to be responsible for this growth has been the increase in car ownership within the Union. On the basis of trends since 1975, the number of cars in the EU is expected to increase by 25-30% from 1990-2010 (CEC, 1992b, p.14).

The growth of transport in Europe has led to pressures on infrastructure such as road and rail networks, with infrastructural capacity being reached, especially on strategic transport corridors. This has resulted in congestion and environmental damage. At the same time other modes of transport have been underutilised. The EC refers to this as *modal disequilibria*; an imbalance in the share of transport which favours road. It sees inadequate or incomplete transport networks causing bottlenecks and preventing the integration of peripheral areas within the Single European Market. These inefficiencies are considered as a threat to the development of the Union, hindering the process of economic integration and affecting the international competitiveness of the EU (CEC, 1992b, p.31).

A common transport policy

Each Member State of the Union has developed a national transport system to meet national interests. National transport markets have differed in structure with, for example, the smaller Benelux countries developing road freight transport which is more profitable over short distances, transporting bulk goods by inland waterways.

In contrast, in Germany and France rail has a higher competitive advantage over longer distances (Erdmenger, 1983). The different national systems have led to conflicts between Member States which have to be resolved at the Union level. Erdmenger (1983) suggests that:

> ... closer examination of international transport in Europe can be seen to be full of subtle irrationalities and obstacles which arise from differing national systems, which not only make transport itself more expensive but also distort and impede the common market for goods and services.

The 1957 Treaty of Rome recognised the benefits of having a common transport policy, although it said very little about the nature of CTP and left it to the Commission to elaborate policy (Whitelegg, 1979). The first proposal for a Common Transport Policy was published in April 1961 in the *Schaus Memorandum* (named after the first Transport Minister), which outlined principles and guidelines for action. The guiding principle of the CTP outlined in the Memorandum stated that:

> ... transport undertakings and users should benefit from the advantages of competition (CEC, 1973).

The Memorandum identified four special aspects of the transport sector which hinder normal competition, and the action which was needed to remove or neutralise these effects. These included the high degree of public intervention in the provision of infrastructure; obligation to large traditional public services; complex relationships between transport and other sector objectives; low supply and demand elasticities which (supposedly) led to unstable prices (Gwilliam, 1980, p.48). The Schaus Memorandum was to be a blueprint for transport policy in the European Community for more than a decade. In the following year an Action Programme covering the period up to 1970 was adopted which was to initiate a wide-ranging discussion of options open to the CTP. Its purpose was to ensure that, over a period of time, measures to promote the expansion of the transport market kept in line with measures to organise and harmonise it. The Action Programme had three objectives: liberalisation, harmonisation and organisation.

The first, liberalisation, was to eliminate obstacles which distort the natural functioning of the free market. The second, harmonisation, was to integrate transport activities (technical, fiscal, social) on a community level, for example, weights and dimensions of road vehicles and taxation. The third was the organisation of the transport system with an initial proposal for a forked tariff - a minimum/maximum carrier tariff which a carrier must not exceed (Despicht, 1969, p.48).

During the period 1958-1969 Community institutions outlined non-binding guidelines for the development of a Community Transport Structure. The ambitious aims for parallel measures to liberalise, organise and harmonise the transport market were abandoned. Instead, a number of minor measures were introduced to facilitate transport operation. A comprehensive series of measures were developed to reform gradually the structure of inland transport in the Community. These include steps to harmonise competitive conditions for rationalising railway operations and a new system of allocating infrastructure costs (Despicht 1969, p.56).

Erdmenger (1983, p.11) refers to the period from 1958 to 1973 as the first stage in the development of the CTP, when the EC concentrated efforts on creating a Common Transport market for road, rail and inland waterways towards a common competition oriented market. The lack of guidance in the Treaty of Rome influenced the formulation of the CTP in this first stage. By 1973 Great Britain, Denmark and Ireland had joined the EEC. A number of economic and geographical changes had taken place in the transport sector, which required a further contribution to the CTP in addition to the guidelines set out by the Council in 1965 and 1967. The Paris Summit held in October 1972 emphasised that Community policy should have a human factor and should be directed to regional development and the protection of the environment. On 25 October 1973 an EEC Communication to the Council of Ministers on *Common Transport Policy: Objectives and Programmes* was published and stated (CEC, 1973: paragraph 19) that:

> The efforts which have been made to eliminate impediment to trade and to create a common transport market have not fully succeeded, and the common transport policy is in an impasse.

The Communication expressed a need to move in the direction of closer links with other Community policies (paragraph 28), while at the same time maintaining the special characteristic of the CTP. The main contribution which transport could make to the attainment of the objectives of the Paris Summit was efficiency; operations should take place at the lowest possible cost (paragraph 29). Whitelegg (1979) argues that this belief is based on the assumption that market mechanisms, income and welfare distribution are efficient enough to improve the transport sector. This efficiency is believed to lead to economic growth, the benefits of which would be passed on to all concerned, although this has not always been the case.

The Communication provided further guidelines to organise transport's contribution to the attainment of the objectives which were defined by heads of State and Government at the Paris Summit. The Summit stressed that transport should strengthen the Community by forming an economic and monetary union, thus enabling regional disparities to be reduced by economic expansion and improvements to quality of life, as well as giving special attention to protecting the environment (CEC, 1973, p.11). The Action Programme accompanying the 1973 Communication emphasised the need:

1. To develop an optimal transport network in accordance with an agreed master plan.
2. To calculate the costs of using the transport infrastructure.
3. To define the role of the railways in the future transport system and solve financial problems.
4. To progress in the development of inland transport markets.

(CEC, 1973, Whitelegg, 1988, p.15)

The new Member States influenced the development of a CTP which had been concerned mainly with one or two modes and the competitive nature of transport, rather than with general transport problems on a European scale (Whitelegg, 1988, p.14). The CTP had been surrounded in bureaucracy and red tape associated with fixing of tariffs and cross-frontier movement which stunted the growth of the CTP. Post-1973 developments of the CTP included extending the scope of Community interest to air and maritime modes. Transport began to be considered in a wider context with links to regional, fiscal, industrial, environmental and energy matters.

The creation of a Common Transport Policy involves taking the individual transport systems of Member States and developing them into a Community transport system. This would consist of a common transport system and a common transport market (Erdmenger, 1983, p.16). New infrastructure (for example, high speed train networks) would need to be integrated into existing infrastructure on a European-wide scale. It is therefore necessary to co-ordinate national infrastructure development programmes within a CTP framework. Yet the importance given to different modes varies in each Member State and in part reflects the nature of their transport sector and its contribution to the national economy. The UK and the Netherlands, for example, are dependent on road haulage and may argue that road construction is necessary for access to a European market. To develop infrastructure and

31

remove bottlenecks, the Community has granted financial assistance to projects of Community interest.

The development of the CTP has tended to be slow. This is surprising, given the important role which transport plays in the European economy. Due to the vague nature of the Transport Title in the Treaty of Rome, the Court of Justice has had to intervene a number of times on the basic interpretation of the transport provision stated in the Treaty.

In 1973 the Commission believed a CTP could be achieved over a ten-year period, but this was over-optimistic (Erdmenger, 1983, p.21).

The Commission has implemented a number of Action Programmes, with the first covering the period 1973-1977 as discussed above. In November 1977, another programme was submitted to the Council to cover the period 1978-1980, which listed a number of priorities to be adopted regarding EC transport policy. The Council did not adopt the programme, but took note of the priorities which had been listed. However, in March 1981 the Council adopted the following ten main points for the 1981-1983 work programme (Erdmenger, 1983, p.23):

1. improving the situation of railways;
2. continuing measures to harmonise conditions of competition;
3. implementing measures in the field of transport infrastructure;
4. developing combined forms in transport;
5. facilitating frontier crossing;
6. improving the operation of the transport market, in particular international transport;
7. improving the efficiency and safety of transport;
8. bettering social conditions in the transport field;
9. continuing the work in hand on sea and air transport in accordance with the conclusions reached by the Council at its previous meetings; and
10. solving the problems likely to arise in connection with intra-Community transit via non-member countries.

On 9 March 1982, a decision was taken to extend the programme to run to 1984-1985 which was outlined in the communication: *Progress towards a Common Transport Policy - Inland Transport* on 9 February 1983 (CEC, 1983). The objective which was contained in the Schaus Memorandum and the 1973 Communication, i.e. to achieve an efficient transport system as a crucial part of establishing and further developing a single market, also characterised the 1983 publication.

Difficulties in the development of a CTP can be attributed to two main reasons - the absence of direction and power in the Treaty of Rome and the differences in national policies (Bayliss, 1979, p.31). Bayliss suggests that the failure to organise a wide-reaching CTP has been due to the fact that it was not perceived by Member States as being detrimental to the European ethos. Compromise tended to result in net costs rather than benefits, with Member States regarding their transport policy as appropriate to their own needs in the absence of any 'Grand Design'. However, the development of a CTP has further progressed with the adoption of the 1985 Single European Act and the 1992 Maastricht Treaty

Single European Act

The result of not having a common market has been seen by the EU as creating extra costs both in qualitative and quantitative terms. This would make European business less competitive when compared with its American and Japanese counterparts (European Documentation, 1989, p.15). The achievement of a complete internal market in Europe was an aim of the original treaty. In June 1985 the Commission published a White Paper which outlined a programme to take the final steps towards achieving a Single European Market by 1992. The paper was comprehensive and put forward about 300 legislative proposals for the removal of existing physical, technical and fiscal barriers. In December 1985 the Single European Act was agreed and came into force on 1 July 1987. It contained major amendments to the Treaty of Rome and outlined measures with regard to the establishment and functioning of the Single Market after 1992. It formed the institutional framework for adopting and negotiating the majority of the Single Market legislation. The adoption of the Single European Act reflects the renewed political will of the Community to halt economic fragmentation and to complete, within a given time period, the objectives of the original treaties (European Documentation, 1989, p.6).

The Single European Act outlined the aims of the European Community: to promote a harmonious and balanced development of economic activities throughout the Community, to provide sustainable and non-inflationary growth which protects the environment, and to provide a high level of employment and social protection, enabling improvement in the quality of social and economic life in Member States (CEC, 1992b, p.18).

In 1985 the Court of Justice declared that transport of goods and passengers should be open to all Community firms without discrimination. This decision coincided with the White Paper on CTP. The provision of transport was seen by the Commission as important if other restrictions on the abolition of technical, social, fiscal and customs barriers were to be abolished. Since the adoption of the Single European Act, progress of the CTP has developed quickly to achieve a single market in transport services. It has improved competitiveness, financial performance and efficiency of transport, together with measures to improve the environment as well as provision of a trans-European network to achieve better social and economic cohesion.

The Single European Act has marked an important point in the development of a CTP. This includes the elimination of frontier controls which had previously been enforced by national requirements for hauliers and safety of vehicles. Intra-Community transport had been subject to national 'quotas' which resulted in stringent checks, at national frontiers. These quotas were replaced in 1988 when the Council adopted a quota for the whole Community. In principle, this will enable hauliers to operate freely throughout all the Community without the need for controls at frontiers (European Documentation, 1989, p.36).

European Union

The main Treaty which has further influenced the development of the EU is the Treaty of Political and European Union. The Treaty on European Union was signed on 7 February 1992 in Maastricht, the Netherlands and was seen as providing stability in a fast-changing Europe. In the course of 1992 10 Member States completed the procedures for the ratification of the Maastricht Treaty.

The aims of the European Union contained in the Treaty include:

- promoting stable and lasting economic and social growth through an internal market and economic and monetary union;
- affirming its identity on the international scene through a common defence and security policy;
- protecting the rights and interests of its citizens by establishing a Union citizenship;
- establishing close co-operation in legal and internal security matters;
- maintaining the *acquis communautaire* and adapting the Treaties where necessary to improve their performance; and
- respecting subsidiarity when implementing the Union.

The main aspects of the Treaty include the transition to full economic and monetary union and the creation of a single currency which will bring price stability, the development of a political union which would include EC institutional reform and the launching of a Common Foreign Security Policy and intergovernmental co-operation on justice and home affairs.

The three elements of the EU strategy for the industrial sector include, firstly, liberalisation, which is based on the free movement of goods, people and capital services. The second element is to adopt a five-year Research and Development programme which aims to achieve the Union's Single Market priorities. The third element is technical harmonisation and standardisation, which is also seen as being important for the free movement of goods and services (European Research Associates, 1992, p.55). To achieve an internal market the Union identified a need for creating a European transport network. This would require trans-national co-operation in large infrastructural projects such as the Channel Tunnel and the High Speed Train Network and further research in transport technology such as automatic driving systems, as well as the liberalisation of transport services between and inside Member States, which involves the opening up of markets in road haulage and air transport.

The development of an internal market requires the elimination of obstacles to the free movement of goods, capital, services and people. However, the benefits received from eliminating these obstacles will, according to the Commission, not be optimised if a compatible infrastructure of continental proportions does not exist (CEC, 1989a, p.3). In October 1988 the Commission proposed a Council regulation for an Action Programme in the field of transport infrastructure with a view to the completion of an integrated market in 1992. This was submitted by the Commission to the European Council on 23 June 1988 (COM (88) 340 final). Article 1 of the regulation expressed the Community's commitment to developing EC transport infrastructure within an Action Programme. The programme would eliminate bottlenecks and integrate areas which are geographically landlocked or on the periphery of the Community. This would involve the reduction of transit costs, the improvement of links on land/sea routes and the provision of high quality links to urban areas and high speed rail links. In December 1989 the Commission adopted a Communication entitled *Towards Europe-wide Networks: objectives and possible applications*. The Communication stated that a particular priority should be given to the development of trans-European networks in the areas of transport, energy, telecommunications and training, with a view to inter-operability and inter-connection (CEC, 1989a). On the basis of the Communication, the Council invited the Commission to submit a work programme by the end of 1990. In July 1990 the Commission published a progress report, *Towards Trans-European Networks*. The final Community Action Programme was published on 10 December 1990 (CEC, 1990b).

The need for EU infrastructure is due to four main factors which are related to the development of a single market, firstly, the predicted increase in intra-Community trade unimpeded by physical, technical and fiscal barriers;

secondly, the need for existing infrastructure and services to be interconnected to match new dimensions of the market; thirdly, the increased need for adequate service and quality throughout Europe; fourthly, the need to bring together all elements of the Community into one space (CEC, 1990c, p.6).

Existing European infrastructure has not been designed to cater for large amounts of movements between Member States, which has led to inadequate interconnections. The development of a trans-European network requires 'missing links' to be established and bottlenecks to be resolved. A coherent network throughout the entire Community to ensure optimal use of these networks and the removal of inhibiting national provisions is considered necessary for European harmonisation (CEC, 1990c, p.8). The planning of the networks would be co-ordinated and outlined in coherent master plans.

The Action Programme provides four main lines of action for the development of trans-European networks (CEC, 1990c, p.37, European Research Associates, 1992, p.81):

1. regular establishment of a master plan for trans-European networks transport, energy and telecommunications;
2. annual standardisation programmes to ensure the harmonious development of the trans-European grid;
3. data collection for the evaluation of constraints which inhibit the linking of existing networks and the development of new networks; and
4. execution of feasibility studies to identify projects of European interest.

The contents of the Community Action Programme cover *inter alia* road and rail transport, combined transport, inland waterways, sea shipping and telecommunications and telematic services. For road transport, it identified a number of projects for the interconnection of existing networks which will be subject to financial support from the Community. The road projects include links across the Pyrenees: Toulouse-Madrid and Bordeaux-Valencia and Toulouse to Barcelona via the Puymorens tunnel. To open up peripheral regions, the following projects have been suggested: a road link to Ireland (A5/A55 link between Crewe and Holyhead), a link from Lisbon to Madrid, Brindisi - Patras - Athens. For rail transport, attention has been concentrated on the development of high speed rail links during the period 1990-2010. In the North, high speed links will be developed between Paris-London-Brussels-Amsterdam-Cologne. In the South, links between Seville-Madrid-Barcelona-Lyon-Turin-Milan-Venice will also be developed. For combined transport, the programme supports the implementation of Council Resolution of 12 November 1990 on a European combined transport network, which establishes a coherent pattern of lines and terminals. This work has concentrated mainly on road and railway modes and will be extended to include inland waterway and maritime transport. The Community will give financial priority to the development of a trans-European network. Priority will be given to feasibility studies, loans for projects with long-term operability, contributions to other projects, as well as funding from structural funds, which will also contribute to the development of a Community network. Loans available from the European Investment Bank will facilitate the emergence and development of such initiatives (CEC, 1990c, p.30).

With regard to the environmental aspects of the programme, the Commission aims to establish a long-term comprehensive scheme for multi-modal infrastructure, allowing a shift from one mode to another without technical difficulties. It states that the approach proposed for the trans-European transport and energy networks should in itself make a significant contribution to protecting the environment, by supporting an integrated approach to various modes of transport and energy interconnections at the Community level, which will enable optimum use of the Community infrastructure. The Community acknowledges the environmental impact of transport and provides for the development of different modes as its solution. In terms of the impact of building new transport infrastructure, it refers to the Directive 85/337/EEC on Environment Impact Assessment as providing a framework for decisions to be taken. It also places the responsibility of environmental protection on the local and regional authorities of Member States (CEC, 1990c, p.9).

Master plan on a Trans-European road network

In 1993 the Commission published a Master Plan for the European Network entitled; *Trans-European Networks: Towards a Master Plan for the Road Network and Road Traffic*. This was a response to the Maastricht Treaty which incorporated the principle of master plans for transport networks under the Title XII on Trans-European networks. The development of a master plan would have a number of benefits for society. It would reduce accidents, congestion, pollution and contribute to sustainable mobility. For Europe the master plan would facilitate the Single European Market and contribute to the free movement of goods and people and would strengthen economic and social cohesion and reinforce European competitiveness (CEC, 1993a).

The road network in the European Union is 2,900,000 kilometres long, but does not comprise a uniform system. Table 3.6 shows the average annual growth in motorway traffic from 1985-1989. The largest growth has been in Portugal, Spain and the UK respectively.

Table 3.6
Annual average growth in motorway traffic, 1985-1989
(vehicle kilometres)

Country	% annual average growth
Belgium	10.0%
France	10.0%
Germany	7.4%
Greece	6.0%
Italy	7.0%
Portugal	16.4%
Spain	13.5%
United Kingdom	11.3%

Source: CEC, 1993a, p.19

Growth in traffic could lead to greater congestion on strategic corridors. The Commission states that the average annual Union traffic rate per day could increase from 19,000 to 34,000-44,000 vehicles between 1990 and 2010. Growth on motorways could be even higher, with an increase from 25,000 to between 38,000 and 49,000 vehicles (CEC, 1993a, p.23). The need for some regulation of transport demand is seen as important to ensure the smooth operation of the internal market. The EC believes unrestricted demand could jeopardise the competitiveness of the Union and prevent it from achieving economic and social cohesion. The master plan develops a systematic approach to the European road network and sets out policy on road traffic, modernisation of the network, better recognition of external factors and changes in infrastructure financing.

A Trans-European road network is expected to be achieved by the year 2002. The master plan consists of 54,000 kilometres of new roads in the European network linking major communities, of which 37,000 kilometres were in use on 1 January 1992. A further 12,000 kilometres are expected to be completed or upgraded by the year 2002. The developments will take the form of motorway links or express roads and include work to overcome natural barriers and bypass major European conurbations. Initial estimates of the master plan covering the period 1992-2002 suggest the total cost will be ECU 120 thousand million (CEC, 1993a, p.101). The master plan recognises the need to regulate the demand for transport in order to reduce congestion. It advocates a number of measures to be taken in the short and medium term. In the short-term, it suggests better planning of trips and optimisation of existing capacity. In the medium and long-term, the external cost of transport, such as air pollution, should be internalised and reflected in transport costs. Alternatives should be promoted on congested strategic corridors and on a European level with better management of traffic (CEC, 1993a, p.78).

European environmental policy

The Treaty of Rome did not provide any constitutional basis for policy on environmental protection. The word 'Environment' was not mentioned in the Treaty, although the preamble to the Treaty did state that Member States should make efforts to improve the living and working conditions of their people. Article 2 of the Treaty provided for the development of a common market with improved living standards. The initial environmental measures which were taken by the Community reflected a desire to unify the market and facilitate the movement by removing obstacles to trade, to enable equal competition between companies by standardising environmental legislation (Vandermeersch, 1987, p.40). A number of Directives have been adopted by the European Commission, which have covered all aspects of environmental policy.

The first European Action Programme was adopted by the Community in October 1972 in the same year as the United Nations Conference on the Human Environment in Stockholm. Heads of government met in Paris to set out basic principles for the environment. In the conclusion of the Summit they declared that economic expansion was not an end in itself (European Documentation, 1989, p.7).

The first Action Programme was agreed by the Council of Ministers on 22 November 1973. The programme outlined action which the Commission would take to reduce pollution and nuisance; to improve the natural and urban environment problems caused by the depletion of certain natural resources; to promote awareness of environmental problems and education (Haigh, 1991, p.9). Table 3.7 outlines the Action Programmes on the environment. The second Action Programme ran from 1977-1981, the third programme 1982-1986, the fourth 1987-1992. The Fifth Action Programme, which is the most recent, covers the period 1993-2000.

Table 3.7
EC environmental action programmes

	Time Period	Date approved	OJ Reference
First	1973-6	22.11.73	C112 20.12.73
Second	1977-81	17.05.77	C139 13.06.77
Third	1982-86	7.02.83	C 46 17.02.83
Fourth	1987-92	19.10.87	C328 7.12.87
Fifth	1993-2000	1.02.93	C138 17.05.93

OJ: Official Journal of the Commission of the European Communities

The Community's first two Action Programmes contained a large number of measures, mainly remedial, which were deemed necessary at the European level. The Third Action Programme further developed the principles on which present environmental policy has been based. It was at this stage that the preventative approach became a main part of EU environmental policy. A central theme was the consideration of the environment in the formulation of national and Community policy. Haigh (1991, p.10) lists the main principles which were set out in the first Action Programme and subsequent programmes. These have been updated to include the concept of sustainable development and shared responsibility which are features of the Fifth Action Programme (Table 3.8).

Basis of European environmental policy

European environmental policy has been based on Articles 235 and 100 of the Treaty of Rome. Article 100 provides for the harmonisation of Member State laws, and covers issues which might directly affect the functioning of the common market. However, environmental protection could not be assured on the basis of Article 100 alone, for it excludes any measures which bear no relationship to the function of the common market. Article 235 enabled the Union to regulate in areas which are not contained within the Treaty. This Article was used as a legal basis to enable the Union to regulate over environmental issues which are not related to economic activities. Vandermeersch (1987, p.411) argues that the relationship between certain environmental measures taken by the Union and economic conditions has been tenuous. This reflects the institutional problems faced by an economic community when it wishes to regulate in non-economic areas.

Table 3.8
Principles of EU environmental policy

- Precautionary principle; prevention better than cure.
- Environmental effects should be taken into account at the earliest possible stage in decision-making.
- Exploitation of nature or natural resources which causes significant damage to the ecological balance must be avoided. The natural environment can only absorb pollution to a limited extent. It is an asset which may be used, but not abused.
- The Community and Member States should act together with international organisations in promoting world-wide environmental policy.
- Scientific knowledge should be improved to enable action to be taken.
- The polluter pays principle: the cost of preventing and eliminating nuisances must be borne by the polluter, although some exceptions are allowed.
- Activities carried out in one Member State should not cause deterioration of the environment in another.
- The protection of the environment is a matter for everyone. Education is therefore necessary.
- The principle of appropriate level. In each category of pollution it is necessary to establish level action (e.g. national or local) best suited to the type of pollution and to the zone to be protected.
- National environmental policies must be co-ordinated within the Community, without hampering progress at the national level.
- Principle of shared responsibility, the mixing of actors and instruments at different levels.
- Concept of sustainable development.

The Single European Act amended the Treaty of Rome and inserted a new Title VII 'Environment' in part three of the Treaty. The new provision provides a legal basis for action on the environment and covers numbers 130r-130t, which specifies the objectives of the Union's environmental policy. Article 130r outlines the scope of the action taken by the Union which should preserve, protect and improve the quality of the environment, ensuring rational use of natural resources. At the same time action should be taken to protect human health.

41

Article 2 of the Single European Act is devoted to the EC's aims and also provides a legal basis for EU legislation to take account of environmental aspects. The Article states that:

> ... the Community shall have as its task ... to promote ... a harmonious and balanced development of economic activities ... respecting the environment ...

Table 3.9 below outlines the main articles of the Single European Act which provides the basis for European environmental policy.

Table 3.9
Basis of environmental policy in the Single European Act

Article 3k	The activities of the Community shall include an environmental policy.
Article 130r.2	This policy shall be based on the precautionary principle. Environmental protection requirements must be integrated into the definition and implementation of other Community policies.
Article 3b	The principle of subsidiarity is given special emphasis, and the objective of having decisions taken as closely as possible to the citizens is confirmed (Article A).
Article 130s.5	Environmental policy can impose disproportionate costs on Member States so that the Treaty requires that economic and social costs should be taken into account in the formation of environmental policy.
Article 130r.3	In preparing its policy on the environment, the Community shall take account of the economic and social developments of the Community as a whole and the balanced development of its regions.

Source: CEC, 1992b, p.18; Fleming, 1993, p.2

Green paper on the urban environment

In 1990 the Commission published a Green Paper on the Urban Environment which identified the range of difficulties confronted by the urban conurbations of Europe and set out a strategy for the environment of urban areas. The Paper recognised that the Single Market would accelerate economic activity and the process of internationalisation. This would have consequences for social cohesion, economic functioning and quality of life in cities (CEC, 1990d, p.7). The paper examined three main themes: urban pollution (air, water, soil, noise), built environment (roads, streets, buildings, open spaces) and nature (urban greenery and wildlife).

The actions which the Paper suggested should be taken to improve urban transportation included: encouraging city authorities to co-ordinate public transport, road construction and land use planning; development of research on environmentally friendly vehicles and advanced traffic management schemes; an information exchange throughout the Union on urban traffic management, to maximise the benefits of different experiences; the consideration of financing pilot projects; and the potential use of economic instruments such as road pricing to solve the problems generated by urban traffic (CEC, 1990d, p.46).

Although the Paper identified the problem of urban transportation, the actions which it proposed were mainly providing 'encouragement', rather than taking on action to deal with the different aspects of transport and environment. The transport sector was further considered in the Fifth Environmental Action Programme and in a Green Paper on Sustainable Mobility.

Fifth Environmental Action Programme

The Fifth Environmental Action Programme *Towards Sustainability* was adopted in March 1992. As the title suggests, the central theme of the programme is sustainable development, which it identified as having three characteristics: to maintain the overall quality of life, to maintain continuing access to natural resources, and to avoid lasting environmental damage. The programme has two guiding principles for policy decisions - the Precautionary Approach and Shared Responsibility, which includes effective implementation of the 'Polluter Pays Principle'. The concept of shared responsibility involves the mixing of actors and instruments at appropriate levels from the Community, regional, and local level. The objective is to strike a balance between the short-term benefit of individuals and the long-term benefits for society. The approaches of previous Action Programmes adopted a 'top-down' approach; the Fifth Action Programme emphasised a 'bottom-up' approach. It set out a strategy to create a new interplay between main groups

43

or 'actors' such as government, private and public enterprise and the general public and the principal economic sectors: industry, agriculture, transport and tourism. This strategy would be achieved through an extended and integrated range of instruments, for example, financial support systems, legislation and fiscal measures. For each of the main issues identified in the programme, long-term objectives are stated and performance targets are indicated for the period up to the year 2000, and a range of actions are outlined to achieve the targets.

For the transport sector, the EU has recognised that transport policy can no longer be demand led due to environmental constraints. It suggests that the efficacy and sustainability of transport policy in the future will be in direct proportion to the quality of the relationship between transport and the environment (CEC, 1992a, p.34). A strategy is needed which is aimed at reducing or at least containing the overall impact of transport on the environment. The Commission has developed a strategy to achieve 'sustainable mobility' which was published in a Green Paper in February 1992 and is discussed below. The elements which should be dealt with in the transport sector include cleaner cars and fuels, rationalisation of infrastructure and improved driver behaviour.

The Environmental Action Programme outlines seven themes which will receive special attention; long-term objectives are set out, together with intermediate goals and actions to be implemented in the period up to 2000. The seven themes include climatic change, acidification and air quality and the urban environment.

Climatic change The objective for the climatic change theme is to limit CO_2 emissions to the rate at which they can be naturally absorbed. An initial target is to stabilise CO_2 at 1990 levels by the year 2000, followed by progressive reductions by 2005 and 2010. To achieve this target, action will be required to conserve energy, such as environmentally benign energy use and economic measures, with improvements in energy efficiency and substitution of fuel which emits less CO_2 .

Acidification and air quality The objective for acidification is that the critical loads and levels of air quality should not be exceeded. Air quality objectives include the protection of people against health risks from air pollution and allowable concentrations of air pollution should take account of the protection of the environment. Targets for each pollutant are set out in Table 3.10 below. Action taken to achieve these targets include identifying potential or existing problems, monitoring of air quality and control of concentration levels in relation to norms for substances covered by legislation.

Table 3.10
EU targets for air pollution

Nitrogen oxide	Stabilisation of emissions at 1990 levels by 1994. This target will be extended to a 30% reduction by the year 2000.
Sulphur dioxide	35% reduction by year 2000 compared to 1985 level.
Ammonia	Variable targets in accordance with problems in each region.
Volatile organic compounds	10% reduction of man-made emissions by 1996; 30% reduction by 1999 compared to 1990 levels.
Dioxins	90% reduction of dioxin emissions by 2005 compared to 1985 levels.
Heavy metals	70% reduction from all pathways of cadmium, mercury and lead emissions by 1995.

Source: CEC, 1992a

The urban environment The proposals for the urban environment were outlined in the Green Paper on the Urban Environment. The Action Programme therefore focuses on the single issue of noise. The objective of the programme is that no person should be exposed to noise levels which endanger health and quality of life. The target set for the year 2000 requires noise levels not to exceed 85 dB. There should also be no increase in exposure for the population which is already exposed to levels less than 65 dB. To achieve these targets the Action Programme will be taken to develop an inventory of exposure levels in the EU, reduction in noise emissions, measures to influence behaviour, and measures related to infrastructure and physical planning.

Subsidiarity The Commission attempts in the Fifth Environmental Action Programme to translate the principle of subsidiarity in operational terms. Sustainable development requires a concerted action of all relevant actors. The Programme combines the principle of Subsidiarity with the wider concept of shared responsibility (CEC, 1992a, p.73). A particular problem or target action could be undertaken at a number of different levels. The principle of subsidiarity would allow action to be achieved at the most appropriate level to deal with the problem.

Implementation and enforcement To overcome the problems which have hindered the implementation of previous Action Programmes the Commission proposed a number of reforms. These included better preparation of measures, including improved consultation arrangements, more effective integration with complementary measures, better practical follow-up to legislative measures (both administrative and operative), and stricter compliance checking and enforcement (CEC, 1992a, p.75). To implement these reforms the Commission intends to establish a consultative forum or implementation network with representatives of national authorities and an Environment Policy Review Group with representatives of the Commission and Member States. These different groups will enable the promotion of greater responsibility.

The Fifth Action Programme has acknowledged the deterioration in the environment. Within the Union the success of an internal market and economic and monetary union is dependent on the sustainability of policies which are pursued in a number of sectors. The programme has realised the importance of taking action at a number of different levels. For transport, the programme is in accord with the strategy for sustainable mobility which is discussed below.

Sustainable mobility

Action taken to reduce the impact of transport has mainly been in the form of technical fixes. The First Action Programme on the environment included measures to reduce noise and gaseous emissions from motor vehicles and action to reduce marine pollution resulting from sea transport. The second programme included further measures to reduce noise from motor vehicles, motor cycles and aircraft. The third programme emphasised the need for greater concern of the environmental effects of transport. Priority was given to vehicle emissions, aircraft noise and the environmental impact assessment of infrastructure projects. However, it was not until the Fourth Action Programme 1987-1992 that the wide ranging effects of transport on the environment was recognised (CEC, 1992c, p.3). In February 1992 the European Commission produced a Green Paper on *Sustainable Mobility*. It was seen as the next logical step in the growing concern about the environmental impact of transport and its contribution to global environmental issues such as climatic change and acid rain. The aim of the Paper was:

> ... to initiate debate on the issue of transport and the environment and the proposed strategy for sustainable mobility.

The Paper provided an assessment of the overall environmental impact of transport. It presented a common strategy for sustainable mobility which would enable transport to fulfil its economic and social role while containing its environmental impact.

The Paper supported a global approach to developing a strategy to deal with transport and environment. It stated that:

> Transport is never environmentally neutral ... existing trends indicate that transport and traffic, particularly in the road sector, will continue to grow over the next decades and that the demand for transport services, all things being equal, will increase; the impact of transport on the environment will become more significant. It is, therefore, essential that the Community adopt a Common Strategy, which aims to reduce or at least contain the overall impact of transport on the environment in a global and coherent manner (CEC, 1992d, p.22).

The strategy promotes sustainable mobility by integrating transport into an overall pattern of sustainable development. Yet the Paper fails to define formally what constitutes sustainable mobility. In the Paper the Commission states that protection of the environment cannot be achieved by technological progress and technical measures alone. It outlines four initiatives:

1. standardisation to ensure greater environmental performance (e.g. limit standards for air and noise quality, weights and standards of HGVs);
2. market organisation to eliminate distortions and to achieve better utilisation of existing transport capacity (e.g. access to intra-Community road haulage and road passenger transport, limited cabotage in the road sector);
3. cost-charging measures to take account of the external costs of transport (e.g. the introduction of a 'Carbon Tax' and higher vehicle taxation); and
4. research initiatives to eliminate any distortion of competition while encouraging a shift to more environmentally friendly modes of transport (e.g. introduction of traffic management schemes and use of fiscal and economic instrument to influence choice in favour of clean technology).

Although the Community has recognised a need to deal with the transport sector in a coherent and global approach, no framework exists for a common strategy aimed at sustainable development. The Green Paper presented a number of initiatives required for such a framework. These included adopting a whole range of measures for stricter environmental standards for different transport modes and stricter air quality standards and an overall action plan for the transport of dangerous goods, which will enable goods to be carried in the safest possible manner. The Paper also proposed the preparation of guidelines on a range of things such as the development and assessment of community infrastructure projects which would discourage unnecessary transport demand and encourage development of alternatives to roads. Guidelines were proposed for the conversion and upgrading of relinquished infrastructure, the

47

development of urban transport, tourism, Community research programmes which promote the development of 'clean' technology together with information campaigns on the rational use of the car. The framework proposed by the Commission should:

> ... contain the impact of transport on the environment, while allowing transport to continue to fulfil its economic and social function, particularly in the context of a single market, and ensure the long-term development of transport in the Community ... (CEC, 1992d).

The EU acknowledges the importance of the environment and the impact of transport. However, EU policy is based on economic efficiency and the formation of a single market. This means adopting a policy which encourages greater movement of transport and distribution of goods, at the same time protecting the environment.

Environmental impact of the Single European Market

The European Commission's Task Force on the Environment and the Internal Market (CEC, 1990a) predicted that the environmental impact of transport would be one of the most significant effects of the SEM, due to the expected increase in passenger vehicle and road freight traffic. The removal of barriers within Europe would stimulate competition and reduce costs of production through economies of scale. Harmonisation of excises and taxes may result in a fall in fuel prices and the price of motor vehicles in some countries. Transport activity will be further stimulated by the following factors:

- liberalisation of transport services;
- projected decline in car prices;
- removal of barriers affecting the road freight industry; and
- higher incomes and increased demand which have resulted from economic growth in the transport sector.

The Task Force estimated that the SEM will lead to an increase of transfrontier lorry traffic of 30-50%. This growth will have an impact on the environment along strategic transport corridors within the EU. The increase in passenger vehicle kilometres will lead to a higher level of emissions of nitrogen oxides and non-methane hydrocarbons. Table 3.11 shows the predicted emissions of these two pollutants from passenger vehicles in the year 2000.

These predictions are based on an average growth of vehicle kilometres of 2% and 2.5%, which is a difference of more than 10% in the emissions of each pollutant (CEC, 1990a, p.3.16).

Table 3.11
Emissions of NO$_x$ and non-methane hydrocarbons from passenger vehicles in the EC in the year 2000 (Kt/year)

Pollutant	Average growth rate in vehicle kilometrage travelled (% per year)		
	2%	2.5%	% difference
Nitrogen oxides	2835	3140	10.8
Non-methane hydrocarbons	1073	1190	10.9

The completion of an internal market without barriers will inevitably lead to an increase in transport activity. The transport sector, as identified by the Commission's Task Force, will therefore be an important problem to resolve within the European Union.

Towards a common transport policy

The advent of the single market has provided an important turning point for the development of a European Transport Policy. The removal of barriers to trade and the elimination of technical, social and fiscal barriers have been designed to optimise the efficiency of the European transport system. The Maastricht Treaty on European Union has provided a new impetus to the development of a Common European Transport Policy. However, increased growth in demand and the creation of a larger European transport sector will have significant implications on the European environment. The main challenges lie in resolving the conflicting aims of economic growth and environmental protection. It is against this backdrop that the Commission published a White Paper on Community transport policy on 2 December 1992 entitled *The Future Development of the Common Transport Policy* (CEC, 1992b). Although the idea of a CTP has existed for over 36 years, the fact that the White Paper has been prepared after the Single European Act means that it has to have an environmental and social dimension.

The Paper outlines a new policy for European Transport based on sustainable mobility and is in line with the principle of subsidiarity. It is divided into three main sections which examine the completion and functioning of the internal market, eliminating barriers to effective integration and strengthening the external dimension of the CTP. Paragraph 20 recognises the environmental effects of transport and states that:

> The effects on transport of the economic and technological developments over the last two decades have exacerbated the areas of conflict between transport and the environment. These areas of conflict take the form of energy consumption, operational pollution, land-intrusion, congestion and risks inherent to the carriage of dangerous goods (CEC, 1992b, p.12).

Paragraphs 23 and 28 are of particular importance, with paragraph 23 stating that in a 'business as usual' scenario the transport sector is likely to be responsible for a 24.6% increase in energy consumption and CO_2 emissions between 1990 and 2000, while Paragraph 28 states that:

> ... forecasts of growth in transport demand show that in a 'business as usual' scenario with a reasonably favourable economic climate the expansion of the road sector is likely to be buoyant. Under these conditions, a doubling of road transport demand for both passengers and freight seems likely. Although technological progress and measures already taken will mitigate the environmental impact, in the absence of additional policy actions significant worsening of the situation is still likely as regards pollution, notably CO_2 emissions, congestion and accidents. Even if lower economic growth slows the rate of deterioration for a time, the risk of the development of the transport sector being unsustainable in the medium to long-term due to its broad environmental impact remains real (CEC, 1992b, p.15).

The White Paper recognises the implications transport has for the environment and emphasises the importance of transport for economic performance and the integration of the European Union. A fine balance is needed between sufficient transport on the one hand and too much transport on the other, ensuring minimal environmental impact. As Article 2 of the Maastricht Treaty states, the objective of the EC is to achieve 'harmonious and balanced development of economic activities, sustainable and non-inflationary growth respecting the environment'. The incompatibility of economic activities and environmental protection is one of intense debate and some critics have argued that it is impossible to resolve these conflicting interests due to the overriding importance given to economy. Whitelegg (1993, p.147) states that:

EC environmental policy has clearly taken second place to single market policies. The publication of grandiose road construction plans and associated funding mechanism in 1992 before the publication of the transport White Paper demonstrates the primary importance of transport infrastructure arguments and the relative insignificance of both environmental arguments and a balanced transport policy. Quite clearly 'sustainable mobility' does not encompass any diminution of road building nor any weakening of economic growth imperatives.

In its attempt to resolve the transport and environment conflict the EC has promoted the concept of sustainable mobility but fails to define this clearly in its White Paper. Paragraph 36 (CEC, 1992b) provides some indication and states that:

> The development of the CTP has ... to respond to wider issues of depletion of natural resources and environmental degradation at the global level ... (the) Fifth Environmental Action Programme ... has identified the importance of the integration of environment and resources issues into sectoral policies. The transport sector is of particular importance in this respect. For example, the greenhouse effect linked directly to energy use and CO_2 emissions is without question of paramount importance. The Community has itself clear targets for CO_2 stabilisation and the transport sector is a key actor in the efforts necessary to achieve a stabilisation target of 1990 levels by the year 2000.

Given that the EU has set targets on CO_2 emissions and has stated in paragraph 23 that the transport sector contribution is likely to increase, T&E (1992, p.4) argue that the EC has committed itself to rejecting the 'business as usual' scenario. If taken with paragraph 28 which recognises the future growth of the transport sector, the logical conclusion is that a strategy to reduce pollution from the transport sector which goes beyond simply technical fixes is inevitable.

The Union, however, is also committed to strengthening greater social and economic cohesion, especially reducing the disparities between the poorer countries and rest of the EU. To achieve this the White Paper states:

> ... the provision of transport infrastructure, including projects within assisted areas and the development of trans-European networks, should be carefully planned in order to remove imbalances and secure effective mobility (CEC, 1992b, p.18).

It goes on to say that transport efficiency requires the development of trans-European transport networks and that individuals and businesses should have access to means of mobility which meets their needs and expectations. At the same time, transport systems must contribute to the protection of the environment and, in particular, to the solution of major environmental threats such as the greenhouse effect and to the achievement of sustainable development (CEC, 1992b, p.19). The White Paper recognises the challenge it has to face and states in paragraph 92 that:

> The challenge for the Community's transport system is how to provide, in the most efficient manner, the services that are necessary for the continued success of the single market and the mobility of the individual traveller, while continuing success to reduce the inefficiencies and imbalances of the system and safeguarding against the harmful effects that increased transport activities generate. It is possible to meet this challenge, while respecting the basic tenets of the free market, by the introduction of economically efficient transport policies (CEC, 1992b, p.36).

Action programme

The White Paper sets out an Action Programme for the future development of a Common Transport Policy covering the period 1993-1994. The programme has five main components which cover the development and integration of the Community's transport systems on the basis of the internal market; safety, environmental protection; a social dimension, and external relations.

The programme sets out further measures for liberalisation and harmonisation of activities in the internal market. These include measures to liberalise civil aviation, cross-border taxi transport, vehicle hire, and certain specialised international transport operations and services e.g. security transport. Further action is proposed in the rail sector to establish criteria for access to and charging of infrastructure. Paragraph 345 focuses on the internalisation of external costs of transport and states that:

> ... the main emphasis will be on the development of a Community framework for the charging of infrastructure and other costs to users. Such a framework is the essential foundation for the realisation of the objective of sustainable mobility for the Community as a whole (CEC, 1992b;104).

The introduction of such costs would proceed in stages. In the short-term a framework for the imputation of infrastructure costs would be developed.

In the medium-term, proposals will need to be made with regard to the charging of externalities, so that environmental problems will be addressed by the economic mechanism.

Paragraphs 368-372 of the White Paper concern the development of Trans-European networks. Strategic networks for each mode of transport will be developed on a Community-wide basis, including the development of a High Speed Train network. Paragraph 369 states:

> The existing networks will be further developed and complemented. The environmental aspect of road network will be given particular attention as will the need for improved mobility to benefit the Community's peripheral and more isolated regions.

The section on the environment (paragraphs 381-383) states that stringent standards of environmental protection will need to be taken to cover gaseous emissions, energy consumption and noise emissions for different modes of transport. Strategic Environmental Assessment will become an integral part of the decision-making process for transport infrastructure on policies, plans and programmes (paragraph 383). The White Paper fails to address in the Action Programme the main issue of reducing the volume of traffic. As discussed above, the Commission has recognised the difficulty faced in achieving CO_2 targets and the need to address demand. The demand side of the transport equation however, is not given priority in the Commission's Action programme. Instead emphasis is placed on the development of technical fixes and stricter standards.

The European dilemma

The development of what today is known as the European Union began as a purely economic entity. The Treaty of Rome was concerned with the removal of trade barriers to improve competition and the notion of a Common Transport Policy was based on the economic foundations of harmonisation and liberalisation. Transport was, and still is, seen as a means to an end and not an end in itself. Transport growth has been equated with economic growth, a theory which has been universally accepted. EU policy on CTP maintains this belief in paragraph 157 (CEC, 1992b) which states that:

> The transport sector as a whole nevertheless emphasises the key contribution of transport to economic growth as well as economic and social cohesion in the Community.

The failure to develop a CTP has been due to a number of reasons, such as the vagueness of 'transport' in the Treaty of Rome and the differing national transport systems throughout the Union. Each country has developed a transport system which meets its own needs and has given importance to particular modes. It is with these differing transport systems that the EU attempts to develop a Common Transport Policy. The development of a CTP has tended to be slow. The Single European Act and the Treaty on European Union have had new implications for the development of a the CTP. The formation of a Single European Market has brought the issue of transport to the fore, with the need to allow for the free movement of goods and services, and people.

The development of an internal market will inevitably promote greater mobility throughout the Union and, if the SEM successfully develops, it may lead to greater centralisation of particular services in other European countries. This will require goods to be transported over greater distances which will be damaging for the environment.

European policy on transport and the environment reflects the difficulties which are being faced in other countries at the national level. The fundamental problem faced in attempting to resolve the majority of environmental issues is the environment and development debate, i.e. the need to maintain economic growth and minimise the impact on the environment. The concept of sustainable development has attempted to provide guidance to resolve these conflicting interests and was adopted internationally at UNCED. However, the European Commission has developed a schizophrenic approach in its policy on transport and the environment. This has been illustrated to some extent in this Chapter, which has examined the main documents on transport and the environment in Europe. On the environmental side, the Commission has recognised the impact which transport has on the environment in the Green Papers on the Urban Environment, Sustainable Mobility and the Fifth Environmental Action Programme and the White Paper on a CTP. In these policy documents the EC has outlined a number of measures which can be taken to reduce the environmental impact of transport and regulate the demand for transport. These have included optimal use of existing infrastructure, stricter air quality standards, internalisation of the external costs of transport, promotion of better public transport systems and greater co-ordination between land use and transport planning. The EU is clearly aware of the impact which present trends in traffic growth will have on the environment and of the urgency to take action to resolve this problem. The European Commission is in a position to stimulate general improvements in standards and practices within the transport sector on a European-wide level.

Despite this concern in the Maastricht Treaty, the White Paper on a CTP and the Master Plan on Trans-European road networks the European Union has emphasised transport infrastructure and economic growth in a way that conflicts with environmental objectives. In the Trans-European road network Master Plan the EU has advocated the building of 54,000 kilometres of new road to ensure greater economic and social cohesion. The completion of 'missing links' and the removal of natural barriers are given priority in the development of the SEM. The SEM is expected to result in an increase in the volume and type of different transport modes. The harmonisation of taxes on such things as motor vehicles will result in a reduction in the total cost of transport. This in effect contradicts the measures proposed by the EC to internalise the external costs of transport, which will require the cost of transport to increase rather than fall (CEC, 1990a).

The EC has promoted the notion of sustainable mobility, yet fails to define clearly what this actually means, although a partial definition in the White Paper (paragraph 123) suggests that sustainable mobility is efficient, safe transport under the best environmental and social conditions. The SEM is based on free movement and encourages mobility, which, if undertaken by one of the main forms of transport such as road, is in the long-term unsustainable. The challenge is to strike a balance between meeting an individual's need to travel and ensuring minimal damage to the environment. The SEM encourages greater mobility over a wide geographical space. It can be argued that this contradicts concern for environmental protection.

The extent to which the European Commission can influence and affect trends in traffic growth is dependent on the type of transport. The EC is in a position to influence freight transport via taxation, transportation standards and regulations. The extent to which it can influence public transport is less clear. Most urban transport tends to meet local needs, with the majority of trips being less than 5 kilometres. Local initiatives are more likely to be effective in identifying local traffic problems and devising appropriate solutions. The effectiveness of local initiatives has been illustrated in cities such as York and Cambridge in Britain and Delft and Groningen in the Netherlands (see Chapter 4). The principle of subsidiarity, which leaves the primary responsibility and decision-making to the competence of a lower level authority, will be most effective in the case or urban transport. However, EC policy can influence local transport conditions via grandiose programmes such as Trans-European Network or the funding of infrastructure under other EC initiatives for urban regeneration.

The European Union provides the policy framework for the 15 Members States. The aim of this book is to examine the differences between the national transport and environmental policies of two Member States within this European framework.

It will delineate the main difficulties faced in attempting to achieve a sustainable transport system. The next two chapters will examine the approaches taken to transport and the environment at the national level in Great Britain and the Netherlands, which have been chosen to provide examples of contrasting approaches. The Netherlands has gained an international reputation for its transport and environmental policy and has been held up as an example of best practice. In contrast, the British government has been criticised for lacking a coherent transport policy and for its overemphasis on road transport, which has taken the form of numerous road programmes. The different approaches to transport and the environment at the national and local level will be examined in each of the two countries.

4 The road to ruin

The evolution of post-war transport policy in Britain has been dogged by political ideology and influenced by the power of different lobbying groups. The result has been a set of disjointed policies, which have lacked a strategic approach to providing an efficient and sustainable transport system. Britain does not have a strategic transport policy covering all modes. Instead, transport policy has tended to be developed *ad hoc* rather than by a process of strategic planning. Policy has been 'road centric' to the detriment of other less polluting modes, and has been demand driven, with little attention given to demand management measures. There has also been a lack of integration of transport policy with other policies, such as environment and land use, which has partly been a result of the institutional structure of government departments.

The UK government's commitment to the agreements made at UNCED and the increasing number of environment-related Directives from the European Commission has meant a greater effort is being made to achieve a life style which is within the carrying capacity of the environment. Recent UK policy developments have now begun to consider transport in a wider context. The White Paper outlining the UK's Environmental Strategy (1990) and the UK Sustainable Development Plan (1994) have both acknowledged the need to reduce the demand for travel. The Royal Commission on Environmental Pollution (1994) examined the issue of transport and the environment and made a number of recommendations for action to be taken and targets to be adopted, in order to achieve a sustainable transport system. In 1994 the Standing Advisory Committee on Trunk Road Assessment provided evidence to show that induced traffic has contributed to the failure of road schemes to achieve their objectives. The past four years have seen a new awareness developing in government thinking, which recognises the contribution which land use and transport planning can make towards reducing travel patterns.

The aim of this Chapter is to examine the development of British transport and environmental policy and the extent to which it has been developing towards sustainability. It will provide an assessment of conflicts which still exist in British transport policy despite the government's recent commitments.

Transport and the environment in Britain

Transport in Britain has grown significantly over the past twenty years, with motor vehicles and personal car use having the largest growth. This has bestowed greater freedom and mobility on a large sector of society. Figure 4.1 illustrates the magnitude of this growth compared with other less polluting modes, such as rail and buses.

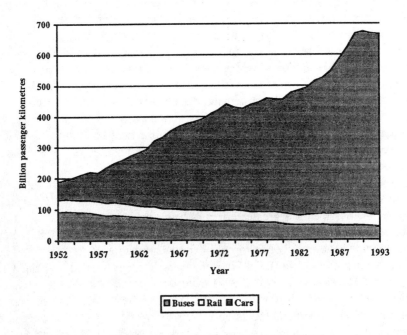

Figure 4.1 Growth in transport in Britain (1952-1993)

Source: DOT, 1993a

Transport is expected to increase by 84-142% from 1989-2010, as outlined in the 1989 Road Traffic Forecasts. Traffic growth will have significant environmental implications, for transport is considered to be the fastest growing sector for carbon dioxide emissions and energy consumption. In 1991 road transport in Britain was responsible for 89% of carbon monoxide emissions, 3% of sulphur dioxide emissions and 21% of carbon dioxide emissions, 46% of volatile organic compounds and 52% of nitrogen oxides emissions (DOE, 1992a). The transport sector accounts for 32% of all energy used by final users in Britain (DOT, 1993a, p.58). Given present traffic forecasts, it is estimated that transport will be responsible for 36% of the UK's energy consumption by the year 2000 (CPRE, 1992a, p.14).

Traffic growth will have implications for air quality. This poses a significant threat to human health and has been linked with respiratory diseases such as asthma and general ill health (Whitelegg et al., 1993). The growth of road-based transport has been a product of government policy over the past forty years, which has tended to favour the motor vehicle and investment in roads over other less polluting modes of transport.

The development of British transport policy

The end of the Second World War saw the Labour Party governing Britain from 1945-1951 with policies directed towards greater state control, regulation of the economy and social welfare. Labour's programme included the nationalisation of railways, road haulage, inland waterways and air transport which was outlined in the 1947 Transport Act. Nationalisation was acknowledged as a political issue as early as 1913, when a Royal Commission was established to investigate its implementation. The outbreak of the First World War led to nationalisation being abandoned until 1947. The nationalisation of transport was seen as providing greater efficiency and co-ordination between each mode, enabling transport to play a central role in the rebuilding of post-War Britain (Barde & Button, 1990, p.41). The 1947 Transport Act transferred the services of railways, canals and road haulage to a newly formed British Transport Commission, creating a federal, rather than a unitary, administration for transport, with each mode having a supporting executive.

In 1946 the road lobby, led by the British Road Federation (BRF), campaigned for the building of a motorway network in Britain. This was adopted by Labour and was seen as complementing their plan of changing the regional balance of employment. However, due to the prevailing poor economic climate, choices on capital investment had to be made. Road plans were postponed while capital was directed to other developments such as the creation of 'new towns' (Starkie, 1982, p.8).

The introduction of motorways in Britain began when the Conservatives came to power in 1951. The change in the economy had provided a favourable climate for greater car ownership. This period saw a rapid growth in traffic on roads from 2.2 million in the 1930s to more than 9 million in 1964 (Starkie, 1982, p.11). The government made a commitment to road investment in the 1953 Transport Act. As well as abolishing the executives created in 1947, the Act returned direct control over road haulage back to the private sector (Bell & Cloke, 1990, p.34). The British Transport Commission became no more than an umbrella organisation for each transport service. In July 1957 five major transport projects were announced: the M1/M6 from London to Birmingham and the North-West, the M2 and M20, the M5, M30 route from Birmingham to South Wales, the M4 from London to South Wales and the comprehensive improvement of the A1 (CPRE, 1992a, p.20).

The 'Motorway Age' was born when the Preston bypass was formally opened in December 1958. This was followed in November 1959 by the M1, which was to become the first long stretch of inter-urban highway. The economic benefits derived from increasing the quality of roads were outlined in a cost-benefit analysis which was greatly welcomed at the time. Campaigning by the road lobby led the British Road Federation to hold a conference on 'Urban Motorways' in 1956, with the objective of creating a network of inter-urban motorways rather than simply a few new roads (CPRE, 1992b, p.24). The government went on to make a further commitment to a five-year rolling road programme to achieve 1,610 kilometres of motorway (Starkie, 1982, p.18). McKay and Cox (1979, p.166) argue that this period was characterised by relative inactivity on the part of the government in other areas of urban transport. Past ideas of integrating transport services were fading, while the Conservatives dismantled the regulations of the 1940s. By the mid 1950s, the building of new roads was seen as a solution to the urban transport problem. This may have been due to underestimating the growth of traffic at the time, for by the end of the decade there was increasing traffic on the roads of Britain. The increase in traffic growth led the incumbent Minister of Transport, Ernest Marples, to aim to squeeze the maximum amount of traffic from existing roads. Marples saw rail as an uneconomic, secondary and duplicate means of transport (Henshaw, 1991, p.117). This led to plans to rationalise the railways and the publication in 1963 of the Beeching Report *The Reshaping of British Railways* following which a significant number of rail lines were closed.

In the early Sixties, inter-urban road building was seen as a solution to increasing car ownership and traffic growth. The 1963 *Traffic in Towns* report, undertaken by a Committee led by Colin Buchanan, focused on land use and transport. The Committee examined the long-term effects of road developments and traffic on the urban environment and warned about the effects of increasing car ownership (McKay & Cox, 1979, p.167). The report has now been seen as a fundamental publication on the impact of the motor vehicle on society. While acknowledging the benefits of motor vehicles, it also identified the negative impacts of noise, visual intrusion and accidents. The report stated that:

> ... the motor vehicle is a beneficial invention with an assured future, largely on account of the great advantages it offers for a door-to-door travel and transport. There is enormous potential demand for its services, and we think a constructive approach to the problem of accommodating it in towns and cities is both required and justified (DOT, 1963, p.191).

The Committee concluded that there was little prospect of a serious alternative to the car emerging. Vehicle numbers were growing at a fast rate and were expected to double within ten years. The report suggested the design of 'compact towns' and cities, based on the principle of 'circulation' to service environmental areas. Based on this principle, rules regarding the pattern, size and character of distributing highways were outlined. The report was accepted in principle by Parliament, with both the Conservative and Labour parties supporting car ownership and the notion of adapting cities to cars. In 1964 the Smeed Report introduced the idea of road pricing for the first time. The report argued that individuals should be charged for the congestion which they cause. Although the economic arguments were accepted, the possibility was rejected for technical reasons, given the unreliability of metering systems and the cost of implementation (Bannister, 1991).

In response to the increasing pressure of car ownership and congestion, greater state involvement was seen as desirable. In 1966 the Labour Party produced a White Paper on *Transport Policy*. It was seen as a first attempt in British policy-making to develop a more integrated transport system. As well as recognising the need for the expansion and investment in roads, small-scale traffic management was encouraged for local authorities. A year later in 1967 another White Paper on *Public Transport and Traffic* was published which outlined the role of public transport. Labour's concern for the co-ordination and integration of transport led to the 1968 Transport Act, which resulted in the creation of passenger transport authorities for major urban conurbations to develop greater integration and co-ordination of transport policy. After local government reorganisation, capital and revenue investment was made available, making possible a more integrated approach to transport (McKay & Cox, 1979, p.173). Investment in roads continued, with the government, in 1969, reaffirming the objectives over the next five years. The 1970 White Paper on *Roads for the Future* outlined a £4,600 million (at 1970 prices) programme over a 15-20 year period. The programme had the broad objective of checking and eliminating congestion on trunk roads and directing long distance traffic from towns and villages (Bannister, 1991).

The 1960s also saw the rise of the environmental movement and concern for the environment becoming a political issue. An increase in the membership of environmental societies took place, such as the Conservation Society whose membership increased from 1,200 in 1969 to 6,474 in 1976, and the National Trust whose membership increased from 176,970 in 1969 to 548,457 in 1976 (Sandbach, 1980, p.11).

The Seventies

By the early Seventies, a number of new environmental pressure groups were formed such as Friends of the Earth (1970) and Transport 2000 (1973) which, among other things, began campaigning against the construction of new roads. Local groups were set up to protest against new road schemes, for example the London Motoring Action Group and the London Amenity and Transport Association. Environmental concern led to the creation of the Department of the Environment and the passing of important environmental legislation such as the Disposal of Poisonous Waste Act (1972), the Water Act (1973), Nature Conservancy Act (1973), and Control of Pollution Act (1974). Environmental awareness, which began to develop in the late Sixties, led to growing opposition to road building in the Seventies, which has continued and increased to the present day.

After being returned to power in 1970, the Conservatives were faced with increasing resistance to urban road building, which resulted in substantial cutbacks being introduced in 1973. An Urban Motorway Committee had been set up in June 1969 due to growing pressure against road building. Its remit was to examine current policies for major roads through urban areas (Starkie, 1982, p.80). In July 1972 the Committee produced a report *New Roads in Towns* which *inter alia* suggested changes in the power of highway authorities to acquire land adjacent to new roads. At the same time, another report was published which reviewed land compensation aspects of road construction. Together they formed a contribution to the 1973 Land Compensation Act. Under the Act compensation was payable where land had depreciated in value due to physical factors such as noise, vibration and fumes.

In December 1972 the House of Commons Expenditure Committee expressed the need to move away from investment in roads to better management of existing resources. This was a boost to the anti-road lobby, which had been campaigning against increased expenditure on roads. New road schemes were stopped and more restrictive management techniques were introduced, as well as the promotion of public transport (McKay & Cox, 1979, p.178). By 1973 there was general opposition to the unlimited use of cars. The 1973 White Paper on *Urban Transport Planning* documents the change in thinking towards transport which took place at this time.

Despite the advances made in transport policy by 1977, there still appeared to be an absence of a proper framework for the co-ordination of public transport, both at national and local levels. The 1977 White Paper on *Transport Policy* suggested more could be done to shift freight from road to rail and to restrict the use of the car with the objective of achieving an efficient transport system (HMSO, 1977, p.1). The paper concluded that more support should be given to public transport and less to road building with greater responsibility being given to planning to meet local needs. It also proposed a drastic reduction in road expenditure together with a small cut in public transport.

Growing scepticism over methods used in trunk road assessment resulted in a review of trunk road decision-making. The Public Inquiry acted as a forum where debates on road building were normally held. The government, however, maintained that a public inquiry could not question public policy on roads or the traffic forecasts made to justify schemes (Bannister, 1991). Dissatisfaction with the procedure culminated in the government setting up a committee in 1976 led by George Leitch, to review trunk road assessment.

On 14 October 1977 the report of the Committee was published and recommended a shift in emphasis from the traditional Cost Benefit Analysis (CBA) to a more comprehensive approach which included social and environmental factors in the assessment of trunk road schemes, as well as the use of a more accurate forecasting model with a better indication of the likely uncertainties involved in forecasting. In 1979 further concern over the environmental impact of lorries resulted in the formation of a committee headed by Sir Arthur Armitage to consider the causes and consequences of growth in the movement of freight by road (HMSO, 1980). In December 1980 the report of the enquiry, *Lorries, People and the Environment* was published. Among its conclusions it suggested an improvement in the safety of lorries and a reduction in noise and vibration. It recommended that heavier lorries should be allowed a maximum gross weight of 44 tonnes, with a variety of axle configurations to distribute load. However, the anti-road lobby managed to block industry's pressures for an increase in gross weight and dimension of goods vehicles. The average size of heavy lorries on roads and loads carried continued to grow (Starkie, 1982, p.114).

The Eighties

In 1979 the Conservatives were returned to power, led by Margaret Thatcher, who implemented policies based on monetarism: strict control of the money supply and free market economics. The government promoted less state intervention, privatisation and competition to achieve greater efficiency (Bell & Cloke, 1990, p.138). Prior to 1979 an increasingly planned, co-ordinated and regulated system of public transport had been developing. The 1980 Transport Act weakened the linkage between each mode and gave further priority to roads. The government saw the solution to the urban transport problem as the removal of unnecessary constraints allowing direct competition. The Act was followed by a White Paper in 1984, which set out the approach for the 1985 Transport Act. This contained four provisions allowing greater deregulation, which included splitting the National Bus Company into 72 constituent companies ready to be sold in the private sector (Bell & Cloke, 1990, p.43-4). After deregulation more bus kilometres were operated while passengers numbers fell (Truelove, 1992, p.65).

With regard to trunk road assessment, the Leitch Committee Report led to CBA being extended to include monetary and non-monetary values. In 1983 the *Manual for Environmental Appraisal* was published, which defined a particular type of framework to be used for trunk road schemes. It outlined the essential elements involved in this framework and provided advice on appropriate methods for assessing environmental effects important in route selection.

In 1989 the government published its White Paper *Roads for Prosperity* in which it planned a greatly expanded programme of motorway and trunk roads to relieve congestion between cities and towns (DOT, 1989a). The government expressed its concern over the increasing traffic on roads (especially on motorways) which had increased by 33% since 1980. It invested in a £23 billion programme to widen existing roads and build new ones. Objectives of previous programmes were maintained - to assist economic growth, and reduce transport costs, and to improve the environment by removing traffic from unsuitable roads in towns and villages and enhance road safety.

A second wave of environmentalism gained momentum in the 1980s, characterised by green consumerism, ethical investment and greater activism from pressure groups such as Friends of the Earth and Greenpeace. At the same time, the environmental disasters of Bhopal and Chernobyl heightened awareness of human impact on the environment. The 1980s also saw the European Commission playing a greater role in the formation of environmental policies directed towards transport. A large number of Directives were adopted covering the areas of air pollution, noise, weight of lorries and Environmental Impact Assessment.

The UK government responded to the climate of environmental awareness by taking steps to improve its environmental credentials. In September 1989 the Government published a progress report on the implementation of sustainable development entitled *Sustaining Our Common Future*. The report was offered as a contribution to the Ministerial Conference held in Bergen, Norway in May 1990 on Sustainable Development. It outlined initiatives to implement sustainable development in a wide range of sectors. For the Transport Sector two policy aims were outlined. The first was to support international efforts to reduce the effects of transport on the environment, especially vehicle emissions such as CO_2, to mitigate pollution and the impact of global warming. The second policy aim involved minimising adverse environmental impacts in the choice of location and alignment of road schemes and applying landscape treatment to reconcile the line of a road with the pattern of the area through which it passes (DOE, 1989, p.24) To achieve these aims, eight measures were outlined which the government had taken. These included the planting of over a million trees and shrubs along trunk roads each year and the design of motorway verges to provide linear nature reserves for a wider variety of species of flora and fauna.

The Nineties - a new realism

In 1990, Britain's first environmental strategy, *This Common Inheritance,* was published, in which the government further stated its support for sustainable development. Since 1990 the government has taken a number of environmental initiatives which it outlined in the White Paper. In January 1991 the report on *The Potential Effects of Climate Change in the United Kingdom* examined the implications of transport for global warming (DOE, 1991a). This was followed by *Policy Appraisal and the Environment* (DOE, 1991b) which provided a guide for civil servants, to increase the awareness within government of the need to examine environmental impacts. The guide offered a systematic approach to the consideration of environmental issues within policy appraisal. This was followed by another report in 1994 *Environmental Appraisal in Government Departments,* which examined the application of environmental appraisal in different sectors (DOE, 1994a).

The 1993 Railway Act outlined plans for the privatisation of British Rail. This has meant separating the responsibility for land, track, stations, signalling and other rail infrastructure from the train operator. The operation of infrastructure, stations and operational land is now the responsibility of 'Railtrack'. The remainder of British Rail is divided into subsidiary companies which will be sold to the private sector. The rolling stock of British Rail will be placed under the control of leasing companies, which will lease it back to train operators. To control and regulate the new rail structure two regulators have been appointed. The first will control rail bodies, including Railtrack, and will license all operators, arbitrate in disputes and be responsible for the application of competition legislation. The second regulator will control the operation of services and franchises, specifying minimum services and controlling the price of fares (RCEP, 1994, p.220).

In August 1993 the government announced a review of the Trunk Roads Programme, which was subsequently published in March 1994 (DOT, 1994a). The government considered that there was a need for a review to provide a clear and manageable work programme for a new Highways Agency, which was established on 1 April 1994, as well as the prioritisation of schemes to speed up delivery. The Highways Agency is responsible for the management of the trunk roads network and the delivery of capital schemes, and is accountable to the Secretary of State for Transport. Of the 371 schemes which were examined in the Trunk Road Review, 22% were given 'Priority 1' and 47% were given 'Priority 2', while 19% were judged not to be needed until later in the programme; preparatory work will therefore be suspended. The remaining 13% of schemes were either withdrawn from the programme on environmental grounds or because they were unlikely to be progressed for the foreseeable future. Additional studies for major routes and corridors were also withdrawn. However, there was little change in the overall scale and nature of the roads programme (RCEP, 1994:84).

Confusion over transport policy

Post-war transport policy in Britain has overemphasised the use of motor vehicles, which in turn has resulted in the provision of roads to meet the insatiable desire for car ownership, and increasing traffic. There has been a distinct absence of a coherent policy, with the benefits of less polluting modes of transport being under emphasised. This has resulted in a transport system which has an over-dependence on roads as a means of transporting passengers and freight.

In essence, the government's policy towards transport is highly contradictory and confusion exists on what actually constitutes Britain's transport policy today. The government has acknowledged that growth in vehicle use should be reduced and it has suggested measures that could be implemented to help reduce the growth in traffic. Until recently, the government was intent on continuing with a £23 billion roads programme which would further encourage travel by car. The privatisation of British Rail has been seen by critics as a step further away from encouraging people to use rail rather than road. The lack of a clear direction from the government reflects the complex nature of the transport sector, and the strong influence of the road lobby and other government departments in influencing transport policy.

What is Britain's transport policy today?

Britain has no single document which outlines a strategic plan to cover all modes of transport. What do exist are a number of White Papers on Roads and government expenditure plans. The failure to develop a coherent transport policy and the present day bias to roads has been a result of a number of factors. Transport policy in Britain has very few explicit objectives and targets and has failed to be integrated sufficiently with other environmental and land use policies. This has partly been a result of the institutional structure of the Departments of Transport and Environment, while the financial assessment of transport has tended to be in favour of roads, to the detriment of rail. The procedure for assessing the environmental impact of transport projects has also failed to give full consideration to the wider implications of further road construction schemes.

Objectives and targets

The government has set out a number of objectives for each mode of transport in its transport expenditure plans for 1993-4 to 1995-6. The strategic aims of the Secretary of State for Transport are to achieve a transport market that is efficient and competitive, which serve the interests of the economy and community with a greater emphasis on environment and road safety.

Road The objectives for road transport are to assist economic growth by reducing transport costs, and to conserve and improve the environment by striking a balance between environmental loss associated with construction of new roads and the derived benefits. The government has encouraged the construction of bypasses to remove traffic from unsuitable roads in towns and villages. In 1987-1993 a total of 85 bypasses were constructed in England to relieve congestion in urban centres (DOT, 1993b, p.54). Other objectives include maintaining and managing the road network in a cost effective manner while making the best use of the existing network. To enhance road safety the government has encouraged the construction of safer roads, improving safety of vehicles and encouraging better driver and road user behaviour. In 1987 the government adopted a target of reducing casualties by one third by the year 2000, compared with the average from 1981-1985. Despite a 40% increase in traffic at the end of 1991, fatalities had fallen by 18.4%, serious injuries by 30.8% and all casualties by 3.3%, compared with the average in 1981. To meet the target fully by the year 2000 the total number of casualties needs to fall by a further 30% (DOT, 1993b, p.49).

Public transport The role of the private sector in the provision of public transport has increased over the past 14 years. The Channel Tunnel, Manchester's Metrolink, taxis, car hire services, British Rail are now all within the private sector.

The aims for public transport include, where necessary, addressing the deficiencies of the market in transport provision, to improve efficiency, extend choice and increase the contribution of the private sector by deregulating the public transport sector and to enable the users of public transport to travel safely, efficiently and reliably. The government recognises the contribution which public transport can make in reducing the impact of transport on the environment. One of its aims involves promoting:

> ... public transport's contribution to the maintenance and improvement of the environment and the reduction of road congestion (DOT, 1993b, p.67).

Land use planning

The absence of a coherent transport policy in Britain has been partly due to the lack of integration of transport policy with land use and environmental policy. The absence of policy integration has been a result of the institutional structure and the relationship between the Department of Transport and the Department of Environment. In the past land use planning has tended to have little effect on transport programmes. The failure to develop a responsive inter-departmental relationship has resulted in policies being pursued which have encouraged greater use of the motor vehicle.

Land use planning has important implications for energy consumption and environmental sustainability. Travel and transport developments have interacted to allow significant land use changes. The result has been the development of more energy-intensive land use and activity patterns. The link between land use planning and transport was recognised as early as the 1960s in the Buchanan Report, in which Buchanan predicted the effect the motor vehicle would have on urban centres and the need for the compact development of towns. Land use planning has been shaped by the increasing dominance of the motor vehicle as the main mode of transport. Developments have tended to become more decentralised, moving to the urban fringe with a boom in the number of out-of-town developments e.g. the Metro Shopping Centre in Gateshead, Meadowhall in Sheffield and large business complexes and housing estates. These developments have tended to accommodate the car user, with few facilities for public transport. There has also been more commuting into town for work in the past decade, with a 6% increase in the population of remote rural areas (DOE, 1994b, p.78). This has been to the detriment of inner city centres, which have been seen as less attractive locations. Policy has failed to deal with increasing road traffic while the lack of integration of land use and transport planning has resulted in a situation where land use developments generate traffic. The absence of policy to restrict traffic growth has led to new developments locating in unsuitable places (CPRE, 1992a, p.21).

A change in the government's approach towards land use and transport was seen in the 1990 White Paper *This Common Inheritance*. In February 1992 the DOE published *Planning Policy Guidance on Development Plans and Regional Planning* (PPG12) in which it stated how planning could contribute to the attainment of sustainable development. PPG12 encourages local planning authorities to pursue policies which promote the use of public transport in identifying areas for new or intensified development. PPG12 provides a checklist of issues which local planning authorities should consider in the formulation of land use policies (DOE, 1992b):

1. development that makes full and effective use of land within existing urban areas without amounting to 'town cramming';
2. development that is closely related to public transport networks - for example, near existing railway stations with spare capacity;
3. location of new development types that *attract* trips (for example, office employment, shopping, higher education, and leisure) at points such as town centres which are capable of acting as nodes for public transport networks, to avoid encouraging substantial increase in car use; and where there may be advantages in enabling one journey to serve purposes;
4. housing (which by contrast to (3) *generates* trips) that is located in such a way as to minimise car use for journeys to work, school and to other local facilities;

5. limitations (by capacity or price) on town centre parking, whether public or as part of other developments, provided that does not encourage development in more energy inefficient locations elsewhere;
6. appropriate interchange opportunities between major public transport networks; and
7. positive encouragement of facilities to assist walking and cycling.

As a result of the White Paper, the Department of the Environment also published a report in 1993 on *Reducing Transport Emissions Through Planning* (DOE, 1993), which examined the extent to which land use planning could contribute to reducing demand to travel, and hence carbon dioxide emissions. The study concluded that planning policies in combination with transport measures could reduce projected transport emissions by 16% over a 20-year period. A 10-15% saving in the use of fuel, and hence emissions from passenger transport, might be achieved through land use changes at the city region scale over a 25-year period (DOE, 1993).

Despite previous separation of transport and land use planning the government is now making attempts to encourage and integrate these in practice. This change in the government's approach to land use and transport planning was further outlined in the 1994 UK Sustainable Development Plan, where the government again emphasised the necessity to minimise the need to travel. The scope for reducing travel is dependent on the size and density of a range of services which are offered in urban areas and are served by public transport as well as local centres within walking distance. The Plan states that:

Local facilities need to be more accessible by a choice of means of transport, with more emphasis on short trips being undertaken by foot and bike (DOE, 1994c, p.62).

New industrial and commercial developments will now be encouraged to locate near to public transport facilities in urban centres rather than on the periphery thus discouraging car use.

In March 1994 the government published further planning policy guidance (PPG13) on transport to meet the commitments made in the Sustainable Development Plan (DOE, 1994b). The guidance aims to ensure that local authorities co-ordinate land use policies and transport programmes, to reduce growth in the number and length of motorised journeys and to encourage alternative modes of transport which have a lower impact on the environment, and thus reduce reliance on private car use.

PPG13 encourages local authorities to implement a form of location policy which requires developments to be sited at places near adequate transport facilities, thus ensuring a greater use of public transport. The guidance promotes a number of transport measures to encourage use of less polluting modes such as walking, cycling and public transport. PPG13 encourages development of urban centres as opposed to peripheral development, by improving the attractiveness and competitiveness of such centres. Measures include restricting the availability of parking, especially for locations which are adequately served by other modes of transport, and for peripheral commercial development which may disadvantage urban centres. The use of parking charges to restrict use and encourage use of other modes, the provision of facilities for pedestrians and cyclists, traffic management and park and ride schemes are all included in the guidance.

Economic assessment of transport

Road construction is seen by the government as contributing to economic growth and has been a main objective of the roads programme. Transport investment has tended to be biased towards roads, with road investment being based on cost-benefit analysis while rail investment has been based on a commercial approach. The modes of transport differ, in that roads and the highway system are provided by the public sector, with the cost of owning, maintaining and operating vehicles met by users. Rail networks have, until recently, been owned solely by British Rail. Each mode of transport is considered by the government as serving different markets with rail making a large number of inter-urban journeys from point to point. Roads have been considered more effective for short distances and rural, cross-country as well as inter-urban journeys. The Department of Transport believes rail and road projects are rarely in practice close substitutes (DOT, 1992a).

Road

Cost-benefit analysis attempts to quantify and place a monetary value on the costs and benefits associated with a road scheme. It estimates the benefits (e.g. savings in travel time) from a new travel facility and compares them with the cost of provision. For example, scheme preparation, land acquisition, construction and maintenance.

To assess the economic impacts of road development the DOT developed a computer program called COBA, which is based on the principle of cost-benefit analysis. The economic costs and benefits which may be derived from the proposed road are compared with the existing network ('Do-nothing'), or with slight modifications ('Do-minimum'). The main variables incorporated within the COBA program include: valuation of travelling time, valuation of accidents, vehicle operating costs, construction and preparation costs, cost of maintenance and discounting. The costs and benefits of the scheme are assessed in monetary terms over a 30-year period and discounted at 8% in real terms. The Net Present Value (NPV) measures the contribution the scheme makes to national economic benefits (DOT, 1992a).

The main construction and capital costs of implementing a road project are *inter alia* due to the costs of surveys, designs, administration and site supervision, acquisition of land to construct the scheme and compensation costs due to severance, noise nuisance, costs of construction and maintenance of infrastructure. To predict the possible delays to traffic during construction, the DOT developed a computer model called QUADRO (QUeues and Delays at ROadworks), which calculates delays and consequences for vehicle operating costs and accidents (IHT, 1987, p.101).

Rail

Assessment of rail schemes has been partly based on commercial criteria. Prior to privatisation British Rail comprised commercial railway (Intercity, freight, parcels and international services). A financial appraisal was undertaken for new rail projects where each project is required to earn an 8% financial rate of return, when compared with the option of withdrawal from the service. Grant supported railway included Network South East and the Regional Railways, London Underground and Docklands Light Railway. Projects for maintaining grant supported services were appraised on the cost-effectiveness of the project, based on the policy requirement that service continues to operate at present levels. Additional cost of improvement was appraised on a financial basis with external benefits taken into account where necessary (DOT, 1992a, p.9). New rail schemes may be eligible for government Section 56 grants (e.g. light rail schemes). These projects are based on financial appraisal as well as CBA for external benefits. New schemes in urban networks may be additionally appraised to full cost-benefit analysis which covers benefits to users and non-users.

In response to the criticism that economic appraisal of road and rail favours road over railways, the DOT claims that different approaches are needed, for in general there is little substitutability between new roads and railways at the level of individual projects. Economic assessment procedures are therefore needed which are appropriate for a particular mode. The bias towards roads has tended to be dismissed by the government and critics believe that roads do not deliver the predicted benefits. The DOT states that for every £1 invested in roads £2.50 worth of benefits are produced. This accounts for a 20% per annum rate of return. These figures, however, do not include environmental benefits or environmental costs due to the bias of CBA (CPRE, 1992a, p.35).

The 1992 SACTRA report examined the economic evaluation of roads and recommended a number of changes, these are discussed further in Chapter 6.

Privatisation of rail may result in greater efficiency and more sensitivity to the demands of the customer. However, if operators concentrate solely on the most lucrative routes, other less lucrative, more socially needed routes may be threatened. Whatever the effects rail privatisation will have on passenger travel, the main objective should be to encourage rail travel rather than discourage it.

Towards sustainable transport in Britain

In response to Agenda 21's call for national government to implement sustainability into practice, the government published its Strategy for Sustainable Development (1994) which covers a 20-year period. The plan builds on the 1990 White Paper, which outlined Britain's environmental strategy and initiatives which the government plans to take in a number of areas related to transport.

To achieve sustainability within the transport sector, economic and social needs should be met without placing an unacceptable burden on the environment. The plan defines sustainable transport policy as one which:

- strikes the right balance between serving economic development and protecting the environment and future ability to sustain quality of life;
- provides for the economic and social needs for access with less need for travel;
- takes measures which reduce the environmental impact of transport and influence the rate of traffic growth; and
- ensures that users pay the full social and environmental cost of their transport decisions, so improving the efficiency of those decisions for the economy as a whole and bringing environmental benefits.

(DOE, 1994c, p.173)

The government recognises that an attempt should be made to reduce the need to travel by the adoption of policies which influence the rate of traffic growth, increase economic efficiency of transport decisions, improve the design of vehicles to minimise impact and provide a framework for individual choice in transport which meets environmental objectives. The measures outlined by the government which are capable of meeting these goals include the internalisation of transport's external costs, land use planning which reduces the need to travel (PPG12, PPG13), market measures to improve the environmental performance of transport and policies and programmes which promote the use of more sustainable modes of transport such as rail and water, especially for freight transport.

The government is now starting to consider transport in a wider environmental context, with the Sustainability Plan outlining steps which the government is taking or plans to take. These include increasing fuel duty by at least 5% a year to reflect external costs of transport and to meet the CO_2 target. Local authorities are being given the power to manage the demand for transport by land use planning and encouraging more sustainable travel, and to develop appropriate demand management programmes. The government has also recognised the need to undertake a strategic environmental assessment of transport programmes.

The government states that the DOT and DOE should work together to increase the understanding of the interaction between transport and environment and to develop policy. The government as a whole should take action to reduce the environmental impact of transport and influence the rate of traffic growth. Local government must undertake measures to tackle transport and land use issues in their areas. In order to do this, they will need to develop sustainable strategies for transport planning and to manage the demand for transport, and to develop clear environmental targets and criteria (DOE, 1994c, p.170).

Air quality

To improve air quality further progress should be taken in the area of acid emissions, photochemical pollution and urban air quality. The main issues identified by the government for sustainability include ensuring that the framework of international targets and programmes based on critical loads operate effectively to limit acid emissions (DOE, 1994c, p.49).

The kind of measures which the government is considering to reduce transport's share of carbon dioxide emissions, in addition to those already stated, include increasing the cost of fuels, incentives for efficiency in choice and use of vehicles, and road pricing, which will increase the marginal cost of transport to the user reflecting the wider costs and improving fuel efficiency of the motor industry (DOE, 1994d, p.70).

Land use

In the field of town and country planning the government aims to shape new development patterns to minimise the use of energy consumed in travel between dispersed development. It is now advocating planning which encourages more compact development, enabling lower energy consumption, by providing a range of services at city centres, which are easily accessible by public transport, as well as at local centres, which are accessible by foot and bicycle (DOE, 1994c, p.161). Industrial and commercial facilities will be located near public transport facilities and near inter-urban transport infrastructure.

The Royal Commission on Environmental Pollution

In 1994 the Royal Commission on Environmental Pollution (RCEP) published its Eighteenth Report on Transport and the Environment. The Commission outlined the main components of an environmentally sustainable transport system and set out clear objectives and recommended, where possible, quantifiable targets. The objectives and targets recommended by the Commission are listed in Table 4.1.

Local government

In order to achieve sustainability in practice, a number of initiatives outlined in the UK Sustainable Development Strategy need to be implemented at the local level. This is where local government will need to play an important role. A number of local authorities have tended to be visionaries in developing their policies on transport and the environment. The Greater London Council (GLC) introduced a number of successful transport initiatives, while Kirklees Council was one of the first local authorities in Britain to produce a state of the environment report and environmental strategy. With the adoption of Agenda 21 local authorities are beginning to take an even greater lead towards developing sustainable policies and practices, sometimes in sharp contrast to national policy.

Under the 1990 Environmental Protection Act local authorities were assigned extra responsibilities for the environment in the areas of air pollution and clearance and control of litter. With these extra responsibilities and increased environmental awareness, local authorities have taken initiatives to develop environmental strategies. These have frequently involved an assessment of policies and practices and the environmental impact they cause in the form of environmental audits, which comprise state of the environment reports and environmental strategies (Haq, 1991). Since UNCED local authorities have begun to take action to implement local Agenda 21.

Structure & local plans

The 1971 Town and Country Planning Act (TCPA) introduced a two-tier system of structure plans and local plans for counties outside metropolitan counties. The 1990 TCPA replaced the 1971 act outlining the main requirements for planning control. Structure plans are written statements which formulate the local planning authority's policy and general proposals in respect of the development and other use of land in the area of the plan. These include measures for the improvement of the physical environment and traffic management. Structure plans set out the main transport strategies and proposals for the county. Policies contained within structure plans may influence private sector proposals for siting new developments near particular transport facilities. Structure plans are subject to approval and amendment by central government, which can have important implications (Truelove, 1992, p.36). Local plans are written statements containing proposals for the development of land use within the area of the local planning authority. They contain a map and illustrations outlining proposals for a particular area. In metropolitan districts the Unitary Development Plan contains both the structure and local plans.

Transport policies and programmes

The Secretary of State for Transport requires all local highway authorities in England to submit to the Department of Transport, on an annual basis, a document containing their Transport Policies and Programmes (TPP). The four aims of the TPP are to facilitate the development of comprehensive transport plans, to eliminate bias between capital and revenue expenditure on transport, to reflect local needs and to reduce government control. The TPP covers a much shorter time period than a structure plan. The bid includes capital expenditure on roads, public transport, road maintenance, safety and public transport revenue support. The document contains a detailed bid for central government to cover a five-year period. The main function of TPPs are to provide the government with information on local highway authorities' proposed plans for highway capital expenditure. This will then form the basis on which Annual Capital Guidelines, Supplementary Credit Approvals and Transport Supplementary Grants are distributed among authorities. Local authorities make their bids in July and, after consideration and detailed justification for planned expenditure, the Secretary of State for Transport announces his decision in December of the same year.

Table 4.1
Objectives and targets for a sustainable transport system

Integrated policy: Objective
To ensure that an effective transport policy at all levels of government is integrated with land use policy and gives priority to minimising the need for transport and increasing the proportion of trips made by environmentally less damaging modes.
Air quality: Objective
To achieve standards for air quality that will prevent damage to human health and the environment.   • To achieve full compliance by 2005 with World Health Organisation health-based air quality guidelines for transport related pollutants.   • To establish in appropriate areas by 2005 local air quality standards based on critical levels required to protect sensitive ecosystems.
Quality of life: Objective
To improve the quality of life, particularly in towns and cities, by reducing the dominance of cars and lorries and providing alternative means of access.
Noise: Objective
To reduce the noise nuisance from transport.   • To reduce daytime exposure to road and rail noise to not more than 65 dBL Aeq. 16h at the external walls of housings.   • To reduce night-time exposure to road and rail noise to not more than 59 dBL Aeq.8h at the external walls of housing.
Use of Materials: Objective
To reduce substantially the demands which transport infrastructure and the vehicle industry place on non-renewable materials.   • To increase the proportion by weight of scrapped vehicles which is recycled, or used for energy generation, from 77% at present to 85% by 2002 and 95% by 2015.   • To increase the proportion of vehicle tyres recycled, or used for energy generation, from less than a third at present to 90% by 2015.   • To double the proportion of recycled material used in road construction and reconstruction by 2005, and double it again by 2015.
Carbon dioxide emissions: Objective
To reduce carbon dioxide emissions from transport.   • To reduce emissions of carbon dioxide from surface transport in 2020 to no more than 80% of the 1990 level.   • To limit emissions of carbon dioxide from surface transport in 2000 to the 1990 level.   • To increase by 40% the average fuel efficiency of new cars sold in the UK between 1990 and 2005, that of new light goods vehicles by 20%, and that of new heavy duty vehicles by 10%.

Table 4.1 (continued)
Objectives and targets for a sustainable transport system

Land use: Objective
To halt any loss of land to transport infrastructure in areas of conservation, or cultural, scenic or amenity value unless the use of the land for that purpose has been shown to be the best environmental option.
Promoting less polluting modes of transport: Objective
To increase the proportion of personal travel and freight transport by environmentally less damaging modes and to make the best use of existing infrastructure.
Personal transport: To increase the proportion of passenger-kilometres carried by public transport from 12% to 20% by 2005 and 30% by 2020. Freight transport: To increase the proportion of tonne kilometres carried by rail from 6.5% in 1993 to 10% by 2000 and 20% by 2010. To increase the proportion of tonne kilometres carried out by water from 25% in 1993 to 30% by 2000, and at least maintain that share thereafter.
Reducing the dominance of motor traffic: objective
To improve the quality of life, particularly in towns and cities, by reducing the dominance of cars and lorries and providing alternative means of access.
Reducing the dominance of motor traffic: To reduce the proportion of urban journeys undertaken by car from 50% in the London area to 45% by 2000 and 35% by 2020, and from 65% in other urban areas to 60% by 2000 and 50% by 2020. Cycling: To increase cycle use to 10% of all urban journeys by 2005, compared to 2.5% now, and seek further increases thereafter on the basis of targets to be set by the government.
Accidents: To reduce pedestrian deaths from 2.2 per 100,000 population to not more than 1.5 per 100,000 population by 2000, and cyclist deaths from 4.1 per 100 million kilometres cycled to no more than 2 per 100 million kilometres cycled by the same date.

Source: RCEP, 1994

The Transport Supplementary Grant (TSG) is the main grant towards the cost of capital expenditure on local authority transport, including roads programmes. The government requires local authorities to carry out capital expenditure improvements, including traffic management measures. TSG is calculated at a rate of 50% of total net expenditure and is paid in four quarterly instalments during each financial year. The TSG is paid as a block to authorities, who are told the amount of expenditure that has been accepted for specific schemes (costing over £1m) and for local safety schemes and structural maintenance. Other funding for local authorities is derived from a combination of other grants, borrowing, capital receipts and revenue. The authority borrowing limit is based on the sum of its basic credit approval (BCA) and supplementary credit approval (SCA). SCA is a credit approval which may be used only to help finance a scheme or be used for the purpose for which it was specifically intended. In some cases SCA is allocated for 50% of the authority's TSG accepted expenditure. Besides the TSG the Department provides annual capital guidelines (ACGs) for each service provided by the local authority as allocated by government departments. The ACGs are then added together by the Department of the Environment which deducts an amount which reflects the authority's ability to finance expenditure for capital receipts. The total of ACGs, less the deduction, is the authority's basic credit approval (DOT, 1991a).

In April 1993 the DOT published a Circular on *Transport Policies and Programmes Submissions for 1994/5* which outlined a 'package approach', providing a more comprehensive assessment of transport needs. This approach differed from previous years which tended to stress roads. Instead the Circular encourages transport infrastructure in general, and a shift from private to public transport and demand management strategies. Local authorities are now invited to submit strategies for urban areas covering roads, public transport, traffic management and parking. Transport Supplementary Grants in the past have only been allocated to highway projects and were not allowed for light rail schemes. Alternative sources were required such as SCA or Section 56 grant. With the package approach, there is parallel appraisal of road building, traffic restraint and public transport options. TSG and Section 56 grants are concentrated on schemes over £2 million with other expenditure met by credit approvals. Local authorities are also expected to outline alternative methods which have been considered for alleviating conditions compared with road building. Public transport proposals for which funds can be allocated include new railway and bus strategies, heavy and light rail schemes in urban areas, bus priority measures and guided buses (LTT, 1993, p.12).

In addition to policy on transport outlined in Structure plans and TPPs, local authorities have been publishing other documents outlining their transport strategies. In 1991 the Association of County Councils published a document entitled *Towards a Sustainable Transport Policy*, in which it outlined a six-point strategy for transport. This strategy was later revised and updated in 1994.

The majority of local transport strategies have adopted similar measures to deal with the transport problem. In London some initiatives have been in response to the *London Assessment Studies* which were initiated in 1984 by the DOT to resolve transport problems within four areas of London. The studies proposed a number of road schemes for the different areas. The studies were criticised for their emphasis on road, with an inadequate emphasis on public transport, and for their failure to provide a comprehensive study and analysis of the problem. This led to the councils of Haringey (1990) and Wandsworth (1989) to propose alternative strategies. Virtually all the schemes proposed by the Assessment Studies were dropped by the then Secretary of State for Transport, Cecil Parkinson, as a result of effective campaigning by local authorities and interest groups (Bainbridge, 1992, p.80).

A number of Scottish local authorities (Central Region, 1993; Lothian Region, n.d.) have formulated transport strategies while English local authorities include, for example, Leeds (1990), Southampton (1992), Nottingham and the Black Country authorities. These local authorities have identified the need to co-ordinate land use and transport planning measures to curb car use, such as parking restrictions, traffic calming, park and ride and the greater use of rail for the transportation of freight. Alternative, less polluting modes of transport have been encouraged, such as walking and cycling, with greater provision of safe pedestrian and cycling facilities. Investment in public transport has been seen by local authorities to encourage a reduction in car use. Manchester has been one of the first cities to introduce light rail, followed by plans in Croydon, Leeds, Sheffield, and interest in a number of large conurbations (Knowles, 1992, p.107). The new 'package approach' adopted by the DOT will now make it easier for local authorities to implement more comprehensive transport strategies which they have been developing.

The increasing domination of urban centres by the motor vehicle is a problem which is also being addressed on a European-wide scale and beyond. In March 1994 a *Car Free City Club* sponsored by the EU was launched in Amsterdam, a city which is making progress to 'ban the car' from its centre (these initiatives will be further discussed in Chapter 5). The Club encourages urban sustainable mobility and allows exchange of experience and information between European cities. The aims of the Club are in accordance with Agenda 21, and the EC Fifth Environmental Action Programme. The British cities which joined the club included Aberdeen, Birmingham, Doncaster, Edinburgh, Leeds and Nottingham.

Assessing Britain's transport policy

Since the 1950s British transport policy has been mono-modal in its approach, with the motor vehicle dominating the direction and emphasis of policy. Land use planning has developed to accommodate towns and cities to the increasing use of the motor vehicle. Despite two attempts to develop an integrated transport policy in Britain by the Labour Party, in 1966 and 1977, a fully integrated transport system has failed to materialise. Transport policy has tended to be disjointed and has developed in a piecemeal fashion according to the political beliefs of changing governments, which have been influenced by a powerful road lobby and to some extent by the environmental lobby.

Despite the predictions of the Buchanan Report in 1963 on traffic in towns, no strategy has been developed to halt the popularity of the motor vehicle. Policies have been pursued which have encouraged the use of motor vehicles and have alienated individuals from other modes. The structure of society and the physical design of towns and cities have been geared to greater use of the motor vehicle. Sustainable modes of transport such as walking and cycling have been threatened by the dominance of motor vehicles in cities and the poor investment in the provision of necessary infrastructure. Post-war transport policy in Britain has followed an unsustainable path which has resulted in ever-increasing amounts of pollution and energy use; a policy which has destroyed the physical and social fabric of cities and towns in its quest to accommodate the car.

The late 1980s and early 1990s have seen a new realism or enlightenment in government thinking on transport and the environment. A number of policy initiatives have been taken by the government. These were first outlined in the 1990 Environmental Strategy, which recognised the contribution land use could make to reducing the need to travel. As discussed earlier, the government undertook a study to examine the potential for reducing CO_2 emissions from land use planning and has provided guidance in the form of PPG12 and PPG13 to local authorities. The result of UNCED led to widespread adoption of sustainable development and the publication of the UK Sustainable Development Plan, which further emphasised a reduction in the need to travel and outlined a range of measures which could be implemented. Due to increasing opposition from environmental groups to the £23 billion roads programme, the government published its 1994 Trunk Roads Review. The Review shelved a third of planned schemes and there was a change in the Government's long-standing belief that roads should be built to accommodate traffic growth.

A number of schemes were dropped for environmental reasons, although some schemes were given priority because of their strategic importance. The review is considered not to have gone far enough in redressing the balance between the different transport modes - road is still the dominant mode.

In some cases local authorities in Britain have tended to be in the vanguard when it comes to developing more sustainable policies and practices. The GLC developed a reputation for its transport initiatives, with a number of local authorities now developing environmental strategies especially with the aim to implement local Agenda 21. The new 'package approach' has to some extent given local authorities the ability to finance a more integrated and comprehensive transport strategy which had in the past been mainly dominated by the funding of road schemes.

There are an increasing number of policy statements outlining government concern for rising traffic growth and the necessity to manage the need to travel. The government, however, has failed to set definite targets. Targets provide a tangible commitment to take action to curb the increasing growth of traffic. They set specific end points to which policy should be directed and enable evaluation to be undertaken to assess progress. The Royal Commission on Environmental Pollution's report on transport attempt to provide targets for a number of areas related to transport. The UK Sustainable Development Plan acknowledged the need to set environmental quality objectives and targets to guide policy, which should be based on sound science and cost-benefit analysis (DOE, 1994c, p.16). Yet the Plan set very few national targets for transport and other environmental media. Britain still has no single document that provides a strategic approach to transport and covers all modes. To gain an understanding of British transport policy it is necessary to examine a wide range of policy documents ranging from White Papers on the roads programme and environmental strategies to transport expenditure plans.

In February 1995 the former Secretary of State (SoS) for Transport, Brian Mawhinney, gave a speech on transport and the environment in which he responded to calls for the adoption of targets in British transport policy. He suggested that the setting of targets, such as those proposed in the RCEP report on transport and the environment, could only be useful if the changes in practice required to meet the targets are clearly outlined. He stated that:

... in the area of transport we cannot rely solely on forcing people to change their behaviour. At least in part they would need to be persuaded (DOT, 1995).

In his discussion of targets he covered the following three points which give an indication of the government's view on the adoption of targets in transport policy:

1. If targets were adopted, they would need to be the right ones, for example, it is not clear that targets which increase the use of public transport would be the best way of reducing the environmental impact of transport. A target therefore would need to be as close as possible to the impact with which it was concerned and be based on thorough examination of benefits, costs and practicality.
2. Although transport is an important and growing source of carbon dioxide emissions this does not justify a carbon dioxide target for the transport sector. The Secretary of State believes that this would result in choices for individuals being constrained. The adoption of such a target for the transport sector would also have a high economic impact.
3. Finally, targets would need to be achievable. There would be no point in setting targets which cannot be achieved.

The SoS stated that:

... setting demand targets would carry the risk of failing to meet them - a problem which my Dutch counterparts are now facing.

The view of the government on target setting is to some extent ambiguous. Although it acknowledges the benefit of targets (see quote below), it seems to be unable to make a commitment to long-term targets for the different aspects of transport to reduce its impact on the environment (DOT, 1995).

Targets for reducing traffic - and other types of targets - could be helpful not simply to Government and local authorities in assessing the effectiveness of their policies. They could also be helpful to businesses, who would be able to judge more clearly whether their decisions on transporting goods and locating factories or offices were tending to help or hinder wider objectives.

What the government will achieve in practice can only be judged over time. It is easy to publish policy statements on what should be done and which kind of action should be taken but it is more difficult to be committed to achieving specific targets. British transport policy has awakened to the concept of developing a more sustainable transport system. It requires, however, a greater number of changes to make up for the increasingly unsustainable path which has been followed over the past 45 years. This could be achieved by making a commitment to specific targets for the different aspects of transport which affect the environment. The next Chapter will examine the approach taken by the Netherlands towards transport and the environment.

5 Going Dutch

The Netherlands is considered to be one of the leading transport and distribution countries in Europe. A high quality transport network, which ensures the future economic development of the country and maintains the position of the Netherlands within Europe is of great importance to the Dutch. Increasing mobility as a result of economic growth and urban expansion has meant greater distances travelled, especially to the work place, with trips within city boundaries increasing. A 70% increase in car use is expected by 2010 compared with 1986 (from 75 billion vehicle kilometres to about 120 billion vehicles kilometres), while the number of cars in the Netherlands is expected to increase from the current 5 million to between 6-7 million by 2010, together with a 70-80% increase in freight traffic on roads. Traffic growth has been a result of greater affluence and mobility and the consequent effects of growth in international road haulage (VROM, 1989a, p.194).

The response of the Dutch government to increasing traffic growth has been to develop a transport policy which is co-ordinated with other policies to deal with the different aspects of the transport problem.

The Dutch have made considerable progress towards defining sustainability, setting ambitious targets and taking measures within the environmental field, and have gained an international reputation for their ideas and approach to environmental management. The comprehensiveness and detail provided in Dutch national policy plans for different sectors is well known. However, the Dutch are faced with the problem of maintaining environmentally damaging transport activities within environmental limits without incurring economic losses.

The Dutch approach to transport and the environment has tended to be based on explicit objectives, targets and direct measures, providing a contrast to the approach in Britain which has been discussed in Chapter 4. This Chapter examines the initiatives taken by the Dutch within the field of transport and the environment. It is used to illustrate a different approach adopted by another Member State within the European Union and provides the policy context for Chapter 8, which will examine the effect of national policy on decisions taken at the project level.

The Netherlands

The Netherlands has an area of 33,936 square kilometres and a population of about 15 million. It is densely populated, with 442 persons per square kilometre. In contrast, Britain has an area of 227,400 square kilometres and a population of about 55 million with 246 persons per square kilometre. Due to its position on the continent the Netherlands has developed within the area of transport and the distribution of goods and services on a European and international scale. The harbour of Rotterdam has become one of the largest in Europe, while Schiphol airport plays an important role in the transport of passengers and goods. The transport sector contributes 7-8% to the Dutch national product.

Three administrative levels exist within the Netherlands: the national level (central government and parliament), the provincial level with twelve provinces (provincial council and executive) and the municipal level, which consists of about 700 municipalities each with a municipal council and executive (see Figure 5.1). Each level has different responsibilities for the provision of transport infrastructure and physical planning. A number of bodies exist at each level which work specifically within the area of physical planning. At the national level these include the national physical planning council and agency with similar bodies at the provincial level, with the town planning department being the main administrative body within the municipalities. The national government is responsible for producing structure plans, while provinces are responsible for regional plans and municipalities for the production of both local structure and land use plans.

The national government is responsible for the main trunk road infrastructure, while the rail company *Nederlandse Spoorwegen* (NS), is a semi-private organisation which owns its infrastructure (see Table 5.1). All shares in the NS are owned by the government and infrastructure investment comes entirely from the state, although plans for the full privatisation of NS are currently being implemented.

Figure 5.1 The Provinces of the Netherlands

Investment in motorways comes from the *Rijkswegenfonds* which uses money from tax revenues. In contrast non-trunk roads are financed by the provincial or municipal authority, while any other infrastructure investment is funded from the budget of the Ministry of Transport, Public Works and Water Management (*Ministerie van Verkeer en Waterstaat*) (MVW).

Table 5.1
Provision of transport infrastructure

Transport infrastructure	Priority setting	Investment funding	Building	Control
Trunk roads	G	RW	R	R
Other roads	G/L	G/L	L	L
Major waterways	G	G	R	R
Other waterways	G/L	G/L	L	L
National railways	G/NS	G/NS	NS	NS
Urban rail systems	G/M	G/M	M	M/PT
Cycle ways	L/M	L/M/G	L/M	L/M

G   Central Government
RW   Rijkswegenfonds
R   Rijkswaterstaat
L   Regional and local government
NS   Nederlandse Spoorwegen
M   Municipality
PT   Public transport undertaking

Source: Gwilliam & Gommers, 1992, p.238

The mobility of the Dutch population has been increasing. During the period 1986-1993 the greatest increase in passenger kilometres was by public transport which rose by 41.8%, followed by car drivers at 13.5%. There was also a high increase in the movement of inland freight by road compared with rail and inland water transport.

Main features of Dutch policy

Dutch policy on transport and the environment is characterised by three distinct features. It is based on explicit objectives, sets specific targets and is integrated with other main national policies.

Policy on transport and environment can be described as 'objective-led', for objectives of policy are explicitly stated and the measures needed to achieve them outlined. Objectives are also stated in British policy, such as those outlined in the Roads Programme. However, these tend not to be as detailed as objectives set out in Dutch policy, which cover all aspects of policy. In order that objectives can be met, specific targets are set to be achieved within a stated time period. This enables the success of policy measures to be evaluated in achieving the targets. Policy areas have been co-ordinated and integrated with environmental, physical planning, nature and water management policy. This provides a coherent and integrated approach to deal with the growth in vehicle kilometres and the many factors which contribute to this growth.

The Netherlands and the environment

Concern for the environment in the Netherlands stems partly from a history of battling against nature. A continual struggle against the sea and the eroding coastline has resulted in the development of land reclamation techniques and the construction of dams, for which the Dutch have become renowned. Environmental concern has also led the Dutch to adopt stringent targets for reducing air pollution and to undertake research to develop renewable sources of energy.

The first wave of environmentalism characteristic of the late Sixties and early Seventies resulted in the Dutch government responding to pressure from environmental groups by undertaking action on environmental protection. In 1971 a new Department for public health and environmental protection was established (*Ministerie van Volkshuisvesting, Ruimtelijke Ordening en Milieuhygiëne*) (VROM). This was followed by the publication of an Environmental Urgency Report in 1972 which formulated environmental policy. The report dealt with regional and local environmental problems on a compartmental basis, emphasising control at source and implementing compartmental legislation to deal with each aspect of the environment. Prior to new legislation, the main act on the environment was the Nuisance Act (1875) which was amended in 1952 and 1981.

The government implemented legislation to deal with each aspect of the environment. This began with the Surface Waters Pollution Act (1969), followed by Air Pollution Act (1971), Chemical Wastes Act (1976), Wastes

89

Act (1977), Noise Nuisance Act (1979), Environmental Dangerous Substances Act (1985) and the Soil Protection Act (1986). The main instrument of the compartmental Acts was licensing, which led to considerable bureaucracy for industry, requiring an industrial plant to apply for several different licences in order to operate. In 1979 the General Environmental Provisions Act (*Wet Algemene Bepalingen Milieuhygiëne*) (WABM) was introduced to provide a more universal procedure for licences. In 1986 WABM was amended to include a section on Environmental Impact Assessment in accordance with the EC EIA Directive 85/337/EEC (Drupsteen & Gilhuis, 1989, p.52).

Although environmental protection has evolved since the late Sixties, the Dutch Constitution did not contain any requirement for the government to take action on the protection of the environment. It was not until 1983 that the Constitution was amended with the introduction of a section on basic human rights, outlining provision to take care of housing, employment, social welfare, and the development of art, culture and education. Article 21 of the Constitution made provision for the care of the physical condition of life and the protection of the environment. The 1983 amendment offered a constitutional basis for environmental legislation. However, Drupsteen and Gilhuis (1989, p.48) argue from a judicial point that the basis of the amendment has not been critical, for environmental legislation had been developed in the past without a constitutional basis.

The second wave of environmentalism which occurred in the 1980s led to further action being taken. Environmental pressure groups emphasised the need for integrating environmental aspects into different policies, such as transport policy. In the second half of the 1980s attention was placed on introducing new environmental policies. In 1985 the first indicative Multi-year Programme for the environment covering the period 1985-1989 was produced. The programme emphasised a more integrated approach which included the following themes: acid deposition, discharge of fertilisers, and diffusion of waste, together with a strategy of target group internalisation, attempting to integrate environmental management into target group activities. The Multi-year Programmes provided a shift in emphasis from the compartmental approach of Dutch environmental policy to a more integrated one (Tellegen, 1989, p.340).

The recognition of the limitations of a compartmental approach led to preparatory work by the Ministry of Environment on the feasibility of adopting a new, more integrated approach. This coincided with the publication of *Our Common Future* by the Brundtland Commission in 1987. The report recognised that continual economic development on a deteriorating resource base was untenable. The Dutch government responded to the Brundtland Report and suggested that it was time for an evaluation of national policy. Environmental issues during this period were of great concern to the Dutch.

This concern was expressed in the 1988 Christmas message of Queen Beatrix in which she stated that:

The earth is slowly dying and the inconceivable - the end of life itself - is becoming conceivable (VROM, 1989, p.61).

In 1989 a strategic plan for the environment, the National Environmental Policy Plan (*Nationaal Milieubeleidsplan*) (NMP), was published, which contained a medium-term policy directed towards the attainment of sustainable development. The strategy was also a response to a publication produced by the research division of the Department of the Environment - the National Institute of Public Health and Environmental Protection (*Rijksinstituut voor Volksgezondheid en Milieuhygiëne*) (RIVM) - in 1988, entitled *Concern for Tomorrow - A National Environmental Survey 1985-2010 (Zorgen voor Morgen)*. The document provided a scientific basis for investigation into existing environmental problems in the Netherlands. It put forward the view that consideration must be given to the possibility of a further deterioration in the quality of the Dutch environment. RIVM concluded that the Dutch environment was far from sustainable. To deal with environmental problems long-term targets were defined, for example, to reduce air emissions of polluting gases. The survey outlined three policy scenarios over the period 1985-2010: scenario A - 'business as usual', no change in present policies; scenario B - intensifying existing policies to provide a reduction in emissions from end of pipes; scenario C - end of pipe emissions from scenario B replaced by implementation of changes in production and consumption processes (Lander & Mass, 1990, p.185).

The NMP outlined action to be taken during the period 1990-1994 and set targets for achieving policy objectives at different levels from the local to the global environment. One of the most controversial recommendations was the imposition of extra cost and new taxes on Dutch citizens, with the removal of tax benefits for car commuters and the direction of revenues to public transport, thus enabling a reduction in fares and improvement in the quality of buses, trams and rail networks and the doubling of tracks to four in most densely populated areas (Gossop, 1990, p.181).

Concern for the imposition of extra costs on driving an automobile resulted in the Liberals within the ruling coalition tabling a motion to oppose these fiscal proposals.

The Christian Democrat Prime Minister, Ruud Lubbers, stood firm, which led to the Liberals withdrawing their support. Lubbers offered the resignation of the government and called a general election. A new government was elected in September 1989 formed by the Christian Democrats and the Labour Party. On taking office the new government (led once again by the Christian

Democrats) issued a policy statement (on 27 September 1989) to the effect that the environment was to be a main element of government policy, alongside action to achieve economic growth with a reduction in both the budget deficit and unemployment. The government stated that it was no longer acceptable to defer environmental problems for future generations to deal with them.

Trends needed to be reversed and this could only be achieved by means of far-reaching measures. In government policy proposals the effect on sustainable development would need to be considered (VROM, 1990, p.16). In order that sustainable development be achieved sooner, long-term objectives which were set out in the NMP were brought forward and outlined in the National Environmental Policy Plan Plus (*Nationaal Milieubeleidsplan Plus*) (NMP+) which was published in June 1990. The NMP+ required additional action to be taken to reduce CO_2 emissions, to prevent acidification, to protect and develop nature, to control the waste flow and to promote energy conservation, together with better co-ordination with other policy, although additional action did not require any strategic changes in the intentions outlined in the NMP. It did, however, require long-term targets to be brought forward to enable sustainable development to be achieved sooner. The NMP+ in addition to the NMP formed a strategy for the period 1990-1994.

National environmental policy plan

The national environmental policy strategy was based on sustainable development which it used to develop the ideas within the Indicative Multi-year Programmes for the Environment. In addition, it took account of the recommendations set out in the Brundtland Commission report - attention to long-term effects for future generations and the need to deal with global environmental problems, and the interrelation of economic development and environmental quality.

The NMP identified five levels affected by human activities: local, regional, fluvial, continental and global. It developed measures used in environmental policy since 1979 which *inter alia* included the 'Polluter Pays Principle' and promotion of the 'Stand Still' principle; ensuring no deterioration in the quality of the environment, abatement of pollution at source, prevention of unnecessary pollution and the application of the 'Best Practicable Means' following development of new technology, the isolation, control and monitoring of waste disposal and the implementation of more stringent source-oriented measures on the basis of effect-oriented quality standards.

The seven main themes of the NMP include climatic change, the need to stabilise the emission of CO_2 by the year 2000 at 1989/1990 levels and the promotion of energy conservation; acidification - to reduce the maximum deposition of 2400 acid equivalents per hectare per year by 2010 to enable the protection of forests and natural areas; eutrophication - to restore the balance between the inputs and outputs of phosphorous and nitrogen in water and soil and reduction of between 70-90% in the emissions of eutrophying substances; diffusion of substances - a reduction in the risk to human beings and environment from toxic substances; waste disposal - setting up and improving the waste disposal structure, recycling and prevention of waste generation; disturbance - to reduce the number of people exposed to noise nuisances by the year 2000 to 1985 levels; dehydration - maintaining dehydrated areas at 1985 levels by the year 2000 (VROM, 1989a, p.24).

The Dutch government sees its role within the area of environmental management as being:

... characterised by formulating quality objectives, creating conditions necessary for environmentally friendly behaviour, stimulating guiding, and investing (VROM, 1989a, p.189).

To develop the conditions under which environmental quality could be attained the NMP set objectives for sources of pollution which would influence decisions taken by various target groups and the behaviour of individual organisations. It also focused on those individuals who make decisions, whether consumer or producer, about new materials, production processes and waste management. The joint activities of both producers and consumers, ultimately affect the quality of the environment (VROM, 1990, p.86). The 1986-1990 long-range environmental programme promoted 'internalisation' of environmental norms within specific target groups. This target group approach was continued within the NMP which added consumers, the retail trade and environmental research institutes to the existing groups of agriculture, industry, public utilities, traffic and households. Each actor involved in the formation and implementation of environmental policy is assigned particular roles. The strategy of internalisation aims at giving environmental management equal weight in the decision-making process. Internalisation supplements the present level of environmental management which exists in the Netherlands, rather than being a substitute for regulation.

To ensure structural solutions are achieved within a stated time period, goals and intermediate standards have been set for each target group. Policy objectives for each target group are set in consultative frameworks directly coupled to the Directorate General for the Environment (*Directoraat-Generaal Milieubeheer*), Inter-Provincial Organisation (*Inter Provinciaal Overleg*), and Union of Netherlands Municipalities (*Vereniging van*

Nederlandse Gemeenten) consultative structure, enabling representations to take up position on behalf of the authorities concerned.

Target group managers are responsible for the following tasks with respect to each target group: to serve as a central point of reference for discussion on environmental policy - with close co-operation and reference points for the target groups of other authorities, to strengthen the co-ordination of environmental policy, to promote awareness of environmental policy within the target group and to stimulate concern for the environment (VROM, 1990, p.62).

Environmental policy and transport

In terms of transport, the NMP and the NMP+ advocated measures outlined in the Second Transport Structure Plan (*Tweede Structuurschema Verkeer en Vervoer*) (SVV2). Objectives of the NMP for traffic and transport include clean, quiet, economic and safe vehicles with parts and materials optimally suited to reuse. Emphasis was placed on the use of public transport and bicycles as well as a reduction of energy consumption, environmental pollution of freight transport, and the co-ordination of work, shopping and living locations to ensure minimal travel (VROM, 1989a, p.194-5). The plan set limits on noise and pollutant emissions from the traffic and transport sector including NO_x, HC and CO_2 as outlined in Table 5.2.

The NMP facilitated policy contained in the Second Transport Structure Plan to ensure that up to 50% cleaner goods vehicles are on the road sooner, and to achieve target emissions set for goods vehicles, improvement of public transport and cycling facilities to provide an alternative to the car, use of the price mechanism and incentives as instruments to influence modal choice and provision of information to encourage businesses, municipal authorities and members of the public to use public transport (VROM, 1989a, p.198).

Table 5.2
Emission limits for NO_x, C_xH_y (thousand tonnes)
and CO_2 (million tonnes) from road traffic

Vehicles	1986	1989/90	1994	2000	2010
NO_x					
Private	163	-	100	40	40
Goods	122	-	110	72	25
CxHy					
Private	136	-	-	35	35
Goods	46	-	-	30	12
CO_2					
Road	23	26.5	26.5	23*	20.7

* CO_2 reduction of about 6.5 million tonnes in relation to current trends.

Source: VROM, 1989a

To achieve sustainable development the NMP emphasised the need for a shift to more environmentally friendly modes of transport. The required action included technical measures to develop cleaner vehicles such as lorries and public transport and the use of alternative fuels. Measures to influence mobility were divided into discouraging car use and encouraging use of environmental friendly modes. To increase the cost of using the car, measures to raise the excise duty on petrol and the implementation of road pricing were outlined, including the abolition of tax deductions for commuter traffic. In conjunction with measures to regulate cars, the NMP included plans for greater investment in passenger transport infrastructure, improvement of public transport facilities and greater regional co-operation between transport regions. The development of transport regions (*Vervoerregio's*) as outlined in the SVV2 requires co-ordinated plans to solve environmental and traffic problems in an integrated way. NMP also outlined action to encourage the movement of goods by rail and water, with additional attention to infrastructural bottlenecks in rail and waterway networks.

Together the NMP and NMP+ set out the main aims of environmental policy for the Nineties (VROM, 1990, p.5). The NMP provided for the abolition of tax allowances for commuters, to use the revenue (650 million guilders per year) to provide cheap public transport, cycle facilities and promotion of transport regions. However, this proposal was reversed in the

95

NMP+ which decided to reduce the tax rather than abolish it; thus cutting the revenue to 240 million guilders per year (VROM, 1990, p.10).

Dutch transport policy

The transport industry in the Netherlands plays an important role in the national economy, contributing over 34 million guilders to national income and employing 340,000 people. An increase in economic growth has resulted in a rise in congestion due to road traffic, thus jeopardising the accessibility of major economic routes within the Netherlands.

Co-ordination of transport and environmental policies first began in 1977, when the Ministries of Transport and Environment published the Structure Plan on Traffic and Transport (*Structuurschema Verkeer en Vervoer*) to provide a basis for long-term policy. Short- and medium-term policy was outlined in the Multi-year Plan Person Transport (*Meerjaren Plan Vervoer Personen*) and the Policy Memorandum on Freight Transport (*Beleidsnota Goederenvervoer*) (Vleugel et al., 1990, p.129). In 1987 a Second Transport Structure Plan was published which focused on setting targets for specific areas.

The first Structure Plan attempted to develop a more integrated approach to long-term transport policy. The plan was criticised for its deficiency in providing policy instruments to give effect to policy and its failure to take and implement action, which resulted in an unclear policy. Consequently, the plan was perceived as failing to set out definite choices and lacked a distinct financial framework (MVW, 1988, p.7).

In December 1987 the government published a Memorandum on Traffic and Environment (*Verkeer en Milieu*), expressing its growing concern for the environmental implications of the increasing volume of traffic. The result of the interim evaluation was the recognition of the impact of traffic on the environment. Emphasis was placed on the need to change policy and set targets to reduce the level of polluting emissions and to develop tighter emission limits for each vehicle. The Memorandum outlined measures which should be taken and divided it into three 'policy tracks': development of vehicle technology, use of vehicles and urban traffic control measures to achieve current objectives and comments on and formulation of future policy objectives.

Since the mid-1980s many developments have occurred within the transport field. Transport has not only been recognised as an important environmental issue, but also as a factor providing economic advantage in the development of the Single European Market. To accommodate these changes, a decision to produce a new structure plan was taken in December 1986. The Second

Transport Structure Plan took into consideration the criticisms of the first structure plan and attempted to develop co-ordination where efforts had been fragmented. Focus was placed on developing a system which would create a balance between individual freedom, accessibility and environmental amenity. The SVV2 attempted to outline clear policies, presenting choices aimed at achieving practical results within a realistic framework. The plan was presented for consultation to the public and advisory bodies to obtain recommendations and develop discussions. This involved key figures within the transport field and included user groups, industry and trade unions. Consultation was seen as providing the basis of agreement with organisations and individuals, enabling the implementation of policies. The consultation process resulted in two further reports: part B - public consultation responses and part C - recommendations from Expert groups. In 1990 part D of the SVV2 (government decision) was issued.

SVV2 (part D) provided a number of shifts in emphasis compared with part A. It contained additional sections on Dutch sea ports and Schiphol airport, together with information technology aspects of policy. The policy was based on the concept of sustainable development, for doubts existed as to whether the strategy in part A could reach a balance between environmental amenity, individual freedom and accessibility, without environmental interests taking second place. Part D accelerated policy on traffic and transport, providing a significant shift in emphasis compared with part A, which *inter alia* includes the nature and scale of the investment. New road construction was postponed and attention was directed towards road maintenance; for instance, the use of noise absorbing asphalt, road safety and improvement of existing road networks and better use of waterways.

There was also a significant increase in investment for the expansion of public transport infrastructure (VROM, 1990, p.49).

Second transport structure plan

The second transport structure plan part D outlined a step-based approach to develop a strategy based on sustainability. The SVV2 set a target to achieve a 35% reduction in the predicted growth in vehicle kilometres travelled by 2010, i.e. reducing the expected growth by about half (Table 5.3). To develop a more balanced solution between transport and environmental amenity the government provided a strategy in the form of five steps of equal importance.

Table 5.3
Index figures for growth of passenger and freight vehicles

1986	1989	1994	2000	2010
100	117	125	130	135

Source: VROM, 1990, p.50

The five steps included tackling problems at source (e.g. implementation of vehicle technology), managing and restraining mobility (e.g. by reducing the number of vehicle kilometres travelled by freight and passenger transport), improving alternatives to the private car (e.g. raising standards of public transport), providing selective accessibility on roads and strengthening the foundations of policy with support measures, such as finance and investment, communication and inter-authority collaboration and the formation of Transport Regions.

The five steps which form the Dutch strategy to deal with transport problems are translated into specific targets. As outlined in both parts A and D, target scenarios have been developed within a series of policy areas - environmental amenity, accessibility and managing and restraining mobility. Targets will be achieved by implementing a coherent package of measures in the three categories above, together with a fourth category on support measures.

Environmental amenity

The main targets for environmental quality are to reduce the emissions of nitrogen oxides and unburned hydrocarbons by 75% and carbon dioxide by 10% by the year 2010. The total areas exposed to noise nuisance and the number of injuries and deaths are expected to be reduced by 50%, 40% and 50% respectively, with no change in the fragmentation of the countryside and the risk associated with the transport of hazardous waste.

The measures taken to achieve these targets are mainly in the form of technical fixes such as improving the fuel efficiency of cars, fitting three-way catalytic converters and using noise absorbing asphalt for roads. Regulative measures are directed towards providing tighter standards for noise and emissions and lowering speeds, together with the education of drivers to drive better and more safely.

Mobility

To reduce the total mobility within the Netherlands measures have been aimed at concentrating housing, employment and public facilities and restricting car parking spaces. The implementation of 'ABC Location Policy' in accordance with the Fourth Report on Physical Planning requires labour intensive employment and public services to be concentrated near public transport facilities. Every major housing development is expected to be served by a high grade public transport system and land use plans will need to ensure that new developments are located according to ABC location policy.

To control parking, norms were set for each location per hundred employees, to be applied to commercial firms and public facilities (see Table 5.4).

Table 5.4
Location policy and parking spaces

Location type	Location	Number of parking spaces
A	Randstad, urban nodes, conurbations	10
B	Elsewhere	20
C	In the Randstad & conurbations	40
D	Elsewhere	40

Measures outlined to increase the variable cost of motoring include increasing the cost of fuel and introducing toll charges in certain sections of the road network at particular times, together with the introduction of a charge for vehicles during peak hours. Other fiscal measures include reducing the tax relief for company cars and consideration of financial incentives to encourage a shift in public transport (MVW, 1990, p.36). Cost to the user of public transport would be less than the private car user. SVV2 (part A) promoted road pricing but received opposition during the consultation process.

Accessibility

To improve accessibility action is directed to three areas: passenger transport, freight transport and sea ports. The main theme is to ensure accessibility of the country in order that the Netherlands can continue to play a prominent role in the transport and distribution sector.

99

Passenger transport Accessibility of passenger transport is divided into collective transport, road, cycling, car sharing, transfer facilities and telecommunications. SVV2 (part D) accelerated the implementation of plans outlined in part A to achieve greater performance in public transport. This requires greater investment to increase reliability and quality and reduce travel time to create an alternative to the car. The aim for collective transport is to increase capacity by 20-100% in peak hours on main transport corridors by 2010 compared with 1986. Greater investment would enable this to be achieved. The plan also sets out policy to encourage cycling by providing safe, comfortable cycle routes and encouraging car sharing for journeys from home to work in order to increase the number of commuters per vehicle from 1.2-1.6 by 2010. In addition, the provision of transfer facilities on the edge of metropolitan areas would allow park and ride schemes.

Bicycle master plan In 1992 the Ministry of Transport, Public Works and Water Management published the Bicycle Master Plan (BMP) which further elaborated the government's commitment to promoting the use of the bicycle as an alternative mode of transport. The BMP provides an integrated plan for cycling as part of the whole traffic and transportation system. As discussed above, the SVV2 aims to provide safe, comfortable and continuous bicycle paths. The BMP took this a step further by setting out specific targets to be achieved. The main concern has traditionally been infrastructure and road safety. The BMP takes a broader view and addresses mobility and the relationship of cycling with businesses, public transport, theft, parking, information and promotion to influence behaviour.

Bicycle use is very high in the Netherlands and the Dutch use bicycles as a mode of transport for about 30% of all movements (MVW, 1992a, p.2). About 60% of all journeys are less than 5 kilometres and 40% of all trips by car are no more than 5 kilometres. Most of these are in urban areas (Welleman, 1992, p.10). The bicycle is therefore seen as providing a realistic alternative to the car for short distances. The main objectives of the BMP are to increase the number of kilometres travelled by bicycle by 30% in 2010 compared with 1986 and secondly, to encourage greater use of public transport by improving the bicycle/public transport transfer. A target increase of 15-20% in the number of kilometres travelled by train by 2010 has been set. The SVV2 target of a 35% reduction in growth in vehicle kilometres is equal to 40 billion kilometres travelled by car. The BMP will enable the bicycle to account for 12.5% or 5 billion kilometres of this reduction (Welleman, 1992, p.10).

In order to achieve the set targets, a strategy has been outlined which has three themes. The first is to create the right conditions for people to cycle. These are mainly regarded as 'pull measures', such as good, safe infrastructure, secure storage facilities and the separation of cyclists and traffic on roads and junctions. The second theme is to encourage cycling by promotion and education, thus, ensuring a permanent policy at all administrative levels; to enable the public to become aware of the advantages and environmental benefits of cycling. The third theme is to undertake demonstration projects, test new designs and ideas and examine the practical effects. Projects would cover areas such as creating a shift from car to bicycle, theft prevention and improving safety (MVW, 1992a, p.24).

Road transport The trunk road network should provide direct links between 40 centres within the Netherlands and other countries. The network is expected to take the form of a coarse-mesh pattern which was initially derived from the first structure place. SVV2 (part A) supported further investment in infrastructure and the construction of new roads and widening of others to ensure efficient use, as well as the implementation of transitional measures at certain bottlenecks in the trunk road network, for example, use of tidal flow systems by utilising the hard shoulder of a trunk road. Principal links within the Randstad would take priority in accordance with the Fourth Report on Physical Planning (MVW, 1988, p.30). SVV2 (part D) (1990, p.47) maintained the notion of a trunk road network between 40 centres and principal routes. It also listed eight links which were to be deleted from the construction programme for environmental reasons. The remaining trunk road schemes were to be maintained and any investment would require specific project studies to be undertaken, in order to discover whether the construction of new routes or improvement of existing routes would be sufficient.

To reduce congestion the SVV2 (part A) (1988, p.47) set a uniform target for the probability of congestion of 2% by 2010 on all of the trunk road network. This means that no more than 2% of all vehicles on a particular road during a working day should be subject to delays in traffic. Delays are defined as slow driving traffic or traffic where there is very little movement. The application of a 2% norm for congestion would reduce the probability of tailbacks and reduce the indirect and direct costs of delay. Part D differentiated the norms to 2% and 5% compared with the uniform standard in part A. This was to ensure those routes important for business and transport were not faced with a probability of more than 2% congestion, especially those routes linking main centres in the Randstad.

SVV2 requires that the share of international freight transport be maintained and the efficiency of road haulage be improved to achieve a 15-20% reduction in the number of vehicle kilometres travelled by 2010. This would be achieved by improving the efficiency and utilisation of road haulage capacity together with an improvement in infrastructure, especially international links to Rotterdam and Schiphol and by being integrated into the European road system. Separate lines are to be provided, especially on prime routes for freight and other categories of traffic, together with accessibility to city centres based on the concept of selective accessibility. In order to maintain the Dutch share of the road haulage market, the government intends to provide a favourable climate of business which will comprise *inter alia* deregulation of road haulage, enabling access to markets especially within the Single European Market, together with promotion and development of logistical and information services.

Rail transport To maintain and increase the Dutch market share of rail freight, the development of high grade links is required between sea port areas such as Rotterdam and its hinterland and the integration of the Dutch railway system into the European rail network. A target to increase rail freight up to 50 million tonnes per year by 2010 has been set for principal routes capable of carrying axle loads of 22.5 tonnes. It is anticipated that rail networks will suffer from capacity shortfalls as the promotion of the public transport begins to take effect. SVV2 (part D) (1990, p.65) identified the necessity of maintaining sufficient capacity of goods traffic on main freight rail lines, especially the Rotterdam via Venlo line to the German border. Extra capacity for rail freight will also be created on new and existing links to Eastern France and Southern France and Spain.

Rail 21 plan In June 1988 *Nederlandse Spoorwegen* published the 'Rail 21' plan as its contribution to the debate on traffic, transport and environment which was taking place at the time. Rail 21 plans to make rail play a greater role in the future, enabling it to contribute to solving the problems related to transport and the environment. The main themes of Rail 21 include the doubling of present transport volume capacity and improving the quality of travel. It outlined ideas for the development of a new train structure based on a system of three types of train replacing the Intercity and local trains. The provision of trains would be greatly improved in terms of capacity, speed and comfort. Table 5.5 shows how the new train system will be divided.

In 1990, following Rail 21, Nederlandse Spoorwegen published its plan for freight, 'Rail 21 Cargo', which disclosed how freight transport could grow in three phases from 20 million tonnes of goods in 1990 to 65 million tonnes by 2010. Nearly all of Rail 21 has been incorporated in government transport policy, with only the first two phases of Rail 21 Cargo being accepted by the Dutch government. NS and the government agreed on swift implementation of the plan, requiring a new timetable of development removing existing bottlenecks and expanding infrastructure (NS, 1991).

Water transport The transport of freight is dependent on the connecting of principal waterways both within the Netherlands and to other countries. To strengthen the position of the Netherlands in Europe, the government sets out the need to develop its waterway network, especially those transport links to Amsterdam, Rotterdam, Western Scheldt, Germany, France and Belgium. There will be an investment of 4 billion guilders to eliminate bottlenecks, increase capacity, improve the reliability and safety of traffic and waterway. Commercial and leisure traffic on principal routes will be segregated and alternative routes for leisure traffic will be developed. Action will also be taken to promote water transport as a viable alternative, by establishing a water transport information bureau.

Transport regions The section on support measures within the SVV2 included the development of administrative instruments to provide a coherent policy at the regional level. In 1992 Transport Regions (*Vervoerregio's*) were established and at present about seven transport regions exist. Transport Regions provide better co-ordination between Central Government, Provinces and Municipalities. The main functions of the regions cover local and regional transport, the road network, parking policy, cycle provision, freight transport and integration of transport and land use policy (MVW, 1990, p.86).

Policy is outlined in Regional Transport Plans (*Regionale Verkeer en Vervoersplannen*) (RVVPs) and once a region has produced a plan the Ministry of Transport will agree upon whether it will contribute to national policy. The extent of the plan's contribution will depend on the projects and whether they will achieve national goals. The agreement will cover the scheduling of projects and will include the level of funding to be received from central government as is stated in the Multi-year Infrastructure Transport Programme.

Table 5.5
The Rail 21 plan

Eurocity/Intercity
These trains will connect the five national metropolitan areas of the Randstad and the 15 regional centres located outside the Randstad. The European High Speed network would form part of this network, with lines being constructed Southwards to Belgium and France and Eastwards to Germany. The trains will run at a maximum speed of 160-200 km per hour, with trains being provided every hour on each service.
Express Inter-regional
The main function of Express inter-regional trains is to provide access to the Randstad and links within it. They would also provide a fast link between 65 centres which are considered important for the country. The maximum speed of inter-regional trains would be 140-160 km/hour. The trains would run twice per hour and in some cases they will provide connections on an hourly basis.
Regional/Suburban Trains
The regional or suburban trains would provide frequent connections over short distances. These kinds of trains may travel at maximum speeds of 120-140 km/hour and services will run twice per hour, at least four per hour around large urban districts.
Compared with the initial plan in 1988 a number of changes have been implemented, with speeds for short travel being updated and reduced from 200 km/hour to 160 km/hour. The plan was based on 18 billion kilometres which travellers were expected to cover by 2015. The NS now expects 20 billion passenger kilometres by 2010.

Source: NS, 1991

Physical planning

Environment and transport policy in the Netherlands has been closely co-ordinated with physical planning policy. Physical planning makes an important contribution to reducing the need to travel by implementing concepts such as 'Compact City' and 'ABC Location Policy'.

The preparation of government policy at the national level is the responsibility of the Minister of Housing, Physical Planning and Environment. The Minister normally publishes the main principles of Dutch national spatial policy in the form of reports. The first report on physical planning was published in 1960 followed by the second in 1966. The third report consisted of three parts which were published over the period 1973-1977 and included the Orientation Report (background and points of departure), Urbanisation Report and the Rural Areas Report. The fourth report was published in 1989 and was followed by the fourth report extra. The fourth report was considered necessary due to the rapid changes in social development which were not apparent ten to fifteen years previously when the third document was being prepared.

Fourth report on physical planning

On 17 March 1988 the Fourth Report in Physical Planning (*Vierde Nota Ruimtelijke Ordening*) (4NRO) was published, exactly eleven years after the publication in 1977 of the third and final part of the third policy document, which in turn was published eleven years after the second policy document of 1966. The fourth report consisted of three parts: part A - policy intention; followed by parts B and C which were the results of consultations with the public and specialist organisations. The final government decision (part D) considered the social changes taking place and the implications for physical planning in the Netherlands. It highlighted the 'internationalisation' of the Dutch economy, the effect of removing trade barriers in the Single European Market and the economic changes in Eastern Europe. The report replaced the third report on physical planning and develops greater co-operation with the public sector and various levels of the market (VROM, 1988, p.3).

The population of the Netherlands is expected to rise from 15 million to 16.5 million by 2015. This increase will have consequences for housing, amenities and the level of personal mobility. Economic development will be mainly derived from the Randstad and the four major urban regions of Amsterdam, the Hague, Utrecht and Rotterdam. It is expected that the total number of jobs in the Randstad will grow by around 530,000 by the year 2015 at an economic growth rate of 2% (VROM, 1989b, p.7). The economic development of cities, combined with a population increase, will lead to a need for more office locations, business sites and housing stock and a need for the concentration of building and offices in urban regions. The fourth report set out priorities to remove bottlenecks in international transport corridors and to use the introduction of infrastructure measures to guide mobility in the proper direction, especially with regard to transport links to Schiphol and Rotterdam and linking these to the hinterland and economic centres by providing infrastructure within the Randstad.

In May 1989 the fourth report was supplemented by an additional report. The Fourth Report on Physical Planning Extra (VINEX) emphasised the use of physical planning to take advantage of the unique features of the Netherlands in promoting economic development, for example, the spatial diversity of the Netherlands compared with the rest of Europe and its position in the area of international transport. The policy outlined in VINEX was directed at two levels, focusing on the daily living environment of the Dutch and on the international context of the country. The former is based on the principle of maintaining the physical environment, a clean environment with safe surroundings and spatial diversity.

The report designated 28 urban regions, which are areas around big cities, in its attempt to concentrate urban function, to make efficient use of urban space and to diminish the need to travel. New residential, work and recreational areas will be sited at the shortest location from the centre, making it easily accessible by public transport and bicycle traffic. The role of urban renewal is important to enable existing urban areas to be fully utilised, together with the development of open spaces in urban areas (VROM, 1989b, p.15). To improve living conditions and ensure accessibility for freight transport, the report set out measures to reduce mobility, identifying the need for the integration of transport, environment and physical planning policy. It developed a future scenario based on three variables - location policy, provision and promotion of public transport. Due to the changes in the international position of the Netherlands, the report outlined a scenario aimed at strengthening the economic features of the country, taking advantage of these factors in the development and retention of environmental assets, and enhancement of spatial diversity, thus further utilising and strengthening the individual qualities and economic potential of different parts of the country. The report focuses on the need for the development of Rotterdam and Schiphol airport as distinguished main transport axes for goods transport whose function should not be hampered.

Location policy

An increase in suburbanisation has resulted in an increase in distances travelled on the home to work journey, with residential areas being located in the suburbs. In the past the long-term implications of choosing a particular site were given little attention, resulting in poor accessibility due to large volumes of traffic. This was mainly seen as a problem to which the government should respond via the provision of new road infrastructure. The location of businesses near transport links, however, has become increasingly recognised as a means of increasing the use of public transport. The location of companies at railway stations had the effect of reducing the use of motor vehicles.

A reduction in the growth in traffic and an increase in the use of public transport can be achieved by a greater co-ordination of land use and transportation facilities (Hilbers & Verroen, 1992). Location policy enables siting of new businesses and services in appropriate locations which are accessible by both car and public transport (Table 5.6). The 4NRO elaborates the policy, which is in line with SVV2. Each company has its own transport needs. The role of location policy ensures the transport needs of a company are sufficiently met at the location at which it is sited, while encouraging the use of public transport as much as possible. Companies with a high number of employees, for example, are sited near public transport facilities. Conversely, companies which require greater use of motorised vehicles such as freight would be best sited near motorway exits.

The main instruments which are used to match the companies and locations are accessibility and mobility profiles. The latter determines the mobility characteristics of a company, while accessibility profiles assess the multi-accessibility of a location.

By co-ordinating transport needs and opportunities, it is possible to ensure minimal use of the motor vehicle to achieve an optimal location for each company.

Table 5.6
Categorisation of A, B, C locations

A-Locations
Very accessible by public transport such as locations near main transport facilities like central stations in large urban areas. Accessibility by motor vehicles is of secondary importance; commuting by car is restricted (no more than 10-20%).
B-Locations
Sites which are reasonably accessible by both car and public transport. Situated on main urban trunk roads or near motorway exits. Parking geared towards business and services with a moderate dependence on motor transport.
C-Locations
Mainly car-oriented locations which are situated near motorway exits on the fringe of urban areas and are poorly accessible by public transport. Limited number of employers directed towards supply and distribution of goods by road.

Source: Verroen & Jansen, 1991; VROM, 1987

The formation of transport regions has provided an organisational structure which can implement location policy, by ensuring ABC location areas are identified and transport links provided. However, implementation of location policy by municipalities may mean economic losses if an insufficient number of locations for certain types of businesses exist. An A location company, for example, may want to site within an area where the municipality has no A sites available. This may result in municipalities having to turn away businesses, or take action to improve the transport facilities of the particular area. In some instances, municipalities may try and claim to have more A and B locations than really exist, by changing criteria used. The enthusiasm of municipalities to implement location policy is an important factor if the policy is to be effective. The municipalities may need to be made more aware of the potential benefits of location policy.

Local initiatives

Amsterdam

The city of Amsterdam has 80,000 residents and is considered to be one of the largest and most intensely used historic cities in Europe (Polestra, 1993). The city centre covers 7 square kilometres most of which was developed in the seventeenth century. On 25 March 1992 the city council held a referendum on whether action should be taken to make the city 'Car Free'. Just over 52% of the residents of Amsterdam voted for a car free city. Although the result was not by any means conclusive, it was endorsed by the city council. The city council proposed a plan to reduce car use which outlined a step by step approach. On 9 February 1994 the city council agreed a comprehensive traffic and street layout plan for the period between 1995-2005. This examines the extent to which car traffic can be reduced by 35%. The plan proposed the following instruments to reduce car traffic: parking policy, traffic management and the redesign of urban space (Lemmers, 1993).

Parking policy will influence the number of car journeys by reducing the number of parking spaces available and increasing the cost of parking. The cost of parking will be higher in the city centre than on the edge of the city, the cheapest parking spaces being available on the outskirts of the city near public transport facilities. Traffic management measures will be taken to reduce the amount of traffic by developing a one-way system on main radial streets. This will allow space to be made available for public transport improvements and bicycle lanes. By discouraging the number of vehicles entering the city, streets and canals may be designed to cope with less traffic. The plan contained

108

preliminary designs of streets with new tramlines and bicycle routes (Lemmers, 1994).

The implementation of the Traffic and Street layout plan in Amsterdam will enable the targets for air and noise pollution to be met. It will be some time before the benefits and effectiveness of Amsterdam's plan can be assessed adequately. The City has, however, made the first few steps towards becoming a car free city.

Delft

The city of Delft has gained an international reputation for the initiatives which it has implemented to promote the use of the bicycle. The 1980-1984 Multi-year Programme for Personal Transport included action to construct urban cycle networks. The Transportation and Traffic Engineering Division of the Ministry of Transport undertook three evaluation studies on urban cycleways. The first evaluation study was in 1975 and acted as a demonstration project on urban cycle routes.

This study concerned bicycle routes which had been established in the Hague and Tilburg. The second demonstration project concerned bicycle routes along main roads of towns within the provinces of Gelderland and Limburg. The study concluded that one of the effects of these routes was that people use their bicycles more, especially during their spare time. However, this had no effect on the modal shift from the car to the use of the bicycle (Hartman, 1990, p.194).

In 1980 the Ministry proposed the creation of an urban bicycle network to build upon the previous projects, and chose to provide a subsidy for the plan presented by the Municipality of Delft. A 'before study' was undertaken in 1982 to provide a baseline on which the effectiveness of the implementation of an urban cycle network could be assessed. The study covered the North-West of Delft and this was where most of the improvements were undertaken within the study period. The control area was the Wippolder district where no improvements were made. In July 1987 the final evaluation report was published, which sought to answer three questions. Firstly, does the implementation of a comprehensive bicycle network result in an increase in the use of the bicycle as a mode of transport? Secondly, does the bicycle network affect traffic safety? Thirdly, in which way do cyclists use the network and what are their behavioural responses? (MVW, 1987).

The Delft bicycle plan showed that, with the provision of a safe, comfortable and continuous bicycle network, it is possible to encourage the use of a more sustainable mode of transport. The improvements in the bicycle network in Delft increased the use of the bicycle by 6%, which was a main aim of the plan. This was due to a shift from the use of the car and walking. At the same time there was no increase in the level of car use. The change in the modal split saw the bicycle increase from 40% to 43%, while the use of the car and walking remained stable at 20%, and the share of public transport decreased from 6% to 4%. However, the decrease in the use of public transport was for the residents in the study area and did not include the use of public transport by non-residents.

The Delft bicycle plan has shown the competitiveness of the bicycle as a daily mode of transport. The results from Delft can be compared with other medium-sized Dutch cities with populations of 20,000-50,000 where bicycle use varies between 20-50% of the modal split (Ten Grotenhuis, 1988). As the study suggests there are a number of measures which can be taken to improve and encourage the use of the bicycle in urban centres. This has important implications since a high proportion of trips by car are considered to be less than 5 kilometres. The bicycle can therefore provide a sustainable alternative for such short trips.

Groningen

Groningen is situated in the North of the Netherlands and is 200 kilometres from Amsterdam and Hamburg. It has a population of about 170,000 and is considered to be the sixth largest city in the Netherlands. The city has taken action to integrate traffic, transport and planning policy. The traffic policy of the City of Groningen is related to its aims to boost its economic position in the Northern region of the Netherlands and improve the quality of life in the city. The aim of Groningen's transport policy is to enable the city to be accessible, while restricting car traffic and promoting the use of alternative, less polluting modes. Public transport and bicycles are given priority, while traffic is restricted selectively. Traffic which is economically necessary (e.g. delivery goods vehicles) is unaffected, while non-essential commuter traffic is curbed. The principal measures which have been taken to achieve the objectives include: town planning based on the concept of a compact city (i.e. to reduce the distances from home to work and recreation and public facilities), creation of special facilities for bicycles and public transport users and the implementation of a traffic management system to restrict the use of the private car (Hasselar, 1993).

The approach of Groningen to deal with traffic growth within the city has improved the quality of the urban environment. The city has encouraged cycling and walking by restricting the use of cars. More pedestrianised areas have been created. It has integrated transport and physical planning to deal with the need to travel from home to work or public facilities. Most of the initiatives which Groningen began to take over a number of years are now part of government policy and advocated for all cities within the Netherlands. The measures have influenced the modal split; 48% of the residents of Groningen travel by bicycle, 31% by car, 5% by public transport and 17% by foot for the journey from home to work or to public facilities. The city council suggests that bicycle use is 10-15% higher than in other cities of comparable size, while the use of the car is 15% lower (Smorenburg, 1992, p.12).

The initiatives taken by Dutch municipalities have not always been part of national policy and have tended to be innovative in their approach. In this respect, local government in the Netherlands and Britain has had a certain amount of freedom to formulate integrated transport strategies. In the case of Britain, local authorities have attempted to formulate transport strategies which have been forward looking and ambitious when compared with national transport policy (see Chapter 4).

Municipalities in the Netherlands have encouraged cycling as a sustainable mode, especially for short distances of less than 5 kilometres. This is not only due to cultural factors, but is a recognition of the role the bicycle can play in providing an alternative to the car. Amsterdam, Delft and Groningen are among the more well-known Dutch cities which have restricted the use of the motor vehicle and given priority to walking, cycling and public transport. Progress towards implementing the concept of a 'Car Free' city has been greater in the Netherlands than in Britain. At the local level, cities have been limited to the extent to which they are able to take measures to restrict car use in city centres. Measures have taken the form of parking restrictions, location policy and promotion of cycling. Measures which are more effective in reducing car use and encouraging a shift to other transport modes need to be taken at the national level e.g. increasing the variable cost of motoring by raising the cost of fuel and implementing strict emission and energy efficiency standards.

Evaluating Dutch transport policy

In September 1993 the Ministry of Transport published its first annual evaluation report of SVV2 policy (*Beleidseffectrapportage 1992*) (MVW, 1993a). This was followed by a second evaluation report in June 1994 and a third report in June 1995. Based on SVV2 the Ministry developed a set of indicators to help measure progress towards the attainment of goals for traffic and transport. The report not only evaluates the effectiveness of individual policy instruments, but presents developments taking place and future forecasts. In this respect, the reports are not based on indicators which are yet totally reliable; improvement in the indicators is expected to be made each year. For a number of indicators data is not yet available and therefore no conclusion can be made on the progress made towards achieving certain

111

targets. With time and the availability of data and improvement of indicators a more accurate picture of progress towards the attainment of policy targets can be gained. As outlined in SVV2 the evaluation reports cover the three main themes: environmental amenity, mobility and accessibility.

Environmental amenity

Environmental quality targets include the reduction of emissions of nitrogen oxides and hydrocarbons by 20% in 1995 and 75% by 2010, compared with 1986. For carbon dioxide emissions the target is to stabilise emissions at 1989/1990 levels by 1995 and achieve a reduction of 10% by 2010. Since 1988 the emissions of NO_x from road traffic have been decreasing, although the 1995 target for a 20% reduction is not expected to be met (Table 5.7).

In fact, an increase of 10 index points past this target is expected. The main contribution to the reduction of NO_x emissions has been the increase in the use of catalytic converters. However, any benefits derived from this technical fix have been off set by an increase in the number of kilometres travelled by car. Nitrogen oxide emissions for freight transport have also decreased. However, the growth in vehicle kilometres has increased the emissions of NO_x (MVW, 1994, p.39).

Table 5.7
Emissions of nitrogen oxides from road transport (thousand tonnes)

Year	1986	1988	1990	1992	1994*
Personal cars	158	164	148	135	119
Buses	9	10	10	9	10
Freight traffic	97	108	110	114	119
Other road traffic	5	4	5	4	3
Total road traffic	269	286	273	262	251
Index of total road traffic	100	106	101	97	93

*provisional figures

Source: MVW, 1994, 1995

A fall in the emissions of hydrocarbons has enabled the 1995 target to be met earlier than expected, in 1991 (Table 5.8). The main contribution to the reduction in emissions has again been the use of the catalytic converter. A reduction in the emissions of hydrocarbons has occurred for both personal and freight traffic, with the greatest decrease of 39% from personal car traffic in contrast to the 14.3% reduction from freight traffic.

Table 5.8
Emissions of hydrocarbons from road transport (thousand tonnes)

Year	1986	1988	1990	1992	1994*
Personal cars	170	164	142	119	104
Buses	3	3	3	2	2
Freight traffic	28	18	26	26	24
Other road traffic	19	19	20	18	20
Total road traffic	220	214	191	166	150
Index of total road traffic	100	97	87	75	68

*provisional figures

After an initial stabilisation CO_2 emissions from motor vehicles have begun to rise and have passed the 1995 target. Emissions are expected to increase by a further 10% past this target. The emission of CO_2 from the freight sector has increased by 39% in the period 1986-1993 compared with an increase of 15.6% from personal car transport (Table 5.9). The freight sector is responsible for a large proportion of the increase in the emission of pollutants.

Table 5.9
Emissions of carbon dioxide from road transport (thousand tonnes)

Year	1986	1988	1990	1992	1994*
Personal cars	14100	15200	15200	15800	16300
Buses	500	500	500	500	500
Freight traffic	6200	7200	7600	8100	8600
Other road traffic	500	500	500	500	500
Total road traffic	21300	23400	23800	24900	25900
Index of total road traffic	100	110	112	117	122

*provisional figures

Source: MVW, 1994,1995

The target for road transport safety is to reduce the number of traffic casualties in 1995 by 15% and in 2010 by 50%, compared with 1986. The number of traffic casualties has fallen since 1986 and the 1995 target (of no more than 1300 deaths) has been reached. For people injured by traffic a 10% reduction by 1995 and a 40% reduction by 2010 are targets which have been set. It is unlikely, however, that the 1995 and 2010 targets will be met (MVW, 1994, p.50).

Mobility

The SVV2 set a target for a 35% reduction in personal vehicle kilometres by 2010 compared with 1986. To measure the progress which has been made towards achieving this target the total number of personal vehicle kilometres were calculated for working days. Between the period 1986-1993 there has been a limited growth in the number of personal kilometres (Table 5.10). The intermediate target (index 125 in 1994) has more or less been met (MVW, 1994, p.65).

Table 5.10
Mobility index

Year	1986	1990	1991	1992	1993	1994
Index	100	115	114	118	119	123

For bicycle use a target for an increase of 30% has been set for the year 2010, compared with 1986. The number of kilometres travelled since 1989 have been stable and a rise is expected in the future. The implementation of the Bicycle Master Plan will enable the 2010 target to be met.

Accessibility

A 2% norm for the probability of congestion has been set for main strategic routes and a 5% norm for all other roads. The indicator used to measure the progress being made towards this target is the section of main roads where the probability of congestion is more than 2% or 5%. These norms are not being met on a large number of roads and at present the SVV2 target will not be achieved.

The price difference between public transport and the motor vehicle should be in favour of public transport. Comparison of the percentage change in fuel prices and public transport fares showed that after some minor fluctuations an equilibrium was reached in 1993 (MVW, 1994).

Freight transport

A number of targets have been directed at freight transport and have dealt with the efficiency and the movement of freight by road and water. The efficiency of freight transport by road should be improved to achieve a 15-20% reduction in kilometres travelled in 2010. In the last two years there has been a stabilisation in the freight kilometres travelled. The development of the railways in the Netherlands is going as planned. By 2010 freight by rail is expected to rise to 50 million tonnes compared with 1986. The target for the transport of freight by inland shipping is 370 million tonnes by 2010. The amount of freight transported by inland shipping has declined by 10% since 1986. Any growth in freight traffic will most probably occur by road. This will have important implications for the environment and emissions of carbon dioxide and nitrogen oxides which have been increasing significantly in the freight sector.

The second national environmental policy plan

In 1994 the Second National Environmental Policy Plan (NMP2) was published by the Dutch government and provided an evaluation of the NMP. One main element of NMP2 is to improve the implementation of measures by target groups which the NMP had difficulty in reaching. This will be undertaken by providing clearer objectives and targets for target groups and the necessary guidance to ensure action is implemented. NMP2 attempts to complete gaps in the objectives and targets for different groups which did not previously exist; for example, NMP2 sets targets for consumers and the retail trade.

The NMP2 acknowledges that a number of targets within the area of traffic and transport are not being met; for example, the target to reduce carbon dioxide emissions and noise disturbance from the private car. The plan set out further action to be taken, which ranges from influencing purchase and driver behaviour to using tax measures. The problem of freight transport was also addressed. As discussed above, freight transport poses problems for the reduction of carbon dioxide and nitrogen oxides. Additional action includes undertaking further consultation with target groups to develop a five-year interim target to achieve a more fuel efficient, less polluting stock of vehicles and to develop a change in the modal split, and the introduction of tighter emissions standards for CO_2, NO_x and noise. In addition, research will be undertaken into the application of new technologies to reduce air and noise emissions and improve fuel efficiency and the possible use of differential rates of vehicle taxation to stimulate the purchase of more efficient vehicles (VROM, 1994, p.35).

115

From rhetoric to reality

The Dutch have outlined their commitment to developing a more sustainable transportation system in a number of key national policy documents, in which they have included a range of measures to reduce the impact of transport on the environment. A distinct policy framework has been developed where NMP, NMP2, SVV2, 4NRO and VINEX policies have been co-ordinated and integrated. These policies have attempted to address each aspect of the transport problem by measures to reduce mobility - e.g. via physical planning policy, improving accessibility and maintaining environmental quality. The setting of explicit objectives has given a clear direction to policy with commitment being further stated in specific targets for a number of factors.

The approach taken by the Dutch within the field of transport and the environment has been a product of Dutch politics and culture. The corporatist approach of seeking wide consultation and co-operation with a number of interest groups has enabled a broad-based policy to be agreed and implemented. The bicycle plays an important role within the Dutch culture and psyche and has developed as a realistic alternative mode of transport. Municipalities within the Netherlands have promoted the use of the bicycle and have taken measures to restrict car use, as seen in the cities of Amsterdam, Delft and Groningen. The development of transport regions has further strengthened the organisational structure to provide an integrated transport policy at the regional level via regional transport plans.

The rhetoric of Dutch transport policy for some factors has become reality. The evaluation of Dutch transport policy has shown that of the total 34 targets, 13 targets will be or are being met, 14 will not be or are not being met, while 5 targets are in between and for 2 targets data is lacking and it is therefore not possible to comment (MVW, 1995). Targets which have been met include the target for emissions of hydrocarbons, while some targets are still within reach, e.g. the intermediate target to reduce personal vehicle kilometres. The extent to which all the targets will be reached and maintained will be dependent on the implementation of policy measures, monitoring programmes and the annual evaluations. Among the 14 targets which will not be achieved are the targets for a reduction of NO_x and CO_2 emissions, the noise impact from motorways and the number of people injured by traffic. The targets to make the price of public transport more competitive in comparison with the car, increasing the average number of occupants per car and a reduction in the number of freight kilometres by road, will not be met. The setting of national targets, however, seems not to have restricted the Dutch continuing with infrastructural developments such as the plans for the extension of Schiphol airport and the expansion of the A2 in the Amsterdam-Utrecht corridor (see Chapter 8).

A problem which the Dutch will need to resolve concerns maintaining their position as a transport and distribution country and protecting the quality of the environment. The Dutch will be required to implement stricter measures which may mean more fundamental changes, if all 34 targets are to be met. Growth of road freight means that air quality targets for CO_2 and NO_x will not be met. Further measures have been proposed in the NMP2 to ensure there is a shift in freight transport from road to rail. The freight sector is an area in which the Dutch will need to prove their true commitment to the environment. Freight transport will require tighter measures and transport developments, which have economic implications, may need to be abandoned or significantly altered. The extent to which this will be undertaken in practice remains to be seen.

The setting of targets enables the monitoring of policy objectives and, where targets are not being met, further action can be taken. This can be in the form of tightening existing measures or identifying in which sector or target group new measures should be focused. Targets have a role to play in the development of a sustainable transport policy and will need to take effect at a number of different levels. The success of policy will be determined by the extent to which it affects or influences action taken at different levels. An important question is how national objectives and targets filter down from above to the project level? The next Chapter will examine the environmental impact assessment of transport projects and the EIA procedure which has developed in each country. It will discuss the limitations of project-based EIA and the benefits of implementing EIA early in the planning process at the strategic level in the formulation of policy.

6 Environmental assessment of transport

The previous Chapters have examined how the concept of sustainability has been translated into transport and environmental policy at the European, national and local level. An important aspect of sustainability is a reduction in the impact of human activity on the environment. Measures will therefore need to be implemented at a number of different levels, from the national to the project level, with action ultimately taking the form of policies, plans, programmes and projects in order to achieve sustainability in practice.

Environmental impact assessment (EIA) has become an important environmental management tool which has embodied the preventative approach to development projects. The 1985 EC EIA Directive (85/337/EEC) was agreed at a time when the notion of sustainable development was just beginning to receive wide recognition, although the concept had not been fully defined. EIA is directed to project-based assessment which provides information rather than determining the final outcome. It enables the environment to be considered within the project cycle and allows a high level of public participation. However, EIA has come under increasing criticism for concentrating mainly on the impacts of individual projects, giving little consideration to wider impacts which projects may cause in aggregate. These criticisms have led to a call for an environmental assessment of strategic policies, plans and programmes (PPPs).

A number of international organisations have recognised the need for Strategic Environmental Assessment (SEA) (UNECE, 1991; OECD, 1994). The European Commission prepared a draft Directive on SEA in 1992 which is currently under discussion. The British and Dutch governments have also advocated some form of policy appraisal.

International agreements and conventions are increasingly setting objectives and targets to achieve sustainability in a wide range of areas. Strategic environmental assessment could provide a systematic way of ensuring these objectives are met. In order to undertake SEA, it is necessary to understand the objectives of PPPs and the impact they will have on the environment. Criticisms of British transport policy have been that it lacks a clear set of objectives for all modes of transport and fails to integrate with other national policy. Critics (Buchan 1992; Transport 2000/IPPR, 1992) have argued that transport planning should be more objective-led, with the Netherlands often cited as an example of a country which has developed a transport policy in accordance with this approach. To achieve sustainability, policy objectives have to be set. Objectives are also important if SEA is to be undertaken to assess the environmental impact of policies, plans and programmes.

The aim of this Chapter is to examine the environment assessment of transport projects, which have been predominantly road schemes. It will discuss the emergence and development of EIA as an environmental management tool and the different EIA systems which have developed in Britain and the Netherlands. Road appraisal methods used in Britain will be discussed in depth. The benefits of undertaking a strategic environmental assessments of transport policies, plans and programmes will be outlined.

Environmental impact assessment

Each definition of environmental impact assessment varies in its depth, emphasis and scope. Munn (1979, p.1) defines EIA as:

> ... an activity designed to identify and predict the impact on the biogeophysical environment and on Man's health and well-being of legislative proposals, policies, programmes, projects and operational procedures, and to interpret and communicate information about the impacts.

Most EIA studies aim to examine and identify the effects which a proposed development is expected to have on 'the environment', including physical, biological, social, cultural and economic impacts, and to engender appropriate mitigation measures in the plans of the development.

An EIA should compare alternatives and determine the best combinations of environmental costs and benefits and examine and select the optimal alternative from the various options available. The EIA process involves the public in the decision-making process, and acts as a decision-making tool to aid the decision maker by giving a clear ranking of the alternatives considered (Ahmad & Sammy, 1985, p.2).

The aims of environmental impact assessment are incorporated in the actual EIA process (Table 6.1) which has a number of steps, the production of an Environmental Impact Statement (EIS) being just one.

Table 6.1
The EIA process

1. Deciding if an EIA is necessary (Screening phase)
2. Determining the coverage of an EIA (Scoping phase)
3. Preparing the EIA report, which includes;   - baseline study   - impact evaluation (quantification)   - mitigation measures   - assessment of alternatives
4. Producing a non-technical summary
5. Reviewing the EIA report
6. Consultation & participation with statutory consultees and the public
7. Synthesising findings from consultation
8. Reaching a decision
9. Post-decision monitoring of impacts

Source: Ahmad & Sammy, 1985, p.9

The origin of EIA

Environmental Impact Assessment stems from the US National Environmental Protection Act (NEPA) of 1969. The Act was introduced during a period when environmental protection was being recognised as a legitimate political objective, when people were demanding greater accountability from politicians generally, and when 'experts' were being challenged to provide technical justification (O'Riordan & Sewell, 1981). The purpose of NEPA was described in Section 2 of the Act; its aim was to declare:

> ... a national policy which will encourage productive and enjoyable harmony between Man and his environment, to promote efforts which will prevent or eliminate damage to the environment and biosphere and stimulate the welfare of man.

NEPA came into force on 1 January 1970. Section 102 (2)(c) of the Act required an Environmental Impact Statement to be produced for major federal actions significantly affecting the quality of the human environment. The EIS required a description of the environmental impacts of the proposed action; any adverse environmental effects which cannot be avoided should the proposal be implemented; alternatives to the proposed action and any irreversible and irretrievable commitment of resources which would be involved in the proposed action should it be implemented.

Since the passage of NEPA over two decades ago, some form of EIA has been adopted by the majority of Western industrialised countries; some Third World and Eastern European countries and a substantial number of international agencies (Lee, 1983, p.6; Wathern, 1988, p.3).

Implementation of EIA in the European Union

The European Union's Environmental Action Programmes have been in operation since 1973 and have covered many aspects of environmental policy, including the basis for the EIA Directive (85/337/EEC), which can be regarded as the embodiment of the preventative approach to environmental protection (Haigh, 1991, p.349). The use of Directives by the EC has been the dominant legislative device in the field of environmental policy, for Directives specify policy objectives but leave the means to achieve them to each Member State.

Research on EIA was commissioned by the EC in 1975 but the publication of a draft Directive did not occur until five years and twenty-one versions later in June 1980 (Wathern, 1988, p.193). The final approval by the EC Environment Council on the draft Directive did not take place until March 1985. The Directive was officially adopted on 27 June 1985 as Directive 85/337/EEC on *The Assessment of the Effects of Certain Public and Private Projects on the Environment*. It was subsequently published in the Official Journal No. 75 on 5 July 1985.

The EIA Directive is a procedural Directive in that it requires environmental information to be gathered and taken into account during the development consent procedure. It does not require consent to be refused in any circumstances, nor does it require conditions to be imposed to protect the environment. The Directive is also a framework Directive because it sets out a general procedure framework, leaving the details to Member States. The Directive consists of fourteen articles and three Annexes, with the mandatory assessment of certain development projects and the assessment of others at the discretion of Member States. Under Article 3, the Directive states that the EIA should:

> identify, describe and assess in an appropriate manner, in the light of each individual case ... the direct and indirect effects of a project on the following factors:
>
> - human beings, fauna and flora,
> - soil, water, air, climate and the landscape,
> - the inter-action between the factors mentioned in the first and second indents,
> - material assets and the cultural heritage.

Within Article 5 (2) of the Directive, the minimum information which should be provided about a development should include:

> - a description of the project, comprising information on the site, design and size of the project,
> - a description of the measures envisaged in order to avoid, reduce and, if possible, remedy significant adverse effects,
> - the data required to identify and assess the main effects which the project is likely to have on the environment,
> - a non-technical summary of the information mentioned in indents 1 to 3.

Annex I of the Directive lists nine groups of projects which require a developer, under Article 4 (1), to submit an EIA. Annex II projects are contained in twelve categories, for which under Article 4 (2) it is left to the discretion of Member States to decide whether an EIA is required. Annex III of the Directive contains a list of information which should be contained within an environmental impact statement. An EIS should also contain a description of a scheme and site, state measures proposed to mitigate adverse environmental impacts, provide data needed to identify and assess the main environmental impacts which the projects is likely to cause, and contain a non-technical summary.

Where it is considered appropriate, an outline of the main alternatives studied by the developer and an indication of the main reasons for his choice, taking into account environmental impacts, should also be included in the EIS.

A description of impacts should cover the direct effects and any secondary, cumulative effects which the project is likely to have on the environment. The impacts included in the description should include those impacts which may result from the existence of the project, use of natural resources, emissions of pollutants, the creation of nuisances and the elimination of waste.

EIA procedures in Britain and the Netherlands

The EIA Directive was translated into the British legal system by the *Town and Country Planning (Assessment of Environmental Effects) Regulations 1988 (SI No 1199)* which integrates it into the planning system. The regulations extended Section 31 of the Town and Country Planning Act 1971 to apply to projects for which an application for planning permission was lodged on or after 15 July 1988, while the three Annexes became Schedules 1, 2 and 3 of the regulations (Figure 6.1 outlines the EIA procedure in Britain).

About eighteen different regulations implementing the Directive and nine documents were produced. The regulations are, out of necessity, complex and difficult to comprehend, although Circular 15/88, which accompanies the regulations, describes the legal requirements and sets out the guidance for the assessment of Schedule 2 projects (Wood & McDonic, 1989).

The Dutch EIA Act came into force on 1 September 1987 and was incorporated into the Environmental Protection (General Provisions) Act (Bulletin of Acts Directive and Decrees 1986 No. 211, Chapter 4a). Figure 6.2 outlines the Dutch EIA procedure which begins with the publication of a Notification of Intent (NOI). The NOI contains the proposed plan for the development, and the objectives and the interests it will serve. Within the NOI alternatives are outlined which can meet the set of goals or objectives. The alternatives which are considered the most preferable will be identified for the proposed activity. According to Dutch EIA law several types of alternatives should be included in each environmental impact statement - the do-nothing or Zero alternative, alternatives to the proposed activity and the Best Environmental Alternative. The Zero alternative provides a description of the existing baseline conditions of the environment and the expected autonomous development. It acts as a reference point against which the magnitude and significance of predicted impacts can be measured. A description of each alternative for the proposed activity is also required, which should include the impact which each of the alternatives will have on the environment (VROM, n.d.).

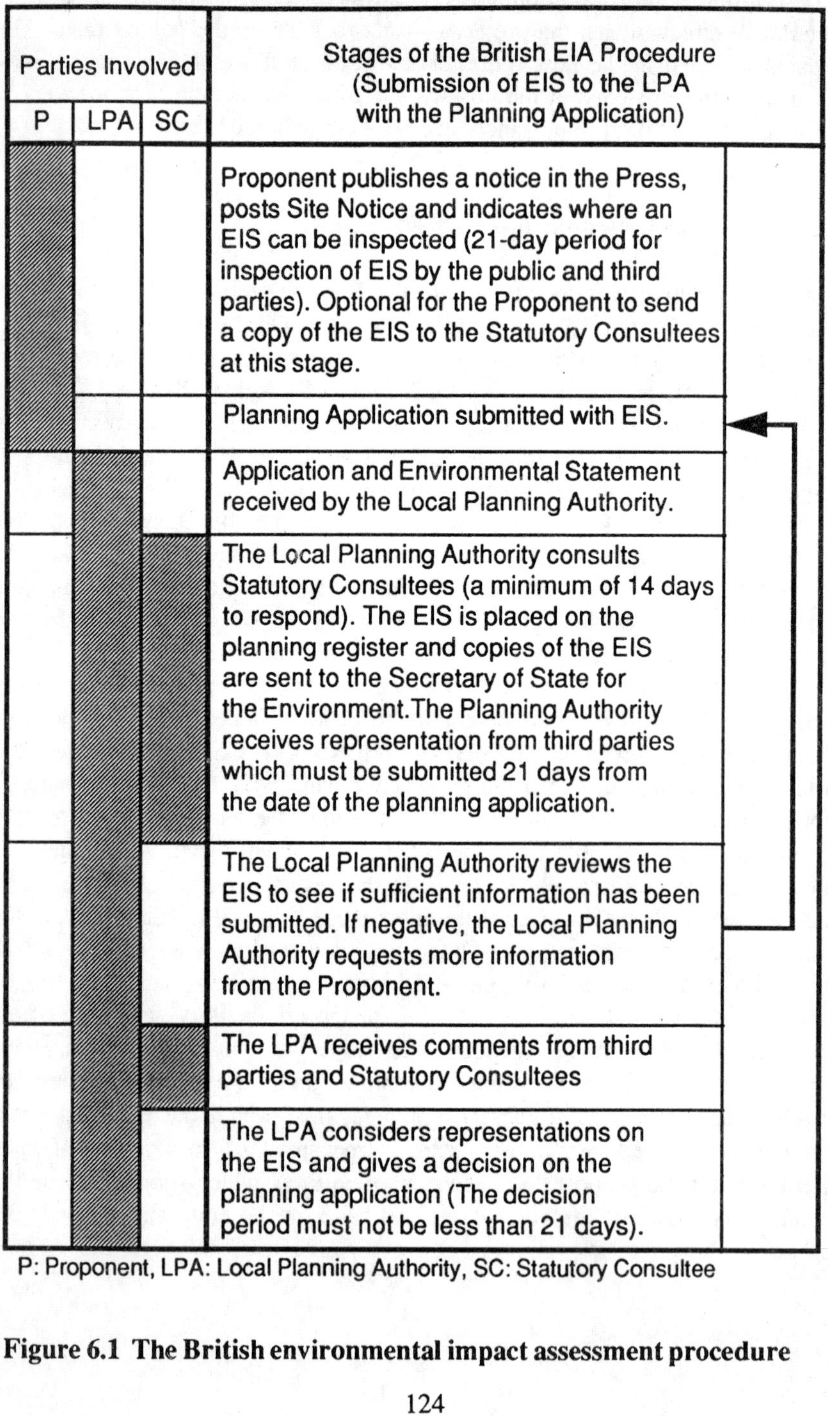

Parties Involved			Stages of the British EIA Procedure (Submission of EIS to the LPA with the Planning Application)
P	LPA	SC	
▓			Proponent publishes a notice in the Press, posts Site Notice and indicates where an EIS can be inspected (21-day period for inspection of EIS by the public and third parties). Optional for the Proponent to send a copy of the EIS to the Statutory Consultees at this stage.
▓			Planning Application submitted with EIS.
	▓		Application and Environmental Statement received by the Local Planning Authority.
		▓	The Local Planning Authority consults Statutory Consultees (a minimum of 14 days to respond). The EIS is placed on the planning register and copies of the EIS are sent to the Secretary of State for the Environment. The Planning Authority receives representation from third parties which must be submitted 21 days from the date of the planning application.
	▓		The Local Planning Authority reviews the EIS to see if sufficient information has been submitted. If negative, the Local Planning Authority requests more information from the Proponent.
		▓	The LPA receives comments from third parties and Statutory Consultees
	▓		The LPA considers representations on the EIS and gives a decision on the planning application (The decision period must not be less than 21 days).

P: Proponent, LPA: Local Planning Authority, SC: Statutory Consultee

Figure 6.1 The British environmental impact assessment procedure

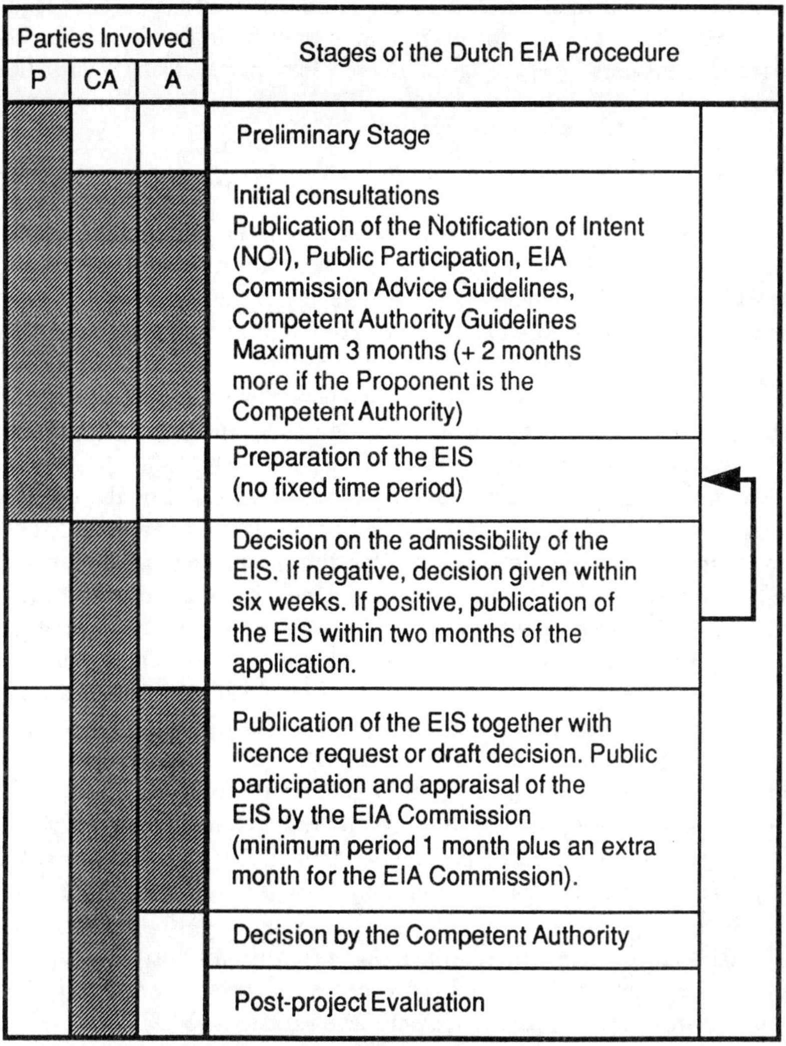

Parties Involved			Stages of the Dutch EIA Procedure
P	CA	A	
			Preliminary Stage
			Initial consultations Publication of the Notification of Intent (NOI), Public Participation, EIA Commission Advice Guidelines, Competent Authority Guidelines Maximum 3 months (+ 2 months more if the Proponent is the Competent Authority)
			Preparation of the EIS (no fixed time period)
			Decision on the admissibility of the EIS. If negative, decision given within six weeks. If positive, publication of the EIS within two months of the application.
			Publication of the EIS together with licence request or draft decision. Public participation and appraisal of the EIS by the EIA Commission (minimum period 1 month plus an extra month for the EIA Commission).
			Decision by the Competent Authority
			Post-project Evaluation

P: Proponent, CA: Competent Authority, A: Advisors

Figure 6.2 The Dutch environmental impact assessment procedure

The Best Environmental Alternative (BEA), under Dutch EIA law, requires environmental protection to be given a high priority. In the BEA alternative, economic considerations are given lower importance than environmental amenity.

The Dutch EIA Commission

In the Netherlands, the EIA Commission assists in the Scoping phase in identifying the environmental parameters which the development may affect. The EIA Commission provides advice guidelines on the production of the EIS which the competent authority can use as a basis for its final guidelines. Taking into consideration the comments from the public review and advice guidelines, the competent authority produces the Final Guidelines, the aim of which is to direct the EIS to the decision-making process, ensuring that important environmental factors are considered.

The initiator of the project uses the guidelines published by the competent authority to undertake the environmental assessment and produce an EIS. The guidelines are not legally binding, but the Proponent must state reasons for wanting to deviate from them. Once the Initiator has submitted an EIS, it is reviewed by the public and the EIA Commission. It is important at this stage for the Commission to examine the EIS for quality and content. It then checks that the statement follows the guidelines and regulations. On the basis of the EIS and public consultation process, a decision is taken by the competent authority on whether a project should go ahead.

The Competent Authority must then state in the decision the role which EIA has played in the decision-making process, information on impacts and alternatives, and comments of public consultation. The decision also includes obligatory post-auditing and monitoring evaluation which needs to be undertaken.

There is no equivalent body to the Dutch EIA Commission in Britain. The absence of a British EIA Commission is one of the reasons why the quality of British environmental impact statements have varied (Wood & Jones, 1991).

EIA and transport in Britain

The application of the EC Directive to trunk road schemes in Britain was given legal effect by amendments to the Highway Act 1980 with Part V(A) of the amendments providing for the environmental assessment (EA) of trunk roads. The DOT Departmental Standard HD 18/88 explains how the Directive and provisions of the Act are to be followed in practice. The Departmental Standard does not require an environmental statement to be undertaken for each of the schemes presented at the earlier public consultation stage, when schemes are presented for discussion. If at the earlier stage any option has environmental effects, significantly different from the preferred scheme, the environmental statement which accompanies the preferred scheme must, in summary, describe the alternatives and give reasons for making final choices (SACTRA, 1992, p.43).

The Departmental Standard states that all new motorway construction schemes must be subject to an environmental assessment. Annex I of the Directive requires an EIA for the construction of motorways, express roads and lines for long-distance railway traffic, and of airports with a basic runway length of 2100 metres or more. The definition of 'express roads' complies with the definition in the European Agreement on main international traffic arteries of 15 November 1975:

> Roads reserved for automobile traffic, accessible only for interchanges or control junctions and on which, in particular, stopping and parking are prohibited.

Express roads equate to the 'Special Roads' under the Highways Act 1980.

Member States are able to decide whether an EIA is required for Annex II projects. Annex II of the Directive contains infrastructure projects which are not listed in Annex I, such as construction of roads, harbours and air fields, tramways, elevated and underground railways and suspended lines or similar lines of a particular type, used exclusively or mainly for passenger transport. Motorway improvements and slip roads to motorways which are added or amended subsequent to the approval of the motorway itself are classed as modifications and are covered by Annex II. The Government requires an EIA for all new roads and major roads improvements over 10 kilometres in length, or over 1 kilometre in length if the road passes through a National Park or through or within 100 metres of a site of Special Scientific Interest, a National Nature Reserve (as defined in the Countryside Act 1949) or a conservation area.

An environmental impact assessment is also required for roads in urban areas where more than 1,500 dwellings lie within 100 metres of the centre line of the proposed road (or of an existing road in the case of major improvements) (DOE Circular 15/88, 1988, p.13). Unlike the *Manual for Environmental Appraisal* for trunk road schemes, no equivalent document exists for the assessment of rail developments. New railway lines are technically exempt from an environmental assessment under the EC Directive since new lines are agreed by Acts of Parliament. The government does recommend that new proposals should be assessed in accordance with the requirements of the EIA Directive.

Appraisal methods for roads are divided into three main areas: traffic appraisal; economic evaluation and environmental appraisal.

Traffic appraisal   The aim of traffic appraisal is to determine current and estimate future flows of traffic on or near an existing road and to decide whether traffic management schemes or improved or new roads are needed. Traffic forecasts should show the impact the scheme will have and predict the traffic using the scheme in future years. Traffic forecasts provide estimates for use in economic and environmental impact assessment and enable a design to be selected which would provide capacity for future traffic (SACTRA, 1986, p.79). Information on traffic flow is obtained by traffic counts, roadside interviews and journey time surveys. The information collected determines how and what type of vehicles use the road and the origin, destination and purpose of journeys. The data collected can then be used to predict future traffic flows by type and purpose of journey for proposed schemes using traffic modelling techniques (SACTRA, 1986, p.37). Traffic forecasts are based on the National Road Traffic Forecasts (NRTF) and are linked to the government's forecasts of expected economic growth. Due to the uncertainties associated with forecasting, the Advisory Committee on Trunk Road Assessment (ACTRA) recommended that the DOT should support a single figure. The DOT responded to this recommendation by introducing the concept of high and low national road traffic forecasts. The high growth forecasts are based on high economic growth and low fuel prices, while the low growth forecasts are based on low economic growth and high fuel prices.

The *Traffic Appraisal Manual* (TAM) was produced as a response to the recommendation made by ACTRA, to produce a manual for inter-urban roads. It sets out the DOT's recommended methods of appraisal. The Manual outlined steps to be undertaken in a traffic study and to define study areas, sources of traffic data, survey methods, traffic growth and calibration, and validation of traffic models (SACTRA, 1986, p.77).

The 1986 report of the Standing Advisory Committee on Trunk Road Assessment (SACTRA) reviewed traffic appraisal methods and recommended that a forecast should be made which shows the immediate impact of the scheme in the first year of operation, and that other forecasts should predict the traffic using the scheme in future years. Due to the uncertainties associated with forecasting, SACTRA recommended that a traffic model be kept up to date with latest information in the assessment process (SACTRA, 1986, p.79). The forecasting period should be for a maximum of fifteen years from the date of implementation of a scheme, or twenty years from the date at which the assessment is made, whichever is the shorter.

The SACTRA Report (1986, p.115), however, recommended the use of a single forecast for traffic growth, based on local data rather than high and low forecasts. If single traffic forecasts fall outside the limits of the regional component of the national traffic forecasts, they should be justified. The implications for the scheme design and evaluation of variation around this single forecast can then be assessed separately.

In 1994 SACTRA addressed the long-standing concern over whether improved road schemes actually unleash suppressed demand and induce more traffic. The accuracy of traffic forecasts is important if economic and environmental appraisal are to be undertaken successfully. The DOT has not considered induced traffic in its road appraisal techniques. Where induced traffic may exist, the DOT believes that it has no consequence for the design and economics of the scheme and should therefore be ignored (SACTRA, 1994). SACTRA identified behavioural responses to improved roads causing more traffic. These included factors such as new trips, redistributed trips, transfer between modes and trips associated with new developments. Trip retiming was considered an important behavioural reaction to the improvement of road capacity. SACTRA (1994) concluded that:

> ... considering all ... [the] sources of evidence, ... induced traffic can and does occur, probably quite extensively, though its size and significance is likely to vary widely in different circumstances.

SACTRA recommended the improvement of traffic forecasts models to include demand responses other than rerouting (SACTRA, 1994, p.190). The government is implementing a research programme to understand further and develop robust modelling techniques to take into consideration demand response (DOT, 1994b).

Economic evaluation Economic evaluation is based on predictions of traffic flow which have been derived from the traffic appraisal. The aim of economic evaluation is to estimate the benefits from providing a new or improved transport facility, compared with the cost of provision. Estimates of cost take account of the costs of scheme preparation, land acquisition, construction and maintenance.

Effects on travelling time are considered for the main categories of travellers - car drivers and passengers, public transport crew and passengers, goods vehicles drivers, motor cyclists and pedestrians. Different types of journey time are distinguished between time spent on travel during the course of work ('working time') and time spent on travel for other purposes such as commuting to and from work ('non-working time') (SACTRA, 1992, p.26).

The DOT publishes values for use in its assessment which are assigned to travel times for each type of journey. Values for working time hours are estimated by the use of average national wage-rates. The National Travel Survey is used to determine rates for both car drivers and passengers, while the New Earnings Survey produced by the Department of Employment is used to determine values for bus drivers and drivers and occupants of commercial vehicles. The value of non-working hours is based on evidence from traveller behaviour and preferences expressed by people in surveys and interviews. Average non-working and working time benefits contribute equally to total benefits of trunk road schemes (SACTRA, 1992, p. 26).

Assessment of new road schemes also consider the effects they have for road safety and the increase in the risk of accidents occurring. The DOT provides values to enable accidents to be costed. The cost is determined by three factors. The first factor is the direct financial cost and cost to the individual and organisation which may be involved, for example, damage to vehicles, police attendance and medical costs. The second factor considers the opportunity cost of lost output to the economy due to individuals being injured or killed. The third factor covers the pain, grief and suffering which may result from personal injury or death (IHT, 1987, p.102).

An economic evaluation computer program called COBA was initially developed for inter-urban roads but has also been applied to urban roads. The main input data of the program are travel costs and time per trip with and without the scheme. These are dependent on the output of traffic forecasting and the modelling exercise, based on fixed demand and variable demand matrices. The former assumes that the development of new road schemes does not affect travel demands in terms of origin and destination of travel, mode of transport and travel time. The variable matrix allows variation in the demand matrices for all situations with and without the proposed road scheme. Any reduction in the perceived (unit) cost of travel will result in an increase in the amount of travel undertaken. The 1986 SACTRA report criticised the method of only using a fixed trip matrix. It claimed:

> ... whilst such an approach is often a reasonable assumption for inter-urban roads where capacity is not reached, it is less likely to be valued for congested urban main roads (SACTRA, 1986, p.88).

A new road improvement could lead to a reassignment of journeys between the same origin-destination and redistribute journeys to different destinations, to take account of greater access to specific parts of urban areas provided by the new route. A modal shift from rail and bus to car, due to the improved road access provided by the new route, could occur as well as journeys being undertaken at different times of the day and the generation of additional trips

(SACTRA, 1992). SACTRA (1994) stated that even the omission of a small amount of induced traffic could lead to the economic value of a scheme being overestimated. This has important effects for the economic assessment of the roads programme.

SACTRA (1994) argued that the level and pattern of demand in the fixed matrix is assumed to be independent of the quality of the network. It showed that in some cases the 'do-minimum' alternative prediction of traffic flows can be too high while in the 'do-something' alternative traffic flows can be too low, with little consideration given to induced demand. The implications of this are that the fixed matrix system can lead to a overestimation of user benefits for a particular scheme. SACTRA therefore recommended that variable demand methods should become part of the normal assessment process of trunk road schemes and should be undertaken in a systematic way and included in the economic and environmental appraisal of road schemes. The government accepted the recommendation and stated that the variable trip matrix will be used for all schemes, except where prior assessment has shown that a trip matrix will not vary significantly as a result of the scheme (DOT, 1994b, p.14).

Environmental appraisal The main guidance for assessing the environmental impacts of a road scheme was outlined in the Department of Transport's *Manual for Environmental Appraisal* (MEA). This was followed in 1993 by the *Design Manual for Roads and Bridges, Volume II: Environmental Assessment*. ACTRA (1977) discovered that factors expressed in non-monetary terms or qualitative terms were given insufficient consideration compared with COBA (ACTRA, 1977, p.57).

Jefferson (Deputy Director of the South West Construction Unit) was requested to draft guidance on the location of major inter-urban road schemes for Road Construction Units, focusing attention on noise and environmental issues. Jefferson produced his report in March 1976 which was for internal use and was unpublished. He concluded that, while inclusion of environmental factors in COBA was impractical, the DOT should adopt a standard format for presentation, covering land-take, noise, vibration, air pollution, severance and accidents. Taking into consideration the Jefferson report, the Committee concluded in 1977 that the Department should adopt a framework for the assessment of trunk road schemes. The assessment would take account of the effects of the scheme on five groups: road users, non-road users directly affected, those concerned with the intrinsic value of the area through which the scheme passes, those directly affected by the scheme, and the financing authority. The framework would be used as a basis to decide between options within a scheme, enabling a judgement to made considering all factors, whether valued in monetary terms or not (ACTRA, 1977, p. 134-5).

The guidance set out in the MEA applied mainly to trunk roads but was also applied to inter-urban roads, which are the responsibility of the highways authority. It was divided into three parts and contained the main elements of the framework for departmental advice on environmental appraisal and methods of assessment. The framework enabled the main effects of a scheme to be brought together within a matrix, so that the effects between different options can be seen, thus permitting the comparison of quantifiable and non-quantifiable costs and benefits in a comprehensive way and ensuring consistency in trunk road appraisal. The framework was divided into to six groups (Table 6.2).

Table 6.2
Interest groups within the MEA framework

Group 1	effects on travellers
Group 2	effects on occupiers of property
Group 3	effects on users of facilities
Group 4	effects on policies for conserving and enhancing the area
Group 5	effects on policies for development and transport
Group 6	effects on financial aspects

The framework provided the public with information on the impacts of a proposed scheme, its alternatives and acted as an aid to decision-making. Group 1 covers time savings and vehicle operating costs savings calculated by COBA. Group 6 included all monetarised factors with the Net Present Value (NPV) presented for high and low growth forecasts for all proposed schemes, compared with the 'do-nothing' or 'do-minimum' option. The Manual considered environmental impacts at the local level and was divided into ten sections: traffic noise, visual impact, air pollution, community severance, construction, view from the road, effects on agriculture, heritage and conservation, pedestrians and cyclists and driver stress. In October 1979 SACTRA produced a report on *Trunk Road Proposals - A Comprehensive Framework for Appraisal*, in which it described the experience gained in using the framework. The report developed further some of the principles set out by ACTRA, which should be used in practice to deal with the choice between alternative routes of a road scheme.

The 1986 SACTRA report on *Urban Road Appraisal* considered techniques for the assessment of environmental and social impacts and examined advice given in the MEA. The report found that:

... coverage and method [was] generally sound, in principle, but in need of some changes of emphasis to make it more suitable for application to a wide range of urban schemes (SACTRA, 1986, p.38).

One of SACTRA's most significant recommendations was to replace the framework, which was considered unsatisfactory and inflexible, with an assessment summary. They modified it into an assessment summary report, which would comprise five parts: objectives and problems, options and consultations, traffic appraisal, economic evaluation and environmental and social impacts. The report stated that the Committee:

... do not recommend the use of impacts which are quantifiable as proxies for other effects which are not quantifiable or which are too difficult to measure. Impacts which cannot be quantified must be assessed on the basis of judgement, not left out. It is often equally important that the basis of judgement is stated explicitly in the supplementary information which will support the assessment (SACTRA, 1986).

The government accepted most of the recommendations made by the 1986 SACTRA report, and agreed in principle to the development of an assessment summary report.

In September 1989 SACTRA was invited to review the Department's methods for assessing environmental costs and benefits. It published its recommendations and conclusions in its report, *Assessing the Environmental Impact of Road Schemes* in 1992. The 1986 SACTRA Report recommended that policy objectives should be explicitly stated to guide the assessment of road schemes. The report defined objectives as having desirable ends, which should be set without preconceptions about how they might be fulfilled. Objectives were distinguished between those at the national level and those at the local level. The use of objectives would act as reference points, against which road schemes could be assessed. The government accepted these recommendations, although the procedure has not been followed in practice. The 1992 SACTRA Report endorsed the view that objectives need to be explicitly stated. The Committee also identified the need for a more strategic level assessment, due to the cumulative impact which individual road schemes may have and their contribution to, for example, global atmospheric pollution.

SACTRA (1992) suggested an assessment should be adequate in its geographical extent (not simply concerned with the immediate vicinity of the new road), in time scale (long-term as well as immediate effects), in its presentation of all alternatives (not just routes, but modes and policies) and in its consideration of interactions (which would include the combined and cumulative impacts of several schemes and policies). The Committee concluded that:

> The system of environmental assessment which we need must therefore derive from explicitly stated environmental policy objectives. It must be comprehensive; based on real evidence; practical; capable of consistent application; and command acceptance of professionals and the public. The resources and time necessary to operate it should not be out of proportion to the importance of the issue involved, or greater than the cost of the outcome. The form of reporting must be clear and non-technical. The value judgements and technical assumptions made, and the methods used, should be explicit, open to scrutiny, challenge and possible revision (SACTRA, 1992, p.92).

In the government's response to the need for an appraisal structure to consider the cumulative impacts of several schemes and policies, it stated:

> The Department accepts that in some cases appraisal needs to cover the combined and cumulative effects of several schemes. Consideration of longer routes or a number of related schemes together may also allow a better choice of alignment and design, in both environmental and traffic approach terms. Increasingly, the Department is trying to ensure this ... is followed, where appropriate. However, since schemes in the programme have been initiated and progressed over different time scales, this is not always possible in practice (SACTRA, 1994, p.189).

SACTRA also expressed concern about the little attention given to the strategic level in the development of the national roads programme and its overall effect on the environment.

Implementation of transport strategies should be set within wider planning strategies dealing with the use and management of land and the state of the environment, at each of the levels from national to local (SACTRA, 1992, p.53). SACTRA stated that the appraisal of individual road schemes will achieve a proper focus only if carried out within a framework of national, regional and local environmental policies and objectives, working in combination (SACTRA, 1992, p.53).

With regard to the planning of trunk roads, SACTRA recommended that no scheme should be admitted into the Roads Programme until its performance against strategic objectives and constraints has been reported in outline. Where local planning authorities have also adopted regional and local objectives, schemes should be tested against these at the Route Identification Stage in the planning process.

Thus, once a scheme has entered the Roads Programme, it would be likely that many of the strategic environmental questions would have been addressed, with the remainder of the assessment process concentrating on regional and local effects which govern the choice between options.

In 1994 SACTRA further endorsed the need for a more strategic approach to road planning in which they recommended that appraisal of schemes be undertaken within the context of strategic area-wide economic and environmental appraisal, taking into account induced traffic. Much more emphasis should be placed on the strategic assessment of trunk road routes within a corridor or at a regional or urban level. They recommended that routes should be assessed in their entirety for environmental reasons and the consequences of road improvements for the pattern of land use development should be considered at the regional or corridor level.

Presentation of the environmental assessment EIA is generally considered to come late in the planning process; with road schemes this is after the Line Orders have been published. SACTRA believed that good practice would require formal assessments much earlier, and this would be a continual process throughout a scheme's development. An environmental assessment of a road scheme should be undertaken at three stages - on its entry into the Roads Programme, after public consultation on the options, and when the Line Orders for the SoS's Preferred Route are published. This is the point at which the Environmental Statement required by statute must be produced. SACTRA proposed that the assessment report would be a free-standing document - Environmental Assessment Report - Road Programme Entry; Environmental Assessment Report - Route Options. The former would be made available to those who undertake the principal work of the environmental assessment, while the Environmental Assessment Report - Route Options would be made available to the public and those directly affected by the scheme for discussion at the public inquiry.

The statutory Environmental Statement will be prepared from the earlier Environmental Assessment Report and would thus relate to the preferred route. It would address those effects which have been judged to be significant, and not all the effects considered at the public consultation stage. SACTRA recommended that the Environmental Statement be divided into five sections - description of the site, description of the scheme and its environmental effects, mitigation of environmental effects, data and methodology, and a non-technical summary.

Due to the implications of the above recommendations for the Manual for Environmental Appraisal, the Committee suggested the Manual be replaced by a manual for environmental assessment, which would be directed exclusively to the preparation of environmental assessments.

In 1993 the Department of Transport updated and expanded guidance on the environmental assessment of new and improved trunk roads, including motorways, in a Design Manual of Environmental Appraisal, which replaced the Manual for Environmental Appraisal. The new Manual retained the idea of a framework table similar to the MEA (Table 6.2), but with a number of changes. In the new Manual the framework tables are now called 'Environmental Impact Tables' and are divided into: Appraisal Groups (local people and communities, travellers, the cultural and natural environment, policies and plans), a Land use Table and a Mitigation Table. The Manual contains guidance on assessing the environmental impact on a number of factors e.g. air and noise pollution, visual intrusion, severance, ecology etc. The new guidance on environmental assessment will hopefully lead to an improvement in the quality of EISs of roads and bridges.

Review of the EC Directive on EIA

Member States were required to implement the EC EIA Directive in the transitional period 1985-1988. In April 1993 a review of the Directive was undertaken in accordance with Article 11 of the Directive, which provided for an assessment of its application and effectiveness covering the period 1985-1991. The review *inter alia* examined the extent of formal compliance by the Member States with the requirements of the Directive, the criteria/thresholds adopted by Member States for Annex II projects and the nature and extent of practical compliance by the Member States with the requirements of the Directive.

Implementation of the Directive required the approval of new regulations and amendments to existing legal regulations. During this period a number of measures were approved in the Netherlands, Spain, Belgium and the UK. The main period of implementation was after July 1988 and especially from 1990-1. The final process of formal compliance was not achieved by all twelve Member States until July 1991.

All projects in Annex I must be subject to an EIA, unless individually determined in exceptional cases. The review found that in the majority of cases formal compliance with Annex I was broadly satisfactory. However, the coverage of Annex I projects may differ to some extent between the Member States due to the scope of classes being interpreted differently. For example, a generally accepted definition of an 'integrated chemical installation' was a particular problem which the review identified.

The number of Annex I and Annex II EISs has differed from country to country with 98% of Irish EISs and 28% of Italian EISs falling in Annex II projects. In the same countries only 2% of Irish and 72% of Italian EISs fall within Annex I (Table 6.3). Where the Member State's thresholds are relatively high, then the number of Annex II projects requiring an EIA will be smaller than average. Where the thresholds are low the number of assessments to be undertaken may be very large (e.g. France). The review found that in the Member States no clear consensus on thresholds levels existed, and that the variability in the consideration of Annex II projects is likely to become an even greater problem if no remedial action is taken (CEC, 1993b, p.20)

Annex III of the Directive outlines the scope of an EIS, leaving it up to the discretion of Member States to develop a procedure for this to be achieved. Belgium (Wallonia), Germany, Luxembourg and the Netherlands have made some statutory provision for Scoping (CEC, 1993b, p.21). Some Member States have encouraged Scoping through non-mandatory guidance via existing administrative procedures.

The review found a number of deficiencies in the quality of EISs. These have been due to failure to begin assessments early in the planning and design of projects, failure to consider a range of alternatives where possible and to identify measures early enough to incorporate them into the project, an unsatisfactory procedure for the scope and coverage of the EIA, and a bias in the assessment and presentation of environmental impacts.

Table 6.3
Number of Annex I and II projects in selected Member States
(% of total EISs)

Member State	Annex I	Annex II
Belgium		
Flanders	37	63
Wallonia	59	41
Denmark	33	67
France	3-4	96-97
Ireland	2	98
Italy	72	28
Netherlands	28	72
United Kingdom	12	88

Source: CEC, 1993b, p.40

137

Member States have tended to rely on existing monitoring procedures and practices to assess the impact of the project once it has been constructed, with the exception of the Netherlands, Italy and Spain. The review of the Directive concluded that the evaluation of environmental impacts of projects takes place too late in the development and planning of projects. This has resulted in less consideration being given to alternatives for the individual project as well as its possible location and route. In the planning and design of the project, mitigation measures are often inadequately integrated into the project.

A considerable variation exists in the number and coverage of EISs undertaken in each country. The review revealed that only a minority of EISs are of satisfactory quality, which is mainly due to the stage at which EIA begins (CEC, 1993b, p.66). Member States have taken a range of measures to achieve a quality standard in the EISs which are submitted. The Netherlands, as discussed above, has an independent Commission, together with Italy and Belgium (Wallonia) (CEC, 1993b, p.45). A study by Wood and Jones (1991) examined 24 British EISs and found that the majority were inadequate, which reflects the concern of Statutory Consultees in Britain with the quality of EISs. They recommended the setting up of an independent EIA review body in Britain to improve the quality of EISs by advising local planning authorities on quality.

During the period 1988-1993 the European Commission received the largest number of complaints from British citizens relating to the implementation of the EC Directive (Table 6.4). Among these were complaints about the application of EIA to transport projects. This led the EC to challenge the UK government with regard to the EIA of the Channel Tunnel Rail Link, the East London River Crossing, the M3 at Twyford Down and the M11 road link. However, EC action related to these projects was subsequently withdrawn, either because the projects themselves were withdrawn or the requirements of the EIA Directive were finally met by the Proponent of the project.

Proposed amendments to the EIA Directive

On 16 March 1994 the European Commission adopted a proposal for a Directive to amend Directive 85/337/EEC in response to the problems identified in the five year review. The proposal follows the co-operation procedure as laid down under Article 189c of the Maastricht Treaty. After the adoption of a common position by the Council, it will be submitted to the European Parliament for a second reading. It is expected that the proposal for amendments to the Directive will be finally adopted by the end of 1996.

The proposed amendments to the Directive include various changes to the Annexes, with a substantial increase in the number of projects included in Annex I and further clarification of both Annex I and Annex II projects. In the amendments Annex II includes modifications to Annex II projects and modifications to Annex I projects.

The main amendments to the Directive are in relation to the Screening of Annex II projects, due to there being no clear consensus in the Member States on the threshold levels used to decide whether a project, which falls under Annex II of the Directive, requires an EIA.

When examining case-by-case projects or setting thresholds or criteria, the Member State will be required to take into consideration selection criteria proposed in a new Annex IIa. Annex IIa will list the factors which should be considered, these are: the characteristics of the project, the location of the project and the potential impact of the project. The proposed amendments attempt to reduce the disparities which arise between the Member States with regard to decisions taken for Annex II projects (Sheate, 1995).

Table 6.4
Complaints received by the EC relating to the EIA Directive
(1988-1993)

Member State	1988	1989	1990	1991	1992	1993	Total
Belgium	1	5	6	3	1	3	19
Denmark	0	0	0	11	3	1	15
France	3	13	17	24	16	15	88
Germany	4	18	15	39	34	15	125
Greece	5	8	21	17	40	23	114
Ireland	2	12	12	12	27	16	81
Italy	5	14	23	12	15	5	74
Luxembourg	0	0	1	-	-	-	1
Netherlands	0	2	1	4	6	3	16
Portugal	4	7	15	5	8	7	46
Spain	8	34	30	27	37	46	182
UK	2	17	29	33	95	29	205
Total	34	130	170	187	282	163	966

Source: CEC, 1993b

Within the proposed amendments greater consideration is given to the 1991 Espoo Convention on Transboundary Environmental Impact Assessment. The amendments detail the procedure to be followed if an project is likely to affect another Member State

Limitations of EIA

Although EIA has become a popular tool to assess the potential impacts of development projects it has nevertheless a number of deficiencies. By the time the EIA stage has been reached, it is often too late to consider different alternatives. With regard to road transport, for example, once a decision has been made to build a road, alternatives considered are normally concerned with the different alignments of the road or other changes in infrastructural design.

Annex III of the EIA Directive requires the consideration of cumulative impacts, although they are rarely considered in practice. Cumulative impacts include the additive effects of the sum of the individual projects within a particular sector. Environmental impact assessment is normally undertaken for project-based developments, once a need and the design of a particular development have been decided upon. Each project is assessed in isolation. For example, each road which makes up the UK Roads Programme is assessed individually. No assessment of the Roads Programme is considered in its entirety

Synergistic impacts occur where one of two factors combine to become more harmful. One example of a synergistic effect is the chemical reaction of the pollutants hydrocarbons and nitrogen oxides in the presence of sunlight to form photochemical oxidants, which enhances the formation of acid deposition and global warming. Indirect impacts occur when a particular development may stimulate secondary infrastructural developments; for example, a new motorway system may give rise to service stations, or encourage out of town-retail-developments. The consideration of cumulative impacts as well as transboundary impacts is, to some extent, limited by lack of knowledge concerning other development proposals and lack of control over them. EIA normally only addresses the direct impacts of a development and does not consider the cumulative impacts of a development project. The 1991 Espoo Convention provided the basis for the examination of transboundary impacts within EIA.

Projects subject to EIA are considered to be limited, for example, most projects decided by Acts of Parliament, are exempt, including projects related to defence and security. EIA is mainly seen as a means to an end by Proponents. No incentive exists to provide a comprehensive EIS, especially within the prevailing time and financial constraints. The level of public participation within the EIA process is to some extent limited, for consideration of public views towards the design and development proposal is considered expensive and time-consuming. Secondly, due to the prevalence of commercial confidentiality, information revealed to the public may be limited. The 1990 Environmental Protection Act, however, did make provision for greater access to information. The actual influence which an EIS has upon the final decision of a project is still not known. The decision-making process is considered to be a black box, with a multitude of influential socio-political factors. To what extent one factor dominates the final decision is a mystery.

Once the EIA has been completed and a decision has been made for the project to be implemented, no follow-up assessment is undertaken. The absence of post-decision monitoring of a project, to ensure predicted impacts are mitigated and to examine whether impact prediction methods were accurate, is a major deficiency in EIA.

Five years after the EC Directive was transcribed by Member States, an assessment review report was produced in the UK (Wood & Jones, 1991). The main conclusions include the following criticisms: the exemption of parliamentary approved projects from EIA, the failure of the Directive to give adequate guidance on Annex II projects, which are left to the discretion of Member States; and public participation only beginning once a formal application is made for a project, not throughout the project planning.

Due to local planning authorities being unfamiliar with EIA, critics argue that EIA has not been consistently applied throughout a broad range of subjects. Discussion of alternatives within an EIS is left to the discretion of the developer. In comparison the Dutch EIA system requires a range of alternatives to be stated, including the 'Zero-alternative' (do nothing) and the best environmental alternative, which ignores any financial constraints.

The content required within an EIA varies between countries. Concern has also been expressed over the objectivity of environmental impact statements which have been produced, especially if the Proponent and Competent Authority are the same, e.g. in the case of the Department of Transport and trunk road schemes which are within the National Trunks Roads Programme. A biased statement may also be due to the Proponent having too much control over the EIS which the consultants produce. Environmental consultants claim to be independent and unbiased. However, due to financial interests critics have questioned to what extent consultants are influenced by the Proponent's needs. Increasing concern over the quality of environmental statements since 1988, has led to action for greater quality. The Institute of Environmental Assessment and the Association of Environmental Consultants in Britain have attempted to develop a more professional standard within the area of environmental consultancy. These organisations have encouraged improvement in the quality of environmental statements, using methods to assess the quality of EISs such as the method developed by Lee and Colley (1990).

141

The difficulties associated with project-based EIA have resulted in increasing support for EIA to be undertaken early in the planning process, and at the strategic level in the formulation of policies, plans and programmes (PPPs).

Strategic environmental assessment

Given the goal of sustainable development, there is a need to assess the environmental implications of policies, plans and programmes. The definition of policies, plans and programmes differ in their use from country to country, but all act as a means of forward planning, enabling resources to be allocated and distributed accordingly.

Wood (1988, p.98) states that a 'tiered' system of forward planning exists, to which EIA should be applied in a chronological sequence of category of action - a tiered system of formulation of policy at the upper level, followed by a plan and programme stage. Wood and Dejeddour (1992, p.8) consider policy as the inspiration and guidance for action, a plan as a set of co-ordinated and time objectives for implementing policy, and a programme as a set of projects in particular areas.

A strategic based EIA was advocated in the World Conservation Strategy (1980) which pinpointed the need to integrate environmental considerations within development. The 1985 Brundtland Report also suggested that the environment should be given consideration at an early stage in planning and the EC Fifth European Action Programme has supports the need for a strategic environmental assessment. The implementation of strategic environmental assessment has a number of advantages (Wood & Dejeddour, 1992, p.7):

1. SEA encourages the consideration of environmental objectives during policy, plan and programme making activities.
2. Facilitates consultations between authorities and enhances public involvement in the formulation of PPPs.
3. May render some EIAs redundant if impacts have been considered adequately.
4. Allows the formulation of basic mitigation measures for later projects.
5. Encourages consideration of alternatives often ignored or not feasible in project EIA.
6. Allows more effective analysis of cumulative impacts and encourages the consideration of synergistic, ancillary and secondary and transboundary impacts.

Some form of SEA system has been in operation in a number of different countries such as Australia, Finland, Germany, Hong Kong, Japan, the

Netherlands, New Zealand and the USA (California). Lee and Hughes (1995) examined existing SEA legislation and procedures in the 15 Member States of the European Union. They discovered that although formal decision-making processes for policies, plans and programmes existed within the EU for a number of sectors (e.g. land use, forestry and transport), the coverage of different sectors and provisions for SEA differ with each Member State. Any SEA instrument adopted at a European level would therefore need to be highly adaptable if it is to be integrated into existing planning procedures.

The EC produced a Draft Directive on SEA in November 1992, in accordance with the Fifth Environmental Action Programme. The 1985 EIA Directive was originally intended to cover both plans and projects, but the final form of the Directive only covers projects in Annex I and Annex II (Wathern, 1988, p.99). Discussion of the Draft SEA Directive is still continuing. Due to political compromise, the final version of the SEA Directive is expected to be a watered down version of the initial 1992 draft. The final SEA Directive is expected to require an environmental assessment of plans and programmes, before submission to parliament or adoption by competent authorities, and the modification of such a plan or programme. A requirement for the SEA of policies is considered to be a politically sensitive issue and is therefore expected to be excluded from the final Directive (ENDS, 1995).

The SEA Directive will be similar to the EIA Directive, requiring an environmental statement to be produced for a number of identified sectors (e.g. energy, land use, transport, mineral extraction, water resources) and consideration to be given to a number of specific environmental factors such as those stated in Article 3 of the EIA Directive. As in the amendments to the Directive 85/337/EEC, it is expected that consultation procedures for transboundary impacts will be given particular attention.

The final SEA Directive will probably be a simple Directive, to ensure its integration into the existing planning procedures of the Member States.

Policy appraisal in Britain

The British Government has slowly begun to acknowledge the need for strategic assessment. The 1990 White Paper *This Common Inheritance* examined the implications of the roads programme for carbon dioxide emissions, protection of the countryside and traffic management schemes, and the effect on policy areas for transport planning. The White Paper concluded that:

... there is scope for a more systematic approach within Government to the appraisal of the environmental costs and benefits before decisions are taken. The Government has therefore set work in hand to produce guidelines for policy appraisal where there are significant implications for the environment (DOE, 1990, p. para 18.6).

The guidelines were published in 1991 in a document entitled *Policy Appraisal and the Environment*. The guide was directed to those in central government who were responsible for advising ministers on policy. This was followed in 1994 by *Environmental Appraisal in Government Departments* which provided further guidance and examined the actions taken in response to the guide. The 1991 guide advocated a systematic appraisal of policy options, identifying, quantifying, weighing up, and reporting on the costs and benefits of the measures which are proposed in the implementation of policy. Table 6.5 outlines the steps of policy appraisal as proposed by the DOE.

The guidelines suggest that the objectives of policy should be clearly specified and priorities assigned at the beginning of the assessment process. The DOE distinguish between 'ultimate objectives' (those which the policy seeks to achieve) and 'intermediate objectives' (the means by which the ultimate objectives are to be achieved). This would enable trade-offs between different classes of objectives to be made explicit (DOE, 1991b, p.2).

It may be too early to determine the real effect which the guidelines will have on government policy. It is inevitable, however, that the environment will be given further consideration in policy formulation simply on the basis of legal obligation, with the signing of international agreements and adoption of European Directives. The environmental appraisal procedure will enable policy to be defined more in terms of aims and objectives and will allow a range of options to be considered.

SEA in the Netherlands

Under Dutch EIA regulations a number of plans are required to be subject to an environmental impact assessment. These include structure plans, drinking water supply, energy and electricity supply and land use plans and provincial plans; waste management and mineral extraction. The EIA Commission has been involved in providing advice guidelines for such plans as the national electricity plans, provincial waste management plans and provincial sludge plans. The Commission suggests that EIA has an added value when applied to strategic decision-making. The NMP outlined a need for a broad-based approach to be taken to achieve sustainability, with co-operation between national government and other authorities and target groups, and with other countries.

144

Table 6.5
Steps in policy appraisal

Summarise the policy issue: seek expert advice to augment your knowledge as necessary. **List the objectives:** give them priorities, and identify any conflicts and trade-offs between them. **Identify constraints:** indicate how binding these are and whether they might be expected to change over time or be negotiable. **Identify costs and benefits:** including the environmental impacts; do not disregard likely costs or benefits simply because they are not easily quantifiable. **Weigh up the costs and benefits:** concentrating on those impacts which are material to the decision. **Test the sensitivity of the options:** to possible changes in conditions, or to the use of different assumptions. **Suggest the preferred option:** if any, identifying the main factors affecting the choice. **Set up any monitoring necessary:** so that the effects of policy may be observed, and identify any further analysis needed at the project level. **Evaluate the policy at a later stage:** and use the evaluation to inform decision making

Source: DOE, 1991b

At the national level environmental aspects need to be considered in all relevant government policy areas. Action 141 of the NMP suggested:

... the government should give an account of how the recommendations contained in the Brundtland Report are to be given substance in each ministry and area of policy. At the same time there will also be an assessment of the extent to which the instruments of the various policy areas contribute to effecting sustainable development (NMP, 1989, p.172).

Action 142 requires that information be provided for those policy proposals which might have important consequences for the environment. Sustainability has been a main component in the NMP+, SVV2 and VINEX.

Existing policy In order to achieve sustainability in policy at the national level, the starting point for the ministries was to assess the compatibility of current policies with sustainable development. In early 1991, the assessment began with the development of a method to guide ministries in drafting reports. In December 1991 the method was approved by the Council of Ministries. The methodology used in the assessment of existing policy involves a checklist of components which contribute to sustainable development (see Table 6.6).

Table 6.6
Checklist for sustainable development

A	Energy consumption (natural gas, oil & coal)
B	Quality of production technologies used
C	Quality of products produced
D	Use of renewable natural resources & raw materials (e.g. timber, fish)
E	Quantity and quality of waste flows and emissions to air, soil and water
F	Use of open space and impact on its existing use
G	Use of non-renewable natural resources and raw materials (such as sand, clay, ground water and spring water)

An assessment of existing policy against these criteria was seen as providing a better indication to attain sustainable development. Those policies which have a greater potential for achieving sustainability are then analysed in more detail. Instruments (legislative and regulative) which are shown to be relevant to the attainment of sustainability will be considered by assessing them against the following questions (Verheem, 1992, p.154):

- How many policy goals have been taken into account?
- Can environmental interests be taken into account in the implementation of policy?
- What are the intended and non-intended (side) effects of use of the instruments on the activities and the behaviour of the target group?
- Do the intended effects lead to the re-use of raw materials, waste prevention and recycling, mobility, energy savings and use of sustainable energy?

Statements are then produced on the impact of the policy area in achieving sustainable development. The report should include the result of all the instruments which have been assessed and conclusions on the combined effect

146

of all the instruments and the consequences for the attainment of sustainable development.

Policy proposals The Dutch have considered the introduction of an 'Environmental Test' for the appraisal of new policy proposals at the national level. The Evaluation Commission on the Environmental Protection Act recommended an environmental review. The Commission recommended *inter alia* that an environmental paragraph be made mandatory for policy proposals which have a significant impact on the environment. Policy proposals exempt from this requirement would include policy which is mandatory under the EIA regulations, policy proposals regarding the NMP and technical budget affairs. The co-ordinating minister of the environmental test should be responsible for the assessment of the need for and quality of environmental paragraphs. This should ideally be recorded in a memorandum to the council of ministers and be included with the policy proposal.

A general criterion for the assessment of a policy proposal is its likely effect on the attainment of other environmental policy goals (Verheem, 1992, p.154). The result of this initial screening indicates whether the proposal is of marginal significance. In some cases more information may be required on the nature of the policy. In order for an environmental test to be effective, information needs to be available to all parties at an early stage in the decision-making process. This is in accordance with Action 142 of the National Environmental Policy Plan. The minimum requirements which have been suggested include (Verheem, 1992, p.154):

- the size, objective of the policy plan, expected secondary effects, policy constraints (such as other policy areas);
- the existing policy and its relationship with environmental issues;
- the alternatives (relating to objectives, instruments and or their implementation);
- the environmental consequences; and
- the compatibility with environmental policy goals and legislation.

The Evaluation Commission also recommended that an Environmental Review Commission be established to evaluate the environmental paragraph as an instrument, to analyse selected policy areas on their contribution to sustainable development, and to introduce an advice desk in the Ministry of Environment to provide support to other ministers on the drafting of the environmental paragraph.

147

Planning for sustainability

EIA has been a useful environmental management instrument, enabling the environment to be given consideration in the decision-making process and providing information to determine the final outcome. However it has not always been clear what effect an EIS actually has on the final decision on whether or not to grant planning permission to a project, and whether EIA has prevented projects being implemented due to the magnitude and significance of predicted impacts. In order that EIA can become a tool for sustainability, it would need to undergo a number of changes. An important question is how can sustainability be implemented from the macro-level to the micro-level, i.e. from the international and national level to the plan, programme and project level? The implementation of sustainability in the transport sector will ultimately depend on the nature of transport policy and whether national transport policy has explicit objectives and targets. EIA would need to examine a wider spatial and temporal dimension. This includes the secondary, synergistic and cumulative effects of a particular activity and its contribution to global environmental problems such as ozone depletion and global warming.

It is widely acknowledged that post-decision auditing and monitoring of a scheme is rarely undertaken after construction. This is a failure of the present EIA system in Britain and is applicable to all types of development projects. A benefit of explicitly stating objectives is that, if a post-decision auditing and monitoring procedure is in place, it can be determined if the scheme achieves its objectives in practice. This would provide valuable information about the scheme and enable mitigation measures to be implemented for new unforeseen impacts which have occurred. Impact prediction methods used in the EIA could also be evaluated for their effectiveness. It would also highlight any misconceptions about the benefits which road schemes are supposed to procure.

Due to EIA coming late in the planning process, no real or other modal alternatives are considered at the project level. Consideration of modal alternatives needs to occur at the beginning of the assessment process when the strategic implications of advocating a particular mode of transport are acknowledged. EIA of road projects is segmented and concentrates on the development of small sections of a particular route. If policy is assessed more strategically, the cumulative impact of developing small sections of a route could be acknowledged.

A more strategic assessment of the environmental impacts of national transport policies, plans and programmes is now being advocated. This would enable the cumulative impacts of the government's roads programme to be assessed. The environmental assessment of policies, plans and programmes can be used to implement sustainability in the transport sector.

Objectives of PPPs based on the concept of sustainable development would need to be explicitly stated and the measures to meet objectives outlined. An environmental assessment of the options proposed to achieve the objectives would be undertaken to determine the most preferred option. A sustainability-led SEA will enable greater consideration to be given to all transport modes at an early stage in the planning process, in the formulation of PPPs. The approaches to policy appraisal taken by Britain and the Netherlands have illustrated the possible procedures available for implementing SEA in practice. The adoption of a European Directive on SEA will encourage a more standardised procedure of SEA to be adopted throughout the European Union.

The final section of this book will examine how British and Dutch national policy influences the decisions taken at the project level and whether either of the approaches is making progress towards developing a more sustainable form of transport planning.

7 Trans-Pennine corridor

This Chapter will examine how national transport policy in Britain influences and directs decisions which are taken at the project level. The Trans-Pennine corridor in the North-West of England is used as a case study to examine the government's approach to deal with congestion on strategic transport routes. A study of the Trans-Pennine corridor was initiated by the 1989 White Paper *Roads for Prosperity*. The Trans-Pennine corridor study provided an opportunity to examine how the government approached the problem of increasing traffic on strategic inter-urban routes, taking into consideration its environmental commitments. The Trans-Pennine area also has a wide rail network linking the major cities of Leeds, Manchester and Sheffield, which provides an alternative to road transport.

The 1989 White Paper announced a greatly expanded motorway and trunk road programme, costing £23 billion, to relieve congestion on main roads between cities and towns in England. The White Paper emphasised schemes which would relieve congestion on most heavily trafficked roads, especially those which were considered important for industrial and commercial communications. The programme concentrated on relieving congestion on trunk roads and motorways, which take the greatest share of traffic, especially heavy goods vehicles (HGVs). High priority is given to meeting the needs of industry and road users and to developing a modern strategic network which would play a role in the competitive challenges of the Single European Market.

During the period 1980-1989 traffic on roads in Britain increased by 35%. Motorway traffic doubled compared with traffic on trunk roads, which increased by half. In the same period the number of vehicles on roads increased by 3 million to over 23 million (DOT, 1989a). The national road forecasts for the period 1988-2025 predict an increase in total traffic of 83-142%, based on the forecasts of economic growth.

National traffic forecasts are used in the appraisal of both motorway and trunk road schemes, and play an important role in assessing whether benefits from a scheme over its lifetime justify initial cost and standard of provision. The government sees road congestion as an important factor which must be resolved to ensure economic prosperity. It stated that:

> Road congestion is bad for the economy. It imposes high costs on industry and other road users, by wasting time, delaying deliveries and reducing reliability. Various estimates have been made of these economic costs of road congestion. There is no way of making accurate overall estimates, but it is clear that the costs are very high (DOT, 1989a).

The government has acknowledged the effects congestion has on the economy, road safety and the environment. The forecasts of higher volumes of traffic will further exacerbate congestion on roads and could result in high costs, which would make British industry less competitive internationally. The Confederation of British Industry estimated that the cost of congestion in London was £15 billion annually (CBI, 1989).

The objectives of the roads programme have remained unchanged; they are to assist economic growth and reduce transport costs, to improve the environment by removing through traffic from unsuitable roads in towns and villages, and to enhance road safety. The 1989 roads programme outlined plans for 43,470 kilometres of new or widened roads to the trunk road network, which would increase the total area of land under roads by about 5%. Just under one fifth of the programme involved new roads through green field sites; about half were for motorway widening and the remainder for rural bypasses (DOE, 1994c, p.173). In 1994 DOT reviewed the roads programme and prioritised some road schemes and deleted others, although there was little change to the overall scale of the programme (see Chapter 4).

In the 1989 White Paper the government did not fully consider alternative options to relieve congestion. Rail was seen as providing a role in reducing the level of congestion. However, the White Paper stated that even with the continued expansion of rail:

> ... it cannot take other than a small part of the increase in demand for transport overall.

The White Paper considered road and rail as mainly serving different markets, and that one mode cannot be readily substituted for the other. Short freight movements would be more suited to roads, since more than 65% of loaded freight journeys are of 80 kilometres or less in length. The government stated that although:

... rail has an important contribution to make ... it is not the panacea for congestion on inter-urban roads.

Traffic management is also seen as playing a role in maximising the safe use of a road network. Its main contribution is directed towards urban centres, although it is considered unable to make any impact on the very high forecasts in traffic. The White Paper concluded:

... the main way in which to deal with growing ... inter-urban road congestion is by widening existing roads and building new roads in a greatly expanded roads programme ..

The roads programme as outlined in the 1989 White Paper, intended to improve the inter-urban motorway and trunk road network which would reduce journey times and increase the reliability of road travel. In addition to the schemes added to the roads programme, the paper highlighted a number of transport corridors which would require further investigation. The studies included the Trans-Pennine corridor, to examine the provision of additional capacity between North Lancashire and South Yorkshire.

Trans-Pennine routes

The Pennine hills are regarded as a barrier to the easy movement of east-west traffic in the North of England. The Pennine region covers the Metropolitan Counties of Greater Manchester, Merseyside, South and West Yorkshire, with neighbouring Shire Counties of Cheshire, Derbyshire, Lancashire and Humberside. The region has a number of major centres of industry and commerce. It was the cradle of the industrial revolution in the late 18th century and has thus continued to play an important role in economic, scientific and social developments. Urban settlements have been located along river valleys such as the Calder Valley. The available modes of transport across the Pennines include road, rail and canal. These have tended to follow the river valleys to link towns and have provided the most accessible routes.

The M62 is the main corridor across the Pennines, in addition to the low capacity and hilly roads which are susceptible to delays due to bad weather. Minor roads are considered to have low traffic capacity and are unsuitable for carrying heavy freight traffic. Poor quality travel communications have been considered by the DOT as a hindrance to the efficient movement of both goods and people, which is believed to restrict economic development within the North-West of England. Five main rail corridors across the Pennines exist - the West Yorkshire-North Lancashire (including the Skipton to Lancaster line),

Preston to North and West Yorkshire, Preston to Halifax and Bradford, Manchester to Sheffield and Manchester to Leeds.

Trans-Pennine studies

In January 1990 the Department of Transport commissioned the transport consultants *Transport Planning Associates* (TPA) to undertake a study of Trans-Pennine routes. The study had five objectives: firstly, to examine the traffic flow and patterns of movements on the existing road network and future problems, taking account of forecasts in traffic growth and proposed developments; secondly, to assess existing and proposed public transport facilities to determine their effects on road traffic; thirdly, to assess the impact of doing nothing to improve the road network; fourthly, to identify potential improvements; fifthly, to assess the economic and environmental impacts of potential improvements. In February 1990 TPA was also commissioned by the Passenger Transport Executives of Greater Manchester, South and West Yorkshire, Merseytravel, Cheshire, Derbyshire, Humberside and Lancashire County Councils together with the Peak National Park, to undertake a rail study. The aim of the rail study was to develop a co-ordinated rail strategy as a means of enhancing economic development on both sides of the Pennines, improving the performance of rail and strengthening Trans-Pennine links.

In April 1991 a Survey Report was published; this was a factual report of the surveys that had been undertaken for the Trans-Pennine study and provided a summary of the main results. The Survey Report was followed in January 1992 by the publication of the Trans-Pennine Rail Strategy Study Report. In June 1992 the Trans-Pennine Study Strategy Report was published and was made available for public consultation. The study examined a range of strategies which could be taken to relieve road congestion on Trans-Pennine routes. In November 1993 the Minister for Roads and Traffic took a decision on the Trans-Pennine Road Study. In May 1995 the consortium of local authorities published another study which further investigated the issues identified in the previous Trans-Pennine studies, with the aim to develop a feasible transport strategy for the area around the Peak District National Park.

Trans-Pennine road study

The study network stretched from the A66 trunk road in the north to the A523 in the south (see Figure 7.1). The main route across the Pennines is the M62 which is a six-lane (2x3) motorway link. To gather information on traffic flows across the Pennines the study undertook a survey to obtain reliable flow and origin/destination information of Trans-Pennine traffic. A review of existing data revealed that little reliable origin/destination information was available and that data which did exist was considered unreliable due to age, especially for the M62. The survey included vehicle roadside interviews, interviews with commercial vehicle drivers, registration matching surveys (to identify the movement of motorway traffic) and manual classification of vehicles and automatic traffic counts.

During the period 1979-89 traffic growth on the M62 increased by 86%. This was significantly higher than the national average on motorways, which increased by 20% during the same period. Over the last ten years, traffic on Trans-Pennines roads in the Peak District National Park has been much lower than the national average and traffic on the M62. However, since 1985 roads in the Park have had a higher rate of traffic growth similar to or higher than national traffic growth, which has partly been due to leisure traffic (TPA, 1991). An examination of the main trunk roads across the Pennines is undertaken in Table 7.1.

Traffic flow on main Pennines road routes

Table 7.2 shows the flow of traffic on main road corridors across the Pennines. The M62 and A59 trunk roads have the highest traffic flow of 78,000 and 13,000 AADT respectively. The number of heavy goods vehicles is highest on the M62 and A628 at 15,600 and 2,900 respectively, with HGVs accounting for a high percentage of the flow on the A628(T) at 27%, A66(T) at 23% and M62 at 20%. The volume/capacity ratio relates to the stable flow of traffic on roads, where a ratio of 0.7 or higher is considered to lead to unstable flows and congestion. The M62, A59(T) and A628(T) have a volume/capacity ratio at peak hour of 0.7, while the A66(T), A65(T), A646 have a ratio of 0.6 (TPA, 1992a, p.4). Table 7.3 shows the main movements by road across the Pennines. The dominant movement is between Greater Manchester and West Yorkshire, which accounts for 24% of the total flow. This is followed by Lancashire and West Yorkshire at 9% and South Yorkshire and Greater Manchester at 5% of the total flows.

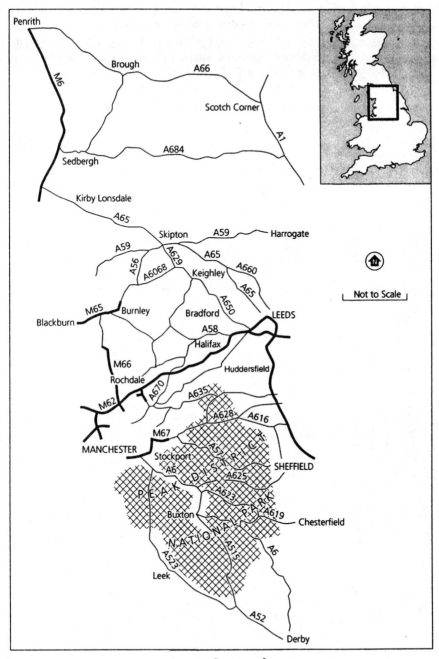

Figure 7.1 The Trans-Pennine road network

Table 7.1
Main trunk roads across the Pennines

M62	The M62 is the most important Pennine corridor and has an Average Annual Daily Total (AADT) of 78,000 vehicles; this represents 40% of all Trans-Pennine traffic. HGVs form 20% or 15,600 of the total AADT flow across the Pennines.
A66	The A66 has an AADT of 10,000, of which 24% are HGVs; it carries a large amount of long distance traffic, which frequently has an origin/destination in Cumbria and the North-East of England.
A65	The A65 is a busy Trans-Pennine road with an AADT of 11,100, of which 9% are HGVs. It links West Yorkshire with Cumbria through North Yorkshire and forms part of the southern boundary of the Yorkshire Dales National Park.
A59	The A59 follows an east/west route between North Yorkshire and Lancashire, crossing the A6(T) at Skipton. It has an AADT of 13,000 of which 11% are HGVs.
A646	The A646 trunk road links the M65 in Lancashire with Halifax in West Yorkshire, it has a AADT of 11,000, of which 7% are HGVs.
A628	The A628 has an AADT of 10,500, of which 28% are HGVs, the A628 has the highest AADT of all the Trans-Pennine routes south of the M62 as well as the highest proportion of HGVs. The route which passes through the Peak National Park is known as the Woodhead route.
A6	The A6 runs mainly within the Peak National Park and has an AADT of 5,700, of which 11% are HGVs.
A523	This road has an AADT of 7,100 of which 11% are HGVs and 78% are private cars of which the majority are home based trips.

156

Table 7.2
Flow of traffic on main Trans-Pennine road corridors

Trunk Road	1990 Flow (AADT)	No. of HGVs (AADT)	% HGVs	Volume Capacity Ratio (Peak)	Average Trip Length (kms)
M62 (J21-22)	78,000	15600	20	0.7	137
A66(T)	10,000	2300	23	0.6	254
A65(T)	11,000	1000	9	0.6	103
A59(T)	13,000	1400	10	0.7	94
A646(T)	11,000	800	7	0.6	39
A628(T)	10,000	2900	27	0.7	119
A6(T)	6,000	700	11	0.3	100
A523(T)	7,000	800	11	0.5	95

Future forecasts on Trans-Pennine road corridors

The study predicted that by the year 2011 traffic flow across the Pennines would increase between 281,000 and 343,000 AADT. By the year 2016 the traffic flow per day would be between 298,000 and 371,000 AADT. The growth would be 46-78% for 1990-2011 and 54-90% for 1990-2016, based on DOT forecasts. How these figures were calculated was not explained in the brief document presented for public consultation on the Trans-Pennine study.

Table 7.3
Main movements by road across the Pennines

Origin/destination	1990 (AADT)	% of Total Flows
Greater Manchester-W. Yorkshire	47,000	24
Lancashire-W. Yorkshire	17,000	9
S. Yorkshire-Greater Manchester	9,000	5
N. Yorkshire-Lancashire	6,000	3
W. Yorkshire-Cheshire	5,000	3
W. Yorkshire-Merseyside	5,000	2
N. Yorkshire-Greater Manchester	4,000	2
Derbyshire-Greater Manchester	4,000	2

Source: TPA, 1991

The study identified five corridors of concern (A66 road through Skipton & Keighley, M62, A628 and roads through South Pennines) taking into consideration the existing and projected traffic patterns across the Pennines, traffic growth and committed planning development and programme of highway schemes over the next twenty-five years.

These five corridors are more likely to suffer from traffic problems, which will ultimately affect movements on strategic routes. The study outlined the conditions which would occur on the five corridors once the highways schemes planned in the current roads programme have been completed and forecasts over next twenty five years have been considered. Table 7.4 outlines the traffic flows on the five corridors up to the year 2016. The A66(T) would experience high flows of long distance traffic, a high proportion of which would be commercial. The present standard of a poorly aligned, mainly single carriageway and limited sections of dual carriageway would result in low speeds, difficulties in overtaking traffic and poor travelling conditions in bad weather. Sections of this route would pass through areas of outstanding natural beauty, which would be affected by an increase in traffic and any infrastructural development.

The routes through Skipton and Keighley, which include the A65(T), A59(T), and A6068, would experience traffic flows of 51,000-64,000 AADT by 2016. The routes pass close to or through the Yorkshire Dales National Park, which would be affected by traffic growth and development of the roads. Due to the existing poorly aligned and hilly single carriageways, the study stated that low speeds, queues and delays would occur in peak periods. A need for a good quality route to link and serve towns within the corridor exists. The poor travel conditions on the route are expected to affect the potential development of the local economy of towns within the corridor (TPA, 1992a, p.8).

Table 7.4
Future traffic flows (2016) on main road corridors across the Pennines

| Road corridor | Traffic flows AADT | |
	Low	High
M62 (J18-25)	122,000	152,000
(between J21 & 25)		
A66(T)	14,000	17,000
Scotch Corner-Penrith		
A65(T), A59(T), A6068	51,000	64,000
Skipton-Keighley		
A628(T), A616(T)	16,000	20,000
Manchester-Sheffield		
A57, A623, A6(T), A515,		
A523(T)	51,000	63,000
Roads through S. Pennines		

Source: TPA, 1992a, p.8-9

Traffic flow forecasts on junctions 21 and 25 of the M62 are predicted to be 122,000-152,000 by the year 2016. As already discussed above, the M62 is the most important Trans-Pennine corridor, carrying large flows of traffic and a high proportion of commercial traffic. However, the study stated that a dual four-lane carriageway would be insufficient to accommodate demand in the peak period. This would result in delays and queues especially during bad weather or periods of road maintenance. The poor travel conditions along the M62 are considered to have implications not only for the regional economy but also for the national economy.

The A628/A616 provides the shortest trunk road route between Manchester and Sheffield which runs through the Peak District National Park. Forecasts predict traffic flows of between 16,000-20,000 AADT by 2016. The route has high flows of strategic traffic and a very high proportion of commercial traffic. However, the existing single carriageway and poor alignment would result in congestion and delays, especially during bad weather. The A57, A623, A6(T), A515 and A523(T) provide the routes through the South Pennines. Traffic flows are expected to increase between 51,000-63,000 AADT by 2016. This would result in flows of long distance traffic on unsuitable routes in environmentally sensitive areas and through small towns and villages. Thus, continuing traffic growth on these routes may result in a deterioration of environmental conditions in the Peak District National Park (TPA, 1992a, p.9).

Trans-Pennine rail study

Within the area covered by the rail study, 16 significant roads and five railway lines exist. The extent to which the car is the main mode of transport in these corridors varies in accordance with the quality of road and rail alternatives. There are about four main corridors within the Trans-Pennine study area. The most northern of these runs from West Yorkshire to North Lancashire and includes the A65 and the Skipton to Lancaster rail line (see Figure 7.2). Rail has a market share of 3% on this corridor, which is due to the low level of rail service on the line (Table 7.5).

The second corridor (Roses Link) runs from Preston to Burnley following the above route, before diverging to the Calder Valley line on to Halifax and Bradford. In parallel to this line runs the A646 trunk road. The rail service was reopened and has secured a 4% share of the market. The third rail corridor is the South Trans-Pennine route from Manchester to Sheffield, which competes directly with both the A628 and A57 and offers an alternative route to the A623 trunk road and A515 and has a market share of 9%.

The fourth corridor within the Trans-Pennine study area consists of the M62 and a number of broadly parallel all-purpose roads such as the A62, together with the North Trans-Pennine and Calder Valley railway lines. Fast services have been concentrated on the North Trans-Pennine route via Huddersfield. The main Trans-Pennine freight route is the Calder Valley line, which is also served by local stop trains. The M62 remains the main high quality all weather road across the Pennines and carries 40% of total vehicular traffic; however, the motorway is susceptible to high levels of congestion on both sides of the Pennines, and to delays which may result from bad weather on the exposed part of the route. Rail has achieved a 7% market share despite the highly competitive nature of the M62.

Table 7.5
Market share in each rail corridor (1990)

Corridor	Rail trips	% Market share (All trips)
Morecambe-Skipton	350	3
Roses Link	680	4
South Trans-Pennine	2430	9
North Trans-Pennine/Calder Valley	5650	7

Source: TPA, 1992b, p.13

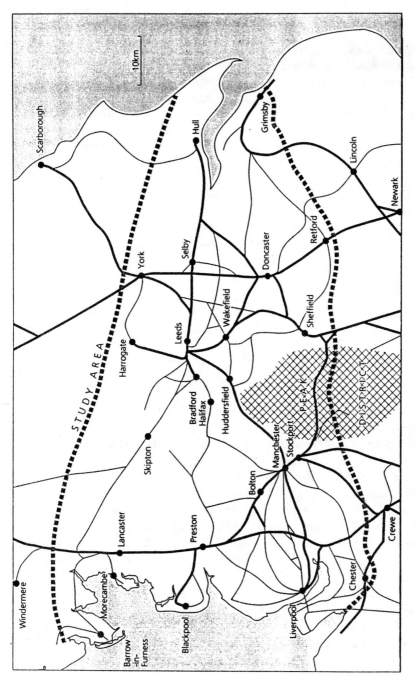

Figure 7.2 The main Trans-Pennine rail routes

North Trans-Pennine services The rail study outlined a number of problems which affect services along the North Trans-Pennine rail services. These include the average speed which, compared with 113 kph on the M62, is relatively low at 72 kph. The study identified the main reasons for these speeds as track curvature and condition of structure and gradients, and the need to make allowance for possible delays at locations where track capacity is at a premium. All such conditions contribute to reducing the maximum speed which could be achieved, with main capacity problems occurring in the areas of Manchester and Leeds.

The Liverpool-York/Manchester Piccadilly trains which cross a main part of Manchester Piccadilly Station obstruct the terminal platform, for local services intensively use the viaduct which runs along the south side of the city centre between Deansgate and Piccadilly stations. Thus, inclusion of any long distance trains in the timetable is considered to have an impact on both local and Trans-Pennine services (TPA, 1992b, p.22).

South Trans-Pennine services The South Trans-Pennine route links Liverpool and Manchester with Sheffield, the East Midlands and East Anglia. Between Manchester and Stockport the maximum line speed is 145 kph; between Stockport and Sheffield it is lower at 113 kph. The line is considered to be well laid and has long sections with no restrictions lower than the line speed. Patronage on the South Trans-Pennine express services vary from 1,600 passengers per day between Liverpool and Warrington to 2,510 between Stockport and Sheffield, where no other fast service exists (TPA, 1992b, p.25). In total, 920,000 passengers per annum use the service on South Trans-Pennine route across the watershed between Chinley and Edale.

The study identified three main problems which exist with the South Trans-Pennine route, relating to capacity, routing patterns and journey speeds. Between Manchester and Stockport limited capacity of signalling exists on this route. Pressures of other services between these two cities can constrain the extent to which service improvements could be implemented. The average speed along this route is low, as on other Trans-Pennine routes, thus leading to longer journey times. The average speed from Liverpool to Sheffield is 71 kph and from Manchester to Sheffield 74 kph. It is anticipated, however, that average speeds may increase in the future. Rail is competitive for movements between the two city centres on this route due to the poor quality of competing roads. The study stated that rail has been able to secure 67% of this market, a share which will increase (TPA, 1992b, p.27).

Calder Valley route The Calder Valley line runs through Manchester Victoria to Leeds via Rochdale, Halifax and Bradford. Through services operate from Liverpool to Leeds using the Chat Moss route via St Helens Junction. The two main problems on the Calder Valley line have been overcrowding and slow journey times. To deal with the problem of overcrowding, the frequency of the service was increased to half-hourly and Calder Valley trains combine with other services to offer a 15-minute frequency between Halifax and Leeds. The average speed on the Calder Valley line is low which has resulted in long journey times between the main cities and towns served on the route.

Bradford, Halifax and Rochdale are important urban centres but experience a slower service compared with equivalent communities on the North and South Trans-Pennine routes. Rail is not a real competitor to the roads serving the communities of Rochdale, Littleborough, Todmorden and Halifax, where the average speed varies from 48 kph to 56 kph. The M62 provides a significantly faster route to the major centres of Leeds, Manchester, Bradford and Liverpool making the Calder Valley uncompetitive for these movements. It is therefore necessary to improve the speed on this line if rail is to provide a viable alternative.

The Roses link The Roses Link stretches from Blackpool to Leeds and York via Preston, Blackburn, Accrington and Burnley. It joins the Calder Valley line at Hall Royd Junction east of Todmorden after it crosses the Pennine Watershed at Copy Pit summit. The maximum line speed is 121 kph between Kirkham and Preston and 113 kph elsewhere, except between Burnley and Hall Royd Junction where the maximum speed is 116 kph (TPA, 1992b, p.32). There is a relatively high proportion of commuting journeys (42%), with leisure travellers on weekdays being below average at 23% and much higher at weekends The daily total number of passengers on the link is 780 passengers per day between Burnley and Hebden Bridge, increasing to 1,120 passengers between Halifax and Bradford.

Lancaster to Skipton This route connects Lancaster and Morecambe with Skipton and Leeds. The number of trains have been steadily reduced and there are only four trains per day in each direction. The service operates from Lancaster, rather than Morecambe at its western end. The line caters for local journeys between West Yorkshire, North Yorkshire and Lancaster, which account for 58% of the total trips made on this line. Passenger volume in 1990, when the service operated from Morecambe, was 400 passengers per day across the Pennine watershed. Trips to and from work account for 21% of the total surveyed, with just over half of trips on the line for leisure. The main problem identified by the rail study on this line was its low frequency of services.

Use of different modes

The use of different modes across the Pennine between Skipton and Sheffield based on the results of both the rail and road studies, are listed in Table 7.6. The Table shows the estimated number of person trips across the Pennines over a 12-hour weekday; estimates make an allowance for an average vehicle occupancy of 1.44.

Table 7.6
Estimated number of trips across the Pennines by mode

Mode	Number	Percentage
Car & motorcycle	134,000	93
Train	9,100	6
Coach	1,300	1
Total	144,000	100

Source: TPA, 1991, p.32

The study calculated that in total 193,000 vehicles AADT (2-way) cross the Pennines, with a high proportion of traffic (40%) using the M62. The next trunk roads which take a high amount of traffic are A66, A65, A646, A628 which between them take 29% of Trans-Pennine traffic.

The main origin/destination across the Pennines is between West Yorkshire and Greater Manchester which accounts for 27% and 20% of all end trips, followed by Lancashire and West Yorkshire (9%) and South Yorkshire and Greater Manchester (5%). Commercial vehicle traffic travelling empty was nearly half on most routes, except for the A628 trunk road and M62 where it was low at 36%. A significantly high proportion of vehicles on roads in the Peak National Park transport building material, including quarry material.

Table 7.6 shows motor vehicles accounting for 93% of all trips across the Pennines with rail at 6%. The forecasts in traffic growth will place greater pressure on Trans-Pennine road capacity, while rail capacity will remain under-utilised if no action is taken to encourage a modal shift from road to rail.

Strategies for the Trans-Pennine Road Corridor

The road study developed strategies for five road corridors, which it identified as having strategic importance and which were likely to suffer from congestion due to traffic forecasts. The corridors were considered individually and as part of a strategy for the whole Trans-Pennine area. The objective of the strategy was:

> ... to increase highway capacity across the Pennines to accommodate future traffic demands in a cost-effective way whilst protecting the environment, particularly in the National Park (TPA, 1992a, p.11).

The road strategy is seen as building upon the investment, construction and improvement of the M62 and trunk road and motorway network, providing good connections to the M62. Six strategies were developed by the study with different combinations and improvements to the five corridors (see Table 7.7). These included major improvement of junctions 18-25 of the M62 to increase capacity, converting the A66(T) between M6 and A1(T) to a dual two-lane road, improving the route of A628(T)/A616(T) with part of the route confined within a tunnel, and traffic constraint measures in the Peak District National Park.

M62

The M62 has undergone widening at junctions 14-17 and 17-18, while the section of the M62 covering junctions 18-25 suffers from high traffic volumes. The study suggested that further widening is needed to address the problems of congestion caused by high volumes of traffic. The study considered that future growth in traffic up to the year 2001 would be more than a dual four-lane (4x4) highway could accommodate and would lead to a higher degree of congestion than on the dual three lane carriageway in 1990. Improvement to other Trans-Pennine corridors together with possible rail improvements would form part of an overall strategy. The study stated that this would bring only limited relief to the M62. Traffic flows on the M62 (junctions 21-22) was 78,000 AADT in 1990, which would increase to 111,000-148,000 by 2016 if strategy A, C or E were implemented with improvements to the M62. Strategies B, D or F, with major improvement, would enable a higher flow of 115,000-157,000 to be accommodated by 2016 (TPA, 1992a, p.13). The study used these figures to advocate a strategy for major improvement to the M62 between 2001 and 2016 to accommodate these flow ranges. Strategies which would provide this relief are B, D and F. The study did not include a preliminary assessment of the environmental impact of the strategies. Instead it identified one or two impacts which it considered important. For example, strategies B, D and F require major widening of the M62. This is likely to have a substantial increase in visual impact in the corridor which is already affected by the M62. Major cutting and structural works would be required in certain sections of the corridor. Strategies A, C and E would be the same as the 'Do-minimum' option, where there would be a slight increase in the visual impact of the road.

A66(T)

In 1990 the traffic flow on the A66(T) was 10,000 AADT. The study proposed widening the A66 to a dual carriageway between the A1(T) at Scotch Corner and the M6 at Penrith, to accommodate future traffic demands, reduce travel times and improve reliability in poor weather conditions. Improvements to the A66 as contained in strategies A, B, C, D, E and F would accommodate a traffic flow of 16,000-20,000 AADT by 2016. Improvement to the A66 would be seen as enhancing the strategic connection between Cumbria and North Lancashire with the North-East of England. The main environmental issue identified by the study for A66 improvements is that it passes through an area of outstanding natural beauty. One solution to this problem put forward by the study was on line widening, which would minimise the environmental impact.

The 'Do-minimum' option for the A66(T) would lead to a 49-85% increase in traffic flows by 2010. This would increase the visual impact of traffic compared with the present. All strategies (A-F) would result in a significant increase in visual impact.

Route from M65 towards A1(T) via Skipton

The study proposed an initial improvement of the route along the A56 from the M65 at Colne to Skipton. This included the dualling of the Skipton bypass, followed by consideration of an eastward extension towards the A1(T). A dual two-lane (2x2) carriageway was considered the most appropriate standard to accommodate the predicted traffic flows. This would give some relief to the M62 and improve journey times for large volumes of traffic between several towns across this part of the Pennines. Traffic flow along the A59(T) just west of Skipton was 13,000 AADT in 1990. Strategies A-F for improvement would accommodate traffic flows of 25,000-34,000 AADT by 2016. Sections of the route are close to the Yorkshire Dales National Park. This would therefore require any alignments to be investigated further, so as to avoid this particular environmentally sensitive area.

Table 7.7
Strategies for Trans-Pennine road corridors

Improvement	Strategies					
	A	B	C	D	E	F
M62 Dual four lanes	✔	-	✔	-	✔	-
Further major improvements		✔		✔		✔
A66 Dual two lanes	✔	✔	✔	✔	✔	✔
Route M65-A1 (2x2)	✔	✔	✔	✔	✔	✔
A628/A616 Dual two lanes with and without traffic restraint measures.	✔	✔	-	-	-	-
Single carriageway with and without traffic restraint Peak Park	-	-	-	-	✔	✔

Source: TPA, 1992a, p.12

If minimal action was taken along this route, then the 67-108% increase in traffic flows by 2016 would result in an increase in the visual impact of traffic compared with the present. Strategies A-F would all have the same environmental impact, which is a significant increase in the visual impact along the A56, with a slight increase along the A59(T) and A629(T), and substantial visual impact east of Skipton.

A628/A616(T)

The M62 and the A628(T)/A616(T) all interact with other roads in the south of the Pennines. The amount of relief brought to the M62 and other roads through the Peak District National Park will ultimately depend on volumes attracted to an improved A628(T) and A616(T). A dual carriageway would attract more traffic and give more relief to other routes, which would result in satisfactory travelling conditions. Any improvement less than converting the road to a dual carriageway would result in the road operating close to capacity, which would attract less traffic, giving less relief to other routes. This is considered to affect the potential for economic growth within the region.

The A628(T)/A616(T) route passes through the Peak District National Park and any major improvement would therefore have a significant impact on the environment in this corridor. The expansion of the road will have significant visual effects, due to the open moor land of Langsett Moors and the climb up to the moors from the head of the Longdendale Valley. The study proposed a tunnel and landscaping on part of the route to reduce the general impact of any road improvement. The disused Woodhead railway tunnel already exists, although the study believed that, due to engineering problems and ownership difficulties, enlarging or modifying this tunnel would not be a viable option. Instead, it proposed the construction of a completely new tunnel, which would remove the road from the most sensitive area of the National Park. However, 10 kilometres of the route would still remain exposed through the National Park where it follows Longdendale Valley. The cost of constructing a tunnel would be £140-240 million (1990) and would thus affect the economic benefits of the corridor improvement.

The 'Do-minimum' option without the tunnel would result in an increase in visual impact, owing to the 68-109% expected increase in traffic. Strategies A and B with and without the tunnel would result in an increase in visual impact in the Longdendale Valley, and across the moors and along the A616(T). Strategies C and D without the tunnel would also result in a significant increase in visual impact in the Longdendale Valley and across the moors. The same strategies with a tunnel would still result in a higher visual impact along the valley, but with a substantial reduction across the moors.

Roads through South Pennines

Dualling of the A628(T) and A616(T) would provide more capacity for all traffic crossing the Peak District National Park and would provide an opportunity to introduce traffic management measures on the Park's roads. The study did not state what form these measures would take. However, the DOT did examine the possible benefits of reducing speed throughout the whole of the National Park. All roads through the Peak District National Park are non-trunk roads and any traffic management measures would be the responsibility of the local highway authorities. Such measures could reduce traffic flows across the Park by up to 40% and would reduce the visual impact and nuisance of traffic in the open countryside and in small towns and villages. Implementation of measures, however, would increase traffic flows on the A523(T) and A52(T) south of the Park. Although this road has a number of improvements planned, the study recommended that, in view of the potential transfer of traffic, it should be re-assessed for any further improvements to accommodate additional traffic. Depending on the type of traffic measures, travel costs could be increased and the net value of the highway improvements reduced (TPA, 1992a, p.17).

Economic appraisal

Table 7.8 shows the calculated Net Present Value (NPV) for all the strategies with different options. Option 1 of traffic restraint and a tunnel for the A628(T) has a negative NPV for each of the strategies. Option 2 which includes traffic restraint with no tunnel has a positive NPV for strategies A and B with a negative NPV for strategies C and D. Option 3 includes no traffic restraint in the Peak Park with the A628(T) tunnel and has a positive NPV for strategies A and B and a negative NPV for C and D. Option 4 with no traffic restraint and no tunnel has a positive NPV for all of the strategies. This highlights the economic costs which would be incurred if a tunnel was built (TPA, 1992a).

Strategies for the Trans-Pennine rail corridor

In the development of rail strategies the rail study concentrated on two issues - the level of infrastructure investment and the pattern of services which operate. For the North Trans-Pennine corridors the study considered three levels of infrastructure development - firstly, an enhanced diesel option involving a limited programme of civil engineering to increase line speeds; secondly, electrification of the Liverpool to York line; and thirdly, extension of electrification to Hull.

Two train service options were considered - present-day service pattern plus limited enhancement, which showed during initial tests to be beneficial, and an enhanced service pattern based on the concept of a 15-minute interval service between Manchester and Leeds.

In total, six rail investment strategies were described by the study, and were compared with a base rail option, which included those changes which would take place without a new development strategy for the route.

Table 7.8

Cost and Net Present Value of road strategies (£ million @ 1990 prices)

Options	Strategies					
	A	B	C	D	E	F
With traffic restraint in Peak Park with A628(T) tunnel.	510	910	483	883	-	-
NPV	-50	-47	-171	-130	-	-
With traffic restraint in Peak Park but no A628(T) tunnel.	350	750	317	717	-	-
NPV	29	31	-89	-49	-	-
No traffic restraint in Peak Park, with A628(T) tunnel.	510	910	483	883	-	-
NPV	4	24	-32	-3	-	-
No traffic restraint in Peak Park and no A628(T) tunnel.	350	750	317	717	198	598
NPV	83	102	50	78	76	94

Evaluation of different rail strategies

The rail study undertook three forms of evaluation to justify whether investment in public transport should proceed. These were financial evaluation, where the financial benefits of the scheme are compared firstly with the cost of implementation; secondly, economic or social cost benefit analysis which examines not only the financial aspects of the schemes but also the wider implications to society as a whole; and thirdly, the evaluation known as 'Section 56', which is used by the Department of Transport to determine grant aid for major public transport schemes.

Financial evaluation The DOT required financial evaluation to be undertaken by British Rail in the assessment of infrastructure and rolling stock investment. Financial evaluation compares the benefits of the schemes, such as increased revenue and cost savings, with the actual cost of implementation. It is advantageous in financial evaluation to maximise the forecast revenue from the project. Relatively high fares are therefore often assumed, even though fewer passengers may benefit from the scheme. Thus, the potential of the service to attract new customers may be reduced.

Economic/social cost benefit analysis Economic or social cost benefit covers a wide range of factors including time savings to users and non-users, and reduction in accidents, operating costs and capital costs of the schemes (TPA, 1991, p.46). Other benefits sometimes include reduction in unemployment and environmental impact. The DOT uses this form of evaluation on which COBA and QUADRO computer programmes are based.

Section 56 grant Section 56 evaluation is used by the DOT to determine grant aid for public transport schemes. Criteria for Section 56 grant require all financial benefits of the scheme, including private sector contribution to the cost, to be maximised. Grant is usually payable for 50% of any shortfall between financial benefits of the scheme and costs, provided that the value of benefits to non-users of the scheme exceeds the total shortfall. The criteria used for the allocation of the grant should be for:

> ... new public transport infrastructural projects where there are exceptional reasons for using specific grant to spread the costs beyond users and local charge payers (DOT, 1989c).

Other criteria which should be met by the authority or company which proposes the scheme are outlined in DOT Circular 3/89 on Section 56 Grant for Public Transport:

- The scheme should be the most effective way, from the viewpoint of the public sector, of achieving the desired objective.
- The present value of total scheme cost should be covered by the revenue from passengers, contributions from other beneficiaries, and direct savings in other areas of public expenditure.
- The scope for fare increases should be fully explored.
- Where the schemes are likely to result in benefits to developers, the possibilities of these beneficiaries making appropriate contributions to the costs should be fully explored; the payment of grant may be made conditional on a certain amount being raised from such beneficiaries reflecting the betterment value accruing to them.
- Benefits to non-users will in most cases arise mainly from the relief of congestion while other external benefits may include environmental improvements. The Department recognises the difficulty of evaluating pollution and amenity benefits and disbenefits. These should nevertheless, be identified and quantified and, if significant, evaluated as far as possible.

A lack of comparability in evaluation tends to benefit road schemes rather than rail projects. Road schemes are evaluated on the basis of social cost benefit analysis, while the DOT applied a combination of financial and Section 56 evaluation to assess rail projects. This results in a bias towards roads. In COBA road investment analysis, a £1 investment is said to give a return of £2.50. The value is mainly attributable to time savings to road users. Rail investment was justified based on the rate of return, not reflecting the wider social and environmental benefits (CPRE, 1992a, p.16).

The rail study adopted the Net Present Value to act as an indicator of the present value of the scheme. The NPV is achieved by taking the difference between discounted benefits and cost of schemes over the life of the project. The study used an 8% discount rate over a 35-year evaluation period from the opening of the scheme (TPA, 1992b, p.47). The time-scale assumed for the major rail investment options was 1997. All benefits were then discounted to 1994, the first year in which significant costs would be incurred. The study, in evaluating the different options, used all three evaluations discussed above. A number of other criteria were considered in addition to the three evaluations; these included level of operating surplus, implications for freight movement, environmental issues, regeneration/development impacts, synergy with other rail schemes, and strengthening of links by increasing patronage through enhanced rail services (TPA, 1992b, p.48).

North Trans-Pennine rail corridor

The study considered six different scenarios for the North Trans-Pennine rail corridor and selected scenarios NT1 and NT3 to be included in the overall strategy (see Table 7.9). Scenario NT1 performed well in the financial, Section 56 and economic evaluation. This scenario, the enhanced diesel option with a base service strategy, was the only scenario which produced a positive financial NPV and a second best economic NPV after scenario NT2 (Table 7.10). Scenario NT1 was preferred due its better financial performance when compared with NT2, because the difference in economic NPVs was only £3.6 million (TPA, 1992b, p.70).

Scenario NT3 (Liverpool-York electrification with a base service strategy) performed better in the economic and Section 56 appraisal compared with other electrification options. Enhanced diesel option (NT1) would lead to 8% more trips over the Pennines than the base option, while the Liverpool-York electrification would lead to a 16% increase. The line to York would gain a 9% increase in fast train patronage with the enhanced diesel option and 17% with electrification.

South Trans-Pennine rail corridor

The rail study considered eight different scenarios for the South Trans-Pennine corridors between the North West and South Yorkshire and Humberside and East Midlands (Table 7.11). The consideration of different scenarios concentrated on a service improvement rather than infrastructural changes. This was for two reasons: firstly, the completion of a programme of upgrading on the line allowing 145 kph operation over most of the route between Stockport and Sheffield which offers an enhanced diesel option, and secondly, due to the high cost of wiring at Sheffield stations the line is not considered for electrification; electric trains would be unable to penetrate further east or south

Table 7.9
Scenarios for the North Trans-Pennine rail corridor

Scenario NT1 *Enhanced* *Diesel Option* *(Base Service* *Pattern)*	The base service pattern of train services, together with enhanced diesel, would provide a hourly service from Liverpool Lime Street to Newcastle, by extending the Liverpool to York service. In this scenario an additional 422,000 passengers per annum would be attracted to rail in 1997. Total daily patronage over the Pennines would rise by 8% (TPA, 1992b, p.57).
Scenario NT2 *Enhanced* *Diesel Pattern* *Revised* *Service* *Pattern)*	The revised service pattern scenario requires the same level of infrastructural investment as in scenario NT1, together with significant changes in service patterns. Compared with the base scenario, the Liverpool-York service would be extended to Newcastle as in scenario NT1. The Bangor-Wakefield Westgate service would be separated into Bangor-Manchester Oxford Road, Manchester Victoria-Stalybridge and Huddersfield-Wakefield Westgate services (TPA, 1992b, p.59).
Scenario NT3 *Liverpool-* *York* *Electrification*	The third scenario for the North Trans-Pennine Corridors is the introduction of electric services, which would allow a number of changes enabling the quality of service to be improved. However, a number of problems would occur where diesel services currently extend beyond the limits of electrification.
Scenario NT4 *Revised* *Service* *Pattern*	The revised service pattern differs from scenario NT3 in three areas. Firstly, the Manchester-Hull service would be split into half hourly semi-fast electric services from Manchester to Leeds and an hourly Leeds-Hull service. The semi-fast train would make the same intermediate stops on the trains equivalent in NT2. The Leeds-Selby stopping service would be revised to operate half-hourly throughout the day.
Scenario NT5 *Liverpool-* *York/Hull* *Electrification*	Base Service Pattern scenario is similar to Liverpool-York electrification. The differences are the electrification of the Manchester-Hull, Leeds-Selby, York-Hull and York-Selby services with resulting journey time savings.
Scenario NT6 *Revised* *Service* *Pattern*	The main differences in this scenario, compared with NT4, include the extension of a half-hourly Manchester-Leeds semi-fast service to Hull, replacing the Leeds-Hull service, as well as the electrification of local services from York and Leeds to Selby and Hull.

than Sheffield, which would result in loss of through journey opportunities (TPA, 1992b, p.72).

Scenario ST3 - Bangor-Cleethorpes option was chosen as the preferred scenario for the South Trans-Pennine corridor to be included in the overall strategy. As shown in Table 7.12, this option has a positive result on financial and economic grounds. This is the preferred option for the development of the South Trans-Pennine route in the short-term. In the long-time, electrification of the Midland main line could provide an environment within which electrification of this route might become a viable option. In the preferred scenario 481,000 cars per year would be removed from the highway, with about half of these being Trans-Pennine movements and representing about 3% of total vehicular movements. This scenario, however, would require a reduction in the number of trains using the section of line between Manchester Oxford Road and Manchester Piccadilly. The study proposed the possibility of providing a Manchester Airport-Cleethorpes service in the short-term (TPA, 1992b, p.84). The section of line between Stockport and Sheffield would see an increase in patronage, with an increase in loading on express services of 36% from 3,970 to 5,390 passengers per day.

Table 7.10
Enhanced diesel and electrification options
for the North Trans-Pennine rail corridor

Criteria	Base NT1	Revised NT2	Base NT3	Revised NT4	Base NT5	Revised NT6
Net Present Value (£ million)						
Financial	+10.8	-3.3	-39.98	-17.6	-36.9	-47.5
Section 56	+19.5	+14.0	+7.9	+6.0	-11.2	-14.4
Economic	+38.5	+42.1	+31.7	+32.1	+19.4	+34.4
Patronage gain ('000 per annum)	422	834	1385	1519	1521	1889
Number of cars removed from the road network ('000 per annum)	393	679	1128	1268	1246	1551

Source: TPA, 1992b

Table 7.11
Scenarios for the South Trans-Pennine rail corridor

Scenario ST1 Manchester Piccadilly to Cleethorpes	Manchester Piccadilly to Cleethorpes would require extending the Manchester Piccadilly-Sheffield fast service to Cleethorpes, calling at Meadowhall, Doncaster and principal stations to Cleethorpes. An additional stopping service would be needed to serve the intermediate stops made by these trains between Sheffield and Doncaster.
Scenario ST2 Manchester Airport to Cleethorpes	The Manchester Airport to Cleethorpes scenario is the same as scenario ST1 above, except that the service from and to Cleethorpes would be extended from Manchester Piccadilly to Manchester Airport.
Scenario ST3 Bangor to Cleethorpes	This scenario requires a direct Bangor-Wakefield service to Manchester Piccadilly, linking it to Cleethorpes via the South Trans-Pennine route. A separate service would be provided between Manchester Victoria and Wakefield Westgate.
Scenario ST4 Manchester Piccadilly to Leicester via Sheffield	The extension of a fast service from Manchester Piccadilly would be required in this scenario, along the Midland main line to Leicester via Derby, thus providing through links from the North-West to Derby and Leicester.
Scenario ST5 Manchester Airport-Leicester via Sheffield	Scenario ST5 requires the extension of the Manchester Piccadilly-Sheffield-Leicester service to run to and from Manchester Airport.
Scenario ST6 Manchester Piccadilly to Leicester via Dove Curve	This scenario provides a through service to Leicester via the Dove curve in addition to half-hourly service between Manchester and Sheffield.
Scenario ST7 Manchester Airport to Sheffield	Scenario ST7 involves providing a service to Sheffield, extending the Manchester Piccadilly service to Sheffield to or from the Airport.
Scenario ST8 Bangor-Sheffield	A through service would be provided although the link from North Wales to South Yorkshire is the same as ST3.

Table 7.12
Scenarios for the South Trans-Pennine rail corridor

Criteria	ST1	ST2	ST3	ST4	ST5	ST6	ST7	ST8
Net Present Value (£ million)	+4.6	+7.5	+13.0	-2.3	-8.0	-9.4	-0.5	+9.0
Financial Section 56	+7.2	+12.5	+19.8	+1.0	+4.3	-6.8	+2.1	+13.0
Economic	+21.2	+36.6	+55.6	+23.8	+37.9	+18.6	+29.9	+22.1
Patronage gain ('000 per annum)	271	499	492	198	448	214	101	316
Number of cars removed from the road network ('000 per annum)	261	484	481	178	435	196	100	310

Source: TPA, 1992b

Northern Trans-Pennine rail corridor

Options for improving Northern Trans-Pennine corridors include service enhancement on the Calder Valley, Roses link and Skipton to Lancaster routes. Enhancing services of these routes as opposed to infrastructural development was seen by the study as offering the best opportunities for developing routes in the short-term (Table 7.13) (TPA, 1992b, p.86).

The preferred scenarios for the Northern Trans-Pennine corridor included in the overall Strategy were Scenario NC3 upgrading the Roses Link and scenario NC4, introducing a Leeds-Windermere through service. As Table 7.14 shows, there is a strong case on both economic and financial grounds. Scenario NC1 (a fast Calder Valley link) would be justified on social cost benefit grounds but would not be financially viable without grant-aid towards the capital cost (TPA, 1992b, p.93). Scenario NT4 has high NPVs in each of the evaluations and would be a viable option. The Southport (NC2) through service would be justified on economic grounds but would not cover the operating costs and was therefore not considered a likely candidate for inclusion in the final strategy.

Table 7.13
Scenarios for Northern Trans-Pennine rail corridor

Scenario NC1 *Liverpool-York Fast Train*	The introduction of a fast Liverpool-York service linking the Calder Valley route, which would call at St Helens Junction, Manchester Victoria, Rochdale, Halifax, Bradford and Leeds in addition to the existing services.
Scenario NC2 *Southport Extension*	The York-Manchester service would be extended in this scenario to and from Southport.
Scenario NC3 *Roses Link*	This option requires converting the service from class 156 units to class 158, resulting in improvements in journey time and passenger comfort. The journeys from Leeds-Blackpool would be reduced by five minutes. An additional service will be introduced to fill current gaps in the hourly service.
Scenario NC4 *Skipton-Lancaster*	This involves restoring a through service to Leeds, which would stop intermittently between Skipton and Lancaster. Alternative destinations at the western end of the route were also examined; it was found that Windermere was the best option for a western terminus, generating greater patronage than Morecambe or Barrow-in-Furness.

Table 7.14
Scenarios for Northern Trans-Pennine rail corridor

Criteria	NC1	NC2	NC3	NC4
Net Present Value				
(£ millions)	-8.3	-4.2	+1.5	+3.8
Finance				
Section 56	-4.8	-1.2	+2.4	+4.5
Economic	+12.6	+19.0	+9.0	+21.1
Patronage gain	380	312	193	268
('000 per annum)				
Number of cars removed from the road network	304	262	160	239
('000 per annum)				

Source: TPA, 1992b

The preferred scenarios from each of the rail corridors were combined to develop three overall strategies for the Trans-Pennine region. The three strategies, A, B and C, are listed below. The benefits envisaged by the study of developing an overall strategy include identifying the best option for each of the corridors that would maximise the benefits of each individual option. Focus was placed on the North Trans-Pennine corridor, as 50% of demand is concentrated in this corridor. Maximising rail performance in this particular corridor would enable rolling stock to be released to develop services in other corridors, where at present there is less scope for major investment such as electrification. Each of the strategies was based on the assumption that any displaced rolling stock in 1997 could be redeployed elsewhere. A summary of the evaluation of the three strategies is contained in Table 7.15.

Strategy A
NT1: *North Trans-Pennine enhanced diesel with base service pattern*
ST3: *Bangor-Cleethorpes through services*
NC3: *Roses link upgrade*
NC4: *Leeds-Windermere through service*
Strategy B
NT3: *Liverpool-York electrification with base service pattern*
ST3: *Bangor-Cleethorpes through services*
NC3: *Roses link upgrade*
NC4: *Leeds-Windermere through service*
Strategy C
NT3: *Liverpool-York electrification with base service pattern*
ST3: *Bangor-Cleethorpes through services*
NC3: *Roses link upgrade*
NC4: *Leeds-Windermere through service*
NC1: *Calder Valley fast service*

Table 7.15
Summary of strategies for the Trans-Pennine rail corridors

Criteria	A	B	C
Net Present Value			
(£ million)	+29.1	+7.4	+0.1
Finance			
Section 56	+46.0	+37.5	+33.7
Economic	+124.0	+120.3	+133.9
Patronage gain	1375	2338	2718
('000 per annum)			
Number of cars removed from the			
road network	1273	2008	2312
('000 per annum)			

Source: TPA, 1992b, p.6

All three strategies in Table 7.15 are financially viable at a 8% discount rate, with strategy C just positive. All strategies have significant net benefits under Section 56 evaluation and very large net economic benefits. Strategy A, based on an enhanced diesel option for the North Trans-Pennine corridor, has greater financial benefits compared with electrification options as outlined in B and C. In the economic evaluation there is little difference between each of the strategies. Strategy C, which includes electrification and a fast service on the Calder Valley line, would have the greatest net economic benefits.

A large number of vehicles will be removed from the highway network ranging from 1.3 million to 2.3 million car trips per annum as a result of the strategies. The study stated that 4% of existing movements across the Pennines would be removed because of the strategies; the rest of the traffic would be removed from the region's highway network (TPA, 1992b, p.3).

The diesel option is the most cost-effective strategy in financial terms. However, high on-going costs are associated with diesel trains. In considering strategies for the Trans-Pennine rail corridor, the study highlighted a number of factors which would favour electrification, but which were not possible to evaluate in the rail study. They included:

1. The potential for increasing fares to match the higher quality of service.
2. The rolling stock which would be released for use in other corridors due to electrification, thereby helping to develop rail service in a wider area.
3. Operational benefits to the Intercity and freight businesses of British Rail as well as to Regional Railways.
4. Economic development, image effects and environmental benefits.

(TPA, 1992b, p.9).

Once these factors are taken into consideration, the study indicated that the electrification option would be shown to be the strategy with the greatest net financial benefits.

Analysis of the Trans-Pennine study

The Trans-Pennine study used the same data sources to assess both road and rail facilities across the Pennines to develop separate strategies. The Trans-Pennine road study was commissioned by the Department of Transport while the rail study was left to the initiative of a consortium of local authorities and Passenger Transport Executives, although the DOT did make a contribution to the cost of the rail study. The commissioning of two separate studies reflects the mono-modal approach of the UK Government towards transport - one that places greater emphasis on road transport as the main mode of transportation. One of the objectives of the study was to assess the existing and proposed public transport facilities and to determine their effect on road transport. The study, however, could not give a comprehensive assessment of public transport facilities because of its focus on road transport. In this respect, the study failed to take the opportunity to examine strategic Trans-Pennine issues within a balanced transportation strategy. The rail study was initiated by the consortium because:

> Each of these proposals (*for rail investment*) is being considered in isolation and little account is being taken of the impact on other services or neighbouring authorities ... In view of these separate initiatives it was felt that there was a need to co-ordinate the activities of individual authorities and develop an overall strategy for rail improvements in the Trans-Pennine corridor.

By developing a coherent strategy the consortium felt that the likelihood of individual schemes being achieved would be higher and would ensure that they were implemented in a way that would maximise the benefits of Trans-Pennine rail services as a whole (TPA, 1992a, p.1). However, as Friends of the Earth (n.d, p.3.4) pointed out:

> ... it is clear that its [the rail study] scope was limited to improvements likely to meet the existing Government criteria for rail investment ... major improvements to the rail network ... were hardly considered.

The Trans-Pennine study would have been more relevant if passenger travel and freight studies had been undertaken to cover all modes rather than the separate analysis of road and rail. The Department of Transport's consultation procedure would have been more constructive if it had included the Trans-Pennine Rail Strategy Study Report. Instead, the consultation process was based solely on the recommended strategies outlined in the road study. The Trans-Pennine study failed to take the opportunity to consider transport problems in the Pennines in a comprehensive and multi-modal way.

Road and rail investment

As discussed earlier, the government uses different methods for investing in road and rail. Road schemes are evaluated on the basis of Social Cost Benefit Analysis while the DOT applied a combination of financial and Section 56 evaluation to assess rail projects. The rail study was seen as having a dual function. Firstly, it was a feasibility study which has led to the development of financially and economically viable investment strategies for Trans-Pennine rail routes. Secondly, it demonstrated that it is both possible and worthwhile to evaluate road and rail schemes on a comparable basis using consistent assumptions (TPA, 1992b, p.97).

The study calculated the benefit to cost ratio for Trans-Pennine rail investment strategies, which ranged from 4.70:1 for strategy A to 2.50:1 for strategy C, with strategy B producing a benefit to cost ratio of 2.8:1. The average benefit to cost ratio for road schemes included in the 1989 White Paper was 2.5:1. The rail study concluded that, while some individual road schemes perform better than this average, the Trans-Pennine strategies would all perform at least as well as the average for trunk road schemes. This indicates that the net benefits of investing in rail schemes are likely to be similar to those from road investments (TPA, 1992b, p.97). If rail is assessed in the same way as road investment is evaluated, then the true benefits of rail can be acknowledged. The inherent bias of assessment criteria for roads make it more difficult for rail projects to be justified on an economic basis. Road projects will nearly always appear better value for money compared with rail.

Road study

The road strategies put forward in the Trans-Pennine study included the widening of the M62 to more than eight lanes. The study stated that future traffic growth would be more than a 4x4 highway could accommodate and would lead to further congestion. Major improvements as outlined in strategies B, D and F are likely to accommodate 115,000-157,000 vehicles by 2016, compared with 111,000-148,000 vehicles if strategies A, C and E and a dual 4x4 lane highway were to be adopted.

The Charted Institute of Transport (1993, p.3) criticised the study for failing to consider the possibility of diverting traffic that may have a choice of mode or route from those links that are approaching saturation, such as parts of the M62 and city centre to city centre traffic. The high volumes of traffic that are expected on the M62 further underline the need to invest in improving the north Trans-Pennine routes. The rail study advocated electrification of the Liverpool to York route which would have a time saving of 19.5 minutes (TPA, 1992b, p.55). Electrification would thus allow rail to compete better with road.

The upgrading of the A628/616 to a dual carriageway was proposed within the Trans-Pennine study. This road passes through the Peak District National Park and would thus have a significant environmental impact. This option, however, was ruled out by the DOT, but the problem of higher volumes of traffic between Manchester and Sheffield still exists. The rail study stated that the average speed from Liverpool to Sheffield was only 71 kph and from Manchester to Sheffield 74 kph. The speed between Manchester and Sheffield is expected to increased to an average of 90 kph. The use of the Woodhead Tunnel to provide a fast electric route between South Yorkshire and Greater Manchester was put forward as an alternative solution.

Environmental impact

One of the objectives of the Trans-Pennine road study was to identify potential improvements and assess their economic and environmental impact. Within the road strategy report consideration of environmental impacts was given little attention. The study identified those roads which pass through or near a National Park as having environmental significance. The objective of the Trans-Pennine study, however, was to increase highway capacity to accommodate future demands while at the same time protecting the environment, in particular National Parks. The study concentrated mainly on visual impact and whether this will increase or stay the same. No consideration was given to the wider implications of road expansion such as pollution and land use patterns, nor to the immediate impact on the local environment, such as the effect on Sites of Special Scientific Interest and conservation areas. No was consideration given to the effects on urban congestion of 'delivering' high volumes of traffic into the cities.

The 1994 Road Review provided little change to the overall roads programme, although prioritising of some schemes into the longer term category means that work will be suspended on them at the next suitable point in their development. Work will not be resumed until other higher priority schemes have been completed and the programme has progressed forward. For the North-West, the revised programme makes better use of existing routes and relieves the congested sections of motorway together with a number of bypasses and improvements. Table 7.16 shows the priority given to the M62 road schemes within the Road Review.

The impact of greater motor vehicle use will further cause a deterioration in air quality. In 1993 a study on vehicle-related air pollution within the North-West of England was published by the Manchester Areas Pollution Advisory Council (MAPAC). The report estimated the emissions from road transport in the North-West of England, as shown in Table 7.17. Carbon dioxide is the pollutant which is emitted in the largest amounts from road traffic in the North-West, followed by carbon monoxide and nitrogen oxides. These pollutants contribute to atmospheric problems such as the greenhouse effect, acid rain and smog. In high concentrations they can also be deleterious to human health. The North-West Regional Health Authority estimates that 36.8% of its population is at risk from the air pollutant, ozone. Ozone is considered as a secondary pollutant which can cause inflammation of the lungs and breathing difficulties (MAPAC, 1993, p.29). The growth in traffic within the North-West and on strategic corridors such as the M62 will add to the present air pollution problems within the North-West of England.

Table 7.16
Priority given to M62 road schemes

Route	Title	Order of Total Cost £ million	Length (kms)	Last Stage
M1/M62	**Priority 1** Lofthouse Interchange Diversion, Leeds MB	31.3	6.8	OP
M62	East-M606 Link Road Kirklees MB	14.8	0.6	
M62	J12-14 Widening Westbound, Bury MB	10.0	4.5	PC
M62	**Priority 2** J18-21 Widening Rochdale MB	116.4	12.8	PC
M62	J12-18 Relief Road, Salford MB, Bury MB*	301.1	17.7	PC
M62	J6-7 Widening, Knowsley MB	4.7	5.3	
M62	J6 Improvement, Knowsley MB	13.4	-	
M62	**Long-term** J12-24 Widening, Rochdale MB. Calderdale MB, Kirklees MB	-	-	-

* Scheme added to the National Trunk Road Programme since 1 January 1990.
PC Public consultation held. OP Draft orders published.

Table 7.17

Emissions from road transport in the North-West of England

Pollutant	Emission (thousand tonnes)	% of UK	Main source
Sulphur dioxide	6.50	0.2	Diesel
Nitrogen oxides	141.97	5.2	Petrol
Black smoke	21.30	4.7	Diesel
Volatile organic compounds	99.70	4.2	Diesel
Carbon monoxide	615.00	9.2	Petrol
Lead	0.23	10.4	Petrol
Carbon dioxide	3,080.00	1.9	Petrol

Source: MAPAC, 1993, p.23

In 1992 SACTRA recommended that a formal environmental assessment of a road scheme should come earlier in the planning process, for example, on its entry into the roads programme. The recommendations made by SACTRA were accepted by the Government. If SACTRA's recommendations were to be implemented, a preliminary environmental assessment of each of the strategies for the Trans-Pennine corridor would have been produced. This report would have undertaken an assessment of the environmental impact of each strategy, rather than a cursory assessment concentrating mainly on visual impact.

The construction of transport infrastructure and protection of the countryside have caused environmental controversy. Critics have argued for better co-ordination of transport and land use planning to minimise the need to travel. The government's 1990 White Paper This Common Inheritance acknowledged the need for planning transport routes to take account of the potential impact on settlement and development patterns. In 1992 the DOE published research on how land use planning could reduce traffic volumes by 10-15%.

A study by the Council for the Protection of Rural England (1992c) examined the M40 corridor between Buckinghamshire and Oxfordshire to determine the local development and traffic effects of motorways and other major new roads. The study concluded that construction of a new section of the motorway resulted in development taking place on land which had not been previously developed and which was not contained within approved development plans. Traffic generated by such new developments added to highway problems in the vicinity, necessitating further improvements to the road network (CPRE, 1992c, p.7). The issue of generated development and

186

traffic, however, is not included in the present assessment of motorways and trunk road schemes.

The 1994 SACTRA report identified the importance of the effects of trip generation associated with road construction. By assessing demand for the use of a particular road, predicting future growth and devising a strategy to meet this growth, the government is maintaining the cycle of increasing demand for road travel, as suppressed demand is unleashed with new road capacity. The Trans-Pennine study ignored the possible effects of fiscal and land use policies on traffic growth. The DOT does not see public transport as an alternative that would significantly reduce the use of the M62, even with feasible improvements. The DOT states:

> ... that if major improvements were made such that travel by rail could be increased by 50% this would be equivalent to only a 3% reduction in travel by road. A 50% increase in rail freight would be equivalent to a 6% reduction in road freight (DOT, n.d).

It is not possible to determine the accuracy of this statement since the DOT does not provide the information on which it is based. If it were taken to be correct, then the DOT has itself identified the need to take further measures to control the demand for travel. If improvements in public travel do not reduce the use of road transport, it is clear that fiscal and land use policies need to be implemented. While the government has acknowledged the potential of particular measures, little progress has be made in practice. The Trans-Pennine study is indicative of the government's supply management approach to transport problems, with no measures to manage the actual demand for travel.

Decision on the Trans-Pennine road study

A decision on the Trans-Pennine road study was taken by the Roads and Traffic Minister Robert Key, on 30 November 1993. The Minister decided that while the M62 remains the main corridor across the Pennines, there will be no improvements above those planned in the present roads programme. The DOT plans to examine the need for increasing capacity on particular sections of the M1 and M62 to cope with increased traffic, to improve road safety and to enhance economic growth in the region (DOT, 1993d). The Minister also decided that there would be no improvement to the A66 and to the routes east of the M65 at Colne. A decision not to upgrade the A628/A616 to dual carriageway through the Peak District National Park was upheld and no additional major schemes will take place in this corridor.

187

The Trans-Pennine study resulted in no new schemes being added to the roads programme and only a limited package of measures will be taken to focus on particular problems, although it did not state what form these measures will take. The Minister stated that:

> The response on the consultations were divided on the desirable way forward. While there were many who saw the need for improvements to the road network in the Pennine region, many rejected any further major road improvements because of the likely impact on the natural environment (DOT, 1993d).

With regard to the Trans-Pennine rail study, in response to the public consultation the Minister examined Trans-Pennine rail links to transfer traffic from road to rail. In his decision the Minister stated that:

> A Trans-Pennine Rail Study undertaken by consultants for a consortium of local authorities and Passenger Transport Authorities has shown that any improvement to the rail network would only have a marginal effect on road traffic flows (DOT, 1993d).

Rail is considered to be limited in solving transport problems and, in practice, close substitutes rarely serve similar markets. The road study resulted in no action to reduce the predicted traffic growth by providing sufficient public transport alternatives. The A628 in the Peak District National Park will not undergo any expansion. The Park is still faced with growing traffic problems and believes that traffic restraint measures should be taken in the Park. However, the Minister stated that traffic restraint measures would not be appropriate for they would increase the pressure on routes to the south of the Park. He claimed that, given the environmental sensitivity of the area, it would be difficult to upgrade further the A523 to cope with the extra traffic.

On 2 July 1993 the Peak District National Park decided that further investigations should take place into Trans-Pennine issues. On 14 July 1993 a meeting was held with the Minister, who decided that the DOT would not be involved in funding and that additional work would not make any difference to the Trans-Pennine Road Study. The Minister stated that:

> I remain convinced that another study would not contribute any new information which would materially affect the decision I have already taken (DOT, 1994b).

Transport policy for the Peak District National Park contained in the 1993 Structure Plan covered cross-park traffic. Traffic developments including traffic management schemes which reduce the amount of cross-park traffic, would be supported. Section T3 of the plan stated that:

> No new road for cross-park traffic will be constructed and with the exception of those schemes ... no existing road will be subjected to major alteration, unless there is a compelling national need which cannot be met by any reasonable alternative means and which is demonstrated to be in the overall public interest ... (Peak District National Park, 1993, p.43).

Despite the Minister's refusal to be involved in further Trans-Pennine studies the National Park and a number of local authorities joined together to undertake a further analysis. In May 1995 *South Pennines Transport Needs Study* was produced by Oscar Faber TPA for the Peak Park Transport Forum, with the aim of investigating further the issues identified in the previous Trans-Pennine studies and of developing a transport strategy. The study examined the area which extended from the M62 southwards to the A52/A523 (Leek-Derby). Traffic forecasts across this area are expected to increase by 71% in the period 1994-2015 which are similar to the National Road Traffic Forecasts of 70% over the same period. The Transport Needs Study proposed a strategy for the South Pennines area which would include (Oscar Faber TPA, 1995):

- The development of a 'box' of highway improvements around the Park to reduce cross-park traffic.
- Traffic restraint measures in the Park which would comprise downgrading of the A635 and A515 from their current 'A' road status, a restriction of 80 kph on roads through the Peak Park, localised speed restrictions at a number of locations in the Park, and traffic calming measures in the villages along the A623.
- The strategy for rail which was proposed in the Trans-Pennine rail study.
- The provision of rail services between Manchester and Derby/Leicester via the Matlock-Chinley line.

The study stated that the rail option alone would not be sufficient to negate the need for a road strategy (Oscar Faber TPA, 1995, p.23). Although the above strategy will have a positive effect on reducing cross-Park traffic this would be at a price. Traffic would be more concentrated on roads surrounding the Park, which would affect the environment of the area. Secondly, the cost involved would be high due to the amount of road construction necessary, which would also have a negative environmental impact. The study recommended further economic and environmental appraisals to be undertaken to identify the benefits of such a strategy. A lower cost strategy was also proposed which could be implemented sooner. This would consist of traffic restraint measures in the Park, together with improvements to the A628. It would also require the implementation of the Trans-Pennine rail strategy and support for the abandonment of the A6 Disley-High Lane bypass from the government's roads programme. The benefits of the lower cost strategy would reduce cross-park traffic on roads other than the A628 and would restrict any environmental impacts to this A628 corridor. This option requires a limited amount of new highway construction and could be included in the plans which presently exist for the improvement of the A628.

To reduce the impact of traffic in the South Pennines area, the Oscar Faber TPA study recommended that the transport strategy should be based on enhanced rail services in the southern region, traffic restraint to minimise traffic growth and the encouragement of the use of rail freight by supporting the provision of railheads at quarries. The Peak District National Park will need to choose which strategies can limit traffic demand within the Park as well as gain government and local authority support in order that the funds can be secured to implement the chosen strategy.

Need for a multi-modal approach

The Trans-Pennine study took a mono-modal approach to examine the problems of increasing traffic on Trans-Pennine routes, despite the efforts of local authorities to provide a rail strategy. It failed to consider fully the potential environmental impacts of developing Trans-Pennine roads. The study was based on the need to deal with congestion because of the threat which this poses to economic development. Throughout the road study the inadequacy of the roads was seen as hindering economic growth. Economic development was equated with infrastructure development and no attempt was made to question this fundamental tenet on which British transport policy has been based.

The strategies proposed in the study promoted greater road development and this in the long-term is unsustainable. None of the strategies proposed in either study was accepted by the Minister. Despite the predicted traffic growth on Trans-Pennine routes identified by the study, no measures to reduce or control the demand to travel were taken. The study failed to consider a comprehensive strategy for Trans-Pennine routes. In many respects it was a waste of time, for it provided no solutions to the traffic growth problems which were identified.

The criticisms made of the Trans-Pennine study are indicative of the direction of national transport policy. No coherent transport policy plan which covers all modes of transport in the UK exists. The UK Sustainable Development Plan marked a change in the government's approach to transport, which recognised the need to control traffic growth. The measures proposed include: ensuring that transport costs reflect the true environmental costs, land use policies to minimise the need for individuals to travel by locating facilities close to public transport, and policies which encourage greater use of public transport. The Plan also outlined a commitment to provide a strategic assessment of roads programmes in response to the 1992 SACTRA report. Despite its environmental concerns, the DOT maintains the view that failure to provide additional road in the absence of demand management measures could result in congestion and divert traffic to less suitable roads. It will continue with a programme of bypasses with traffic management measures (DOE, 1994c, p.175). The Sustainable Development Plan did recognise the need to set specific objectives and targets for different sectors, although very few were contained within the Plan itself. The lack of binding national targets in transport and environmental policy permits greater freedom at the project level. However, the government is unwilling to commit itself to targets for the transport sector (see Chapter 4).

If sustainability is to be achieved, an attempt must be made to implement this concept into the transport sector. Therefore, targets should be set to reflect the carrying capacity of the environment at the local and global level. The absence of such targets, together with the misconception that technology fixes will solve the problem, has resulted in the government following an unsustainable transport policy. In the context of the Trans-Pennine study a more comprehensive approach should have been taken to deal with traffic growth on Pennine corridors. The Trans-Pennine study failed to develop a multi-modal strategy to deal with traffic problems. This led to the Peak District National Park commissioning a study to be undertaken, combining both road and rail. A multi-modal strategy should be developed which has explicit environmental objectives. Measures that could be taken by local authorities in the Pennine region should also be considered, such as land use strategies and measures to restrict car use in urban centres, which could reduce the need to travel and discourage travelling to urban centres by car whether for work or leisure. Such an approach, however, may be unrealistic outside a national framework of transport and environmental policy. It is at the national level that changes in policy are required if a balanced strategy for the Trans-Pennine corridor and the country as a whole is to be developed.

8 Amsterdam-Utrecht corridor

To deal with the problem of increasing traffic congestion on a main strategic corridor linking the cities of Amsterdam and Utrecht within the Randstad the Dutch have developed the concept of a multi-modal 'corridor approach' based on national policy targets. The Amsterdam-Utrecht corridor study is the first study of its kind to be undertaken in the Netherlands and the lessons learnt from this study will enable the foundations to be laid for future studies using this approach. This Chapter examines the theory behind the 'corridor approach' and how this has been applied and implemented in practice. The Amsterdam-Utrecht corridor provides a case study, to examine how policy targets influence decision-making at the corridor level. It serves as a detailed examination of a new approach to transport planning which is currently being developed within Europe.

Transport planning in the Netherlands

Road planning in the Netherlands is outlined in the national transport structure plan, which contains long-term initiatives to develop an integrated traffic and transport system. The plan determines the shape of the road infrastructure in the Netherlands, with new infrastructure construction being limited to those projects within the plan. The 1966 *Wet Uitkering Wegen* law requires the production of a national roads plan (*Rijkswegenplan*), which is revised every ten years (Gwilliam & Gommers, 1992, p.240). The national roads plan sets out the medium-term planning for trunk roads. The first plan was produced in 1968, followed by the second in 1984 together with the first transport structure plan. Short-term planning for transport is outlined in a Multi-year Program for Infrastructure and Transport (*Meerjarenprogramma*

Infrastructuur en Transport) which details plans for infrastructure every five years. It is updated every year along with the *Uitvoeringsprogramma,* which contains the budget for road construction at the operational level.

Once major projects have been selected for inclusion within the transport structure plan, the Ministry of Transport, Public Works and Water Management (*Ministerie voor Verkeer en Waterstaat)* provides a detailed design and work schedule for the project, which is presented within the project note (*projectnota*). The project note initially consisted of a few pages, but since the Sixties this approach has undergone a number of changes, especially with the introduction of environmental impact assessment in 1987. The project note now requires an outline of alternatives in an integrated study, which should consider factors such as safety, accessibility, spatial and economic structures, agricultural aspects, effects on the living and working environment and effects on water supplies and recreational activities (Gwilliam & Gommers, 1992, p.240).

Local government in the Netherlands is required to direct regional and land use plans to the plans of central government making provision for the construction of new trunk roads and the expansion and possible development of existing links (MVW, 1990, p.122). In 1990 the Second Transport Structure Plan (part D) proposed streamlining the existing route determination and planning procedure for new roads and railway lines. Three years later, in May 1993, the government finally submitted to parliament proposals for a new route determination procedure. The new procedure is outlined in the Routing Act, which came into force on 1 January 1994. The Act describes the procedures to be followed in the decision-making process for the construction or modification of national or major infrastructure, such as motorways, railways and waterways. It does not, however, relate to provincial or municipal infrastructure and pipe-lines. The 'corridor approach' is advocated within the new Act, which integrates the steps of the old route determination procedure with the present EIA procedure. The Act will enable a broad agreement for the choice of a route, together with consideration of land use planning, public consultation and protection rights. The decision to choose a route under this new procedure may be subject to an appeals procedure under the Administrative Justice (official decisions) Act before it is included in the land use plan of a municipality.

The main aim of the project or route note under the Routing Act is to determine whether the capacity and quality in the provision of transport can be solved by extending or changing road, rail and waterway infrastructure. Alternatives may comprise a 'do-nothing' option and, in the case of road schemes, a public transport option, together with possible effects of each of the alternatives on mobility beyond the local level.

Factors include traffic forecasts based on travel demand, safety, effects on environmental and residential amenity, economic implications, social, cultural and physical effects of development in a rural and urban context, as well as implications for landscape, town values, archaeological, historical and geographical factors. Although the Amsterdam-Utrecht corridor study was initiated before the Routing Act came into force, it does, however, follow a similar procedure advocated within the Act.

Once the route note has been completed and public consultation has been undertaken by local authorities, it is submitted to the Transport and Public Works Council by the Minister of Transport, Public Works and Water Management. The Council then makes the report available for public consultation for a 4-8 week period. The consultation process results in the production of a report and recommendations, which, together with a summary of the report, is forwarded to the Minister of Transport, Public Works and Water Management. In collaboration with the Minister of Environment, the Minister of Transport then makes a decision based on the recommendations and the responses received (MVW, 1990, p.26).

The concept of a corridor study

After the introduction of EIA in the Netherlands in 1986 there was an increased demand for a range of transport modes to be considered in the EIA of transport projects, to enable a more environmentally beneficial solution to be found to resolve the conflicting interests of accessibility and environmental amenity or liveability along particular transport corridors. The problem of congestion and poor capacity on road and rail routes within the transport corridor linking the cities of Amsterdam and Utrecht provided an ideal opportunity to undertake an integrated study (Dekker et al., 1992, p.3). The infrastructure within the Amsterdam-Utrecht corridor had a number of physical points of contact which needed to be addressed at the same time.

On 5 January 1990 the Amsterdam-Utrecht Corridor Study was initiated. It was to be the first study of its type to be undertaken within the Netherlands. Within the study a corridor is defined as a bundle of main infrastructural provisions with a national and/or international function which deals with traffic and transport flows (both passenger and freight) and where possibilities exist for a shift in the modal split between road, rail and canal (MVW, 1993b, p.5). The original goals of the study were to consider the interrelated problems of accessibility and liveability and to devise solutions and ensure optimal use of infrastructure and receipt of maximum return from new investment on any infrastructural development undertaken. Within the study, liveability covered the impact on nature and landscape, soil, water, air and noise emissions, living

194

environment, traffic safety and the risk from transporting dangerous substances.

In the Netherlands the national motorway network is the responsibility of central government, while the rail infrastructure is the combined responsibility of the government and *Nederlandse Spoorwegen* (NS). In July 1991 representatives from both NS and the Ministry of Transport, Public Works and Water Management (Directorate-General of Public Works and Water Management, Utrecht - *Rijkswaterstaat*) were involved in the preparation of the *Corridor Memorandum* in which they agreed on the main principles of what they termed a 'corridor approach'. The approach promoted an integrated examination of different transport modes, an open planning process whereby the participation of different organisations is encouraged, and transport substitution via a modal shift. The Memorandum stated that:

> ... to solve transport and traffic bottlenecks, all possible avenues [should be] ... explored as a matter of course; not only alternative routes ... or alternative modes of transport but also policy possibilities in the adjacent areas, parking policy, [and] environmental planning. The product of a corridor study ... [would be] a project decision (Dekker et al., 1992, p.4).

The NS subdivided projects into three partially overlapping categories so that the approach could be applied in practice. The first category included projects which form part of a national integrated network, such as those projects contained in Rail 21 which are required to be implemented quickly. In a Corridor Study only the size and phase of such a project would be specified in detail, in that it would be an alternative to expanding the road infrastructure. The second category contains projects which in terms of size and possible benefits are weighted against alternative infrastructure development within the corridor being studied. The third category comprises of projects where there is no clear alternative. These projects would not be considered in a Corridor Study.

The traditional approach taken to deal with transport projects in the Netherlands has mainly been compartmental, with each study examining a specific mode of transport. The concept of a Corridor Study enables an integrated approach and a more comprehensive examination of different modes when considering solutions to specific transport problems. Possible infrastructure solutions would be examined in combination with policy for adjacent areas; for example, pricing policy, location policy and parking policy. In order that solutions might be successful the Minister of Transport, Public Works and Water Management would be required not only to reach a decision on the construction and financing of infrastructure, but would also need to agree on policy for adjacent areas with the transport regions and other

195

authorities concerned (Dekker et al., 1992, p.5). An ideal approach would be a solution to a particular problem being agreed in Regional Traffic and Transport Plans (RVVPs), with policy in the SVV2 providing a framework for these plans to be formulated. The feasibility of implementing an alternative would depend on agreements made and co-operation with the state, provinces and regional transport boards/municipalities.

The second component of the corridor approach is an open planning process, which would enable the participation of municipalities, provinces and chambers of commerce in the organisation of the project. The Memorandum recommended that from the beginning of a study official and administrative discussions should be held to enable reciprocal awareness and understanding of each other's ideas and problems. A discussion of possible infrastructural development at an early point to hear views of all parties concerned would provide a broad base on which a decision could be taken.

The third component of the Corridor Study is the consideration of possible substitution or a modal shift between road, rail and water for both passenger and freight transport. Traffic forecasts in a Corridor Study should therefore indicate the total demand for passenger and freight transport and how demand is divided between each mode. Traffic demand between each mode and policy adopted in adjacent areas would be of great importance in formulating a successful solution. Several policy alternatives would also be formulated together with differing infrastructural solutions. It is therefore important to take into consideration SVV2 policy which focuses on strengthening public transport.

The Second Transport Structure Plan, as discussed in Chapter 5, outlines objectives to resolve the conflicting demands of accessibility and liveability to achieve a sustainable transport system. Policies outlined in the NMP+ and VINEX are important for an integrated and effective approach to transport problems. This is in contrast to the compartmental approach of the past which failed to integrate policy and which dealt with the symptoms of the transport problem rather than the causes. A Corridor Study is therefore intended to provide a regional 'tailor-made' solution to achieving a sustainable transport system, as well as implementing an integrated package of measures from SVV2, NMP+ and VINEX at the regional level (Dekker et al., 1992, p.7).

By starting with the relationship between various modes of transport and transport networks and the most probable planning and economic development which may occur, a corridor study would consider a wide range of alternatives. Policy alternatives based on various assumptions of expected growth in motorised mobility (e.g. a maximum growth of 35% in vehicle kilometres by the 2010 compared with 1986) would enable the consequences for infrastructure and environment to be determined depending on the success of policy. A distinction is made between the strategic and project level as well as between passenger and freight transport. This distinction is important in EIA because of the possibilities of influencing different environmental impacts. Not only is the corridor study seen as being directed towards solving existing transport problems but accessibility and liveability must also be guaranteed in the long-term. Thus, infrastructural decisions can no longer be automatically based on demand-led policy for demand-regulating policy is also required; for example, restricting mobility, pursuing a stringent pricing policy and implementing the principle of selective accessibility. Policy relating to areas within a corridor would be defined by transport regions which would form an essential component of the SVV2 policy package (Dekker et al., 1992, p.7). A corridor study would need to have some co-ordination with regional transport plans, to ensure optimum use of existing infrastructure and promotion of public transport. The implementation of plans such as the corridor study and regional traffic and transport plans would need to be carefully matched.

Within the corridor/EIA procedure a number of steps can be distinguished. The first involves the preparation of the starting memorandum or Notification of Intent (NOI), followed by a corridor note/EIA study, after which the procedure follows the normal EIA process up to and including the decision of the Minister of Transport, Public Works and Water Management (see Chapter 6). If one of the alternatives within the study is accepted, then a further three stages would be followed jointly by the participants in the project depending on need. These stages are not part of the EIA procedure and include the preparation of execution memoranda for the building of infrastructure, following statutory procedures for the building of the infrastructure and implementing plans presented in the execution memoranda.

Amsterdam-Utrecht corridor

The Amsterdam-Utrecht corridor (AUC) is a 27-kilometre transport route which links the cities of Amsterdam and Utrecht via the municipalities of Abcoude, Loenen, Breukelen, Maarssen and Vleutan-De Meern (see Figure 8.1). The route comprises the national A2 road which is a six-lane (2x3) highway, the Amsterdam-Rhine Canal (ARC) and a two-track rail link. The AUC forms part of the main corridor from Amsterdam to Germany passing via Utrecht and Arnhem and is an important link connecting the Netherlands to neighbouring countries. It also provides access to Schiphol airport for passengers and freight (MVW, 1992b).

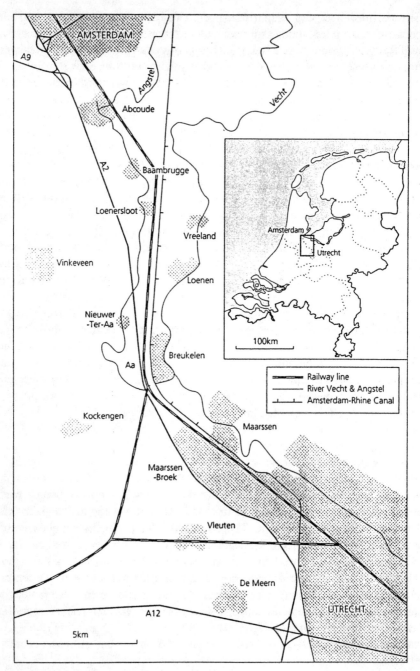

Figure 8.1 The Amsterdam-Utrecht Corridor

The corridor has been identified as an important transport route, and any congestion or delays along this main corridor are perceived to have economic implications for business. The route is also considered to be of economic importance if the Netherlands is to maintain its position as a transport and distribution country within the Single European Market with the tougher competition which is expected to prevail.

Situation (1987-1990)

The corridor study defined the 'present situation' within the Amsterdam-Utrecht Corridor as the period 1987-1990. Within this period a conflict has been developing between the demand of traffic to use the corridor and the capacity of the corridor.

The A2 is overloaded by daily traffic causing traffic congestion and delays during peak hours as well as suffering from safety capacity problems between the motorway junctions of Holendrecht and Oudenrijn. This is seen as resulting in problems for both business and freight traffic. Non-rail public transport is also affected by congestion, especially during peak hours on both the motorway and the local road network. The rail link between Duivendrecht and Utrecht Central Station is used by passenger transport, allowing no possibilities for the movement of freight during this period. Due to rail capacity being at its near maximum, the route is sensitive to disturbances and delays and is considered inadequate to provide a rapid service for both passenger and freight in accordance with the timetable.

The most direct link within the corridor is the Amsterdam-Rhine Canal which is under-utilised and has few drawbacks in terms of safety, but generally offers a fast link for shipping.

Congestion on the A2 and the railway within the corridor is considered to affect the quality of freight transport and the siting of companies within the area adjacent to the corridor. Particular congestion 'hot spots' along the A2 include the section from Abcoude to Vinkeveen, Vinkeveen to Breukelen and Utrecht West to Utrecht. The RW720 road between Abcoude and Maarssen and the S21 road between Aalsmeer and Hiversum are being used by traffic which tries to avoid these congestion points on the A2. The RW720 is also susceptible to poor accessibility due to traffic overspill which tries to avoid bottlenecks on the main transport axes. Public transport using these roads also needs to cope with the delays caused by congestion on the A2. With regard to liveability, the A2 and the ARC are considered as impregnable ecological barriers, while the railway is considered less of a barrier but still has a negative effect on nature.

Table 8.1 below shows the growth in personal transport within the corridor on an average working day between 1987-1990 in both directions. Road traffic on both the A2 and RW720 increased, with the highest increase in rail transport, while regional public transport remained unchanged. Freight transport within this period declined, with an 18% decrease in freight transport by inland waterway (see Table 8.2), while rail freight increased by 9% and road freight by 8%. Table 8.3 shows the growth in traffic specifically on the A2 in both directions over a period of 24 hours for all sections of the A2 and for each different type of motor vehicle. On the same road the chance of congestion increased during the period 1987-1990. The section between Abcoude and Vinkeveen has the highest chance of congestion of 13% (Table 8.4).

Table 8.1
Number of people using the AUC on
an average working day in both directions

Transport Mode	1987 (number)	1990 (number)	Change (%)
Road traffic A2			
Holendrecht-Abcoude	143,000	166,000	+16
Abcoude -Vinkeveen	133,000	155,800	+17
Vinkeveen-Breukelen	121,800	143,200	+18
Breukelen-Maarssen	119,300	140,600	+18
Maarssen- Utrecht West	116,900	136,800	+17
Utrecht West - Utrecht	126,800	149,500	+18
Utrecht - Oudenrijn	141,700	167,200	+18
RW720:			
Abcoude-Baambrugge	4,800	5,500	+15
Loenersloot-Loenen	10,700	12,300	+15
Regional public transport			
A2 & RW720:			
Abcoude-Vinkeveen	3,500	3,500	0
Vinkeveen-Breukelen	4,000	4,000	0
Breukelen-Maarssen	5,000	5,000	0
Rail Transport:			
Bijlmer-Abcoude	40,700	50,500	+24
Abcoude-Breukelen	40,000	49,900	+25
Breukelen-Maarssen	36,800	45,600	+24
Maarssen-Utrecht	37,400	46,200	+24

Table 8.2
Freight transport in the AUC (million tonnes per year)

Mode	1987	Share	1990	Share	Change
Road	27.3	34%	29.5	41%	+8%
Rail	2.2	3%	2.4	3%	+9%
Inland waterway	50	63%	41	56%	-18%
Total	79.5	100%	72.9	100%	-8%

Source: MVW, 1993b, p.27

Table 8.3
Traffic intensity on the A2 in both directions over a 24-hour period

	Cars		Lorries		Motor vehicles	
	1987	1990	1987	1990	1987	1990
Holendrecht to Abcoude	102,100	117,800	12,900	13,200	115,000	131,000
Abcoude to Vinkeveen	95,000	110,600	12,000	12,400	107,000	123,000
Vinkeveen to Breukelen	87,000	101,600	11,000	11,400	98,000	113,000
Breukelen to Maarssen	85,200	99,800	10,800	11,200	96,000	111,000
Maarssen to Utrecht West	83,500	99,100	10,500	10,900	94,000	110,000
Utrecht West to Utrecht	90,600	106,100	11,400	11,900	102,000	118,000
Utrecht to Oudenrijn	101,200	118,700	12,800	13,300	114,000	132,000

Source: MVW, 1993b, p.28

The use of the Amsterdam-Utrecht corridor by traffic has a number of environmental impacts on air quality, noise levels, quality of soil and surface water, road safety, transportation of dangerous substances, and indirect effects on nature and landscape within the corridor. Along the A2 emissions of air pollutants are high especially at Abcoude Lake, Winkel and Utrecht Rheyngaerde where NO_2 limits are exceeded, with high levels also recorded at junctions Holendrecht and Oudenrijn. Noise levels in many places along the A2, the railtrack and the ARC are expected to increase (MVW, 1993b, p.6).

Table 8.4
Chance of congestion on the A2

	1987	1990
Holendrecht-Abcoude	*	*
Abcoude-Vinkeveen	4%	13%
Vinkeveen-Breukelen	0-1%	6%
Breukelen-Maarssen	0-1%	3%
Maarssen-Utrecht-West	0-1%	2%
Utrecht-West-Utrecht	1%	9%
Utrecht-Oudenrijn	*	*

* The chance of congestion was not calculated for this road section due to no
 method being available for slip roads.

Source: MVW, 1993b, p.28

Predicted traffic situation in 2010

The corridor study examined the development of the present traffic problems in the AUC up to the year 2010. The study assumed policy measures contained in the National Nature Policy Plan (*Nationaal Natuurbeleidsplan*) (NBP), NMP+ and VINEX had been implemented. The SVV2 was excluded from consideration due to the proposal within the plan to double the railtracks. Traffic on the A2 is expected to grow by 67% in vehicle kilometres by the year 2010 compared with 1986 (Table 8.5). This is much higher than the SVV2 target which set a maximum growth of 35% in vehicle kilometres by 2010.

Table 8.5
Increase in personal traffic in the study area over the period 1987-2010 on an average working day

	1987	2010
Personal car traffic (Vehicle kilometres)	100	155 (167)*
Public Transport (Passenger kilometres)	100	178(187)*

*index 1986=100 which is the base year for SVV2 targets.
The corridor study took 1987 as the base year.

Source: MVW, 1993b, p.41

The study predicted that the sections of the A2 which are overloaded with traffic will increase from three sections (1987) to five in 2010. An increase in traffic will lead to a greater chance of congestion - 33% instead of the 2% norm set out in the SVV2 for strategic routes (see Table 8.6) (MVW, 1993b, p.42). The rising level of congestion is considered a threat to the economic development of the region, especially the development of Schiphol airport. The northern side of the airport is becoming less attractive for certain types of companies, while the RW720 will be overloaded with traffic from the congested A2. The number of persons travelling by car will almost double in comparison with the year 1987 (Table 8.7) with road-based public transport also being affected by congestion.

The number of passenger kilometres per train in 2010 will have almost doubled and will therefore require new infrastructure. To offer a reasonable quality of service the number of trains in operation will be increased, but due to the limited capacity of the two-track railway this expansion will be restricted. This will mean delays for train passengers, while the share of freight rail per train is expected to decrease as a result of insufficient rail capacity. These bottlenecks are also considered to have negative effects on the economic functioning of the northern part of the Randstad. The predicted growth in mobility will also place pressure on liveability targets (MVW, 1993b, p.8). The doubling of passengers on rail will mean that Nederlandse Spoorwegen will not be able to meet the demand.

Table 8.6
Chance of congestion on A2 (2010)

Road section	Number of lanes	Chance of Congestion 1987	2010
Holendrecht-Abcoude	2x3+	*	*
Abcoude-Vinkeveen	2x3	4%	33%
Vinkeveen-Breukelen	2x3	0-1%	26%
Breukelen-Maarssen	2x3	0-1%	26%
Maarssen-Utrecht West	2x3	0-1%	22%
Utrecht West-Utrecht	2x3	1%	32%
Utrecht - Oudenrijn	2x3+	*	*

* The chance of congestion was not calculated for this road section due to no method being available for slip roads.

Source: MVW, 1993b, p.28

Due to the application of technical fixes, air pollution along the road is expected to decrease. The area of Utrecht Rheyngaerde will remain the area with the greatest traffic bottlenecks. A decrease in the quality of soil, groundwater and surface water along the A2 is also predicted. Noise levels within the vicinity of the main transport axes are expected to increase with traffic growth. Along the A2 noise will increase by 0.5 to 2.0 dB(A) compared with 1987 levels, and 4,206 persons will be seriously affected by noise, while along the railway the noise level will increase by 3 dB(A) with 2,974 persons expected to be affected.

Along the ARC there will be a limited increase in noise levels; nevertheless 461 persons are expected to be affected (MVW, 1993b, p.7). The increasing level of traffic on the A2 will lead to greater traffic intensity and will put further pressure on the underlying road network. Traffic safety and local accessibility will decrease while visual intrusion will increase. The study predicts that the number of traffic accidents within the study area will also increase by 26% compared with 1987; on the A2 there will be an increase of almost 40%.

If present trends continue within the corridor, the SVV2 targets for air pollutants from road transport will not be met by the year 2010. Table 8.8 shows the emission of pollutants from road transport in the year 2010. None of the targets is expected to be met and CO_2 emissions will actually increase by 9%.

Table 8.7
Predicted number of people using the AUC on an average
working day in both directions in 2010

Transport mode	2010 (Number)	Change (%) since 1987
Road traffic A2		
Holendrecht-Abcoude	196,300	+37
Abcoude -Vinkeveen	177,800	+34
Vinkeveen-Breukelen	159,800	+31
Breukelen-Maarssen	159,800	+34
Maarssen-Utrecht West	148,900	+27
Utrecht West - Utrecht Centrum	173,700	+37
Utrecht Centrum- Oudenrijn	175,600	+24
RW720		
Abcoude-Baambrugge	8,500	+77
Loenersloot-Loenen	19,5000	+82
Regional public transport		
A2 and RW720:		
Holendrecht-Abcoude	*	*
Abcoude-Vinkeveen	4,300	+23
Vinkeveen-Breukelen	5,400	+31
Breukelen-Maarssen	7,100	+42
Maarssen-Utrecht C S	*	*
Rail transport:		
Bijlmer-Abcoude	81,200	+99
Abcoude-Breukelen	80,900	+102
Breukelen-Maarssen	71,200	+93
Maarssen-Utrecht C S	76,600	+105

*no details in the traffic model given for these routes

Source: MVW, 1993b, p.40

Table 8.8
Emission of pollutants in the AUC (2010)

	NOx Tonnes per year	%	CxHy Tonnes per year	%	CO_2 Tonnes per year	%
1986 (=100%)	32,000		12,100		2,200	
SVV2 target	8,000	-75	3,025	-75	1,980	-10
2010	18,500	-42	4,800	-60	2,400	+9

Source: MVW,1993b, p.44

The amount of road freight traffic in the corridor is also expected to increase by 84% compared with 1987, with a reduction in freight transported by rail and inland waterway. The share of freight transported by road will increase from 34% in 1987 to almost 50%, which does not meet SVV2 policy (Table 8.9).

Table 8.9
Freight transport in million tonnes per year

Mode	1987 (Number)	2010 (Number)	Increase compared with 1987 (%)	1987 Share of each mode (%)	2010 Share of each mode (%)
Road	27.3	50.1	84	34	48
Rail	2.2	2.2	0	3	2
Inland Waterway	50	52.9	6	63	50
Total	79.5	105.2		100	100

Source: MVW, 1993b, p.41

The predictions suggest that, if present growth in mobility continues unabated, there will be a 67% increase in vehicle kilometres by 2010 compared with 1986. If the corridor undergoes no alternation to the A2 and the doubling of rail track from 2-4 takes place as outlined in Rail 21, the predicted growth in the corridor would not meet the national target of maximum growth of 35% by 2010. In SVV2 (part A) a number of solutions were put forward to deal with accessibility problems along the AUC, including widening the A2 and expanding the rail tracks.

A joint approach to the study of the Amsterdam-Utrecht Corridor was considered necessary if all alternatives were to be examined in a balanced way. This would allow a wide range of solutions to be considered and would assist the Minister of Transport, Public Works and Water Management in the final decision. Due to accessibility and liveability being interconnected, an integrated study was seen as necessary to examine the problems, solutions and effects of these mutual relationships and to consider all the interests involved.

Amsterdam-Utrecht corridor study

On 12 July 1990 the Notification of Intent (NOI) for traffic and transport within the corridor was published by Rijkswaterstaat and Nederlandse Spoorwegen under the General Environmental Protection Act (WABM) which requires an environmental impact assessment to be undertaken. The NOI outlined the goals of the study - to develop a sustainable traffic and transport system within the corridor and its direct area of influence, and to develop this system along the existing main infrastructure. The study made a distinction between the national and international importance of the corridor and the physical effects at the local level. The level at which the study should be aimed - the strategic level or project level - was an important point of discussion. A choice had to be made between the strategic level (policy EIA) concerning the total transport capacity and the modal split to be achieved between various modes, and the project level (project EIA) where questions in relation to route choice and different technical variations had to be addressed.

The NOI identified accessibility and liveability as the two main areas in which problems may arise. To resolve these anticipated problems, the initiators of the study proposed infrastructural development within the corridor, consisting of an expansion of the railway from Duivendrecht to Utrecht Central Station from two to four tracks. This is in line with the Nederlandse Spoorwegen's Rail 21 plan, which proposes a high Eurocity and Intercity network which will connect Amsterdam to Utrecht. The network would act as a fast connection within the urban centres which form the Randstad and between the Provinces of Groningen, Twente, South East Gelderland, Brabant, South Limburg, as well as providing connections from the Randstad to other European urban centres such as Paris. The NOI also proposed the consideration of other alternatives depending on the results of investigations. These included expansion of the railway to six tracks, possible expansion of the road to ten lanes, or maintaining the present six lanes.

The best environmental alternative according to the NOI should encompass measures to improve liveability, such as integrating areas of environmental importance (e.g. fields for migrating birds) next to the corridor, the use of noise absorbing asphalt, noise barriers, installing traffic safety systems, setting speed limits, as well as aligning new infrastructure in close proximity to present transport infrastructure in order to minimise the ecological barrier impact. In addition, measures should be implemented to reduce the impact on nature, landscape and the urban environment.

EIA Commission guidelines

On 10 July 1990 Rijkswaterstaat approached the EIA Commission to provide advice guidelines for the content of an environmental impact statement. From the 16 July to 16 September 1990 the NOI was made available for inspection. Under section 41 n(1) of WABM the EIA Commission is required to provide recommendations within two months after the publication of the NOI. On 30 October 1990 the EIA Commission finally presented its advice guidelines to the Ministry .

The advice guidelines outlined the objectives of the corridor study and provided recommendations to the Ministry on the content of the EIS. The Commission distinguished between two levels within the EIA process - the strategic level and the project level. At the strategic level, the guidelines suggested that the alternatives should be based on measures outlined in the SVV2. The predicted impacts of each alternative should be described and compared. At the project level, the criteria for determining the best environmental alternative were described. The BEA should contain measures to reduce mobility and to reduce peak hour traffic at the strategic level, and mitigation measures should be taken at the project level to improve the quality of the environment.

The Commission recommended that the criteria on which the decisions are to be based should be established and gaps in information listed. In addition to the proposed infrastructural developments, the Commission also suggested an investigation into possibilities of using pipelines for the transportation of raw materials (MER Commission, 1990).

Competent authority guidelines

On 10 January 1991 the competent authority (Ministry of Transport, Public Works and Water Management) published the final guidelines. The guidelines retained the proposals within the NOI of doubling the rail track from Amsterdam to Utrecht together with the widening of the A2. A new development proposal was outlined. This was the construction of the 'Utrecht

Curve' or *Utrechtboog*, a rail connection linking the corridor with Schiphol and the Amsterdam-Amersfoort line.

The proposals outlined in the NOI are required under law to have an assessment of the environmental impacts. The A2 highway serves as a trunk road and is subject to an EIA if the extension of the State road is to be separate from the existing profile (EIA Decree, Part B, 3A; Part C, 1.1). The construction of a new railway embankment at a distance of 25 metres or more from the existing profile of the rail line is also subject to an EIA (EIA Decree, Part B, 3.5; Part C, 2.1). This requirement is applicable to the proposal for the Utrecht Rail Curve and a rail curve near Breukelen which may need widening.

The EIA Commission in its draft guidelines suggested two EIA studies in order that both national and local interests be addressed. The initiators of the study, however, objected to this and a decision was made on one integrated study in which both the strategic and project levels would be addressed together (Dekker *et al.*, 1992, p.10). The final guidelines suggested that a range of alternatives for the expansion of road and rail should be included in the EIA. The guidelines presented a number of measures which should be investigated in order to reduce mobility. These comprise parking policy, restructuring of city areas to discourage car use, enhancing telecommunications, spreading of peak hours and the promotion of public transport and cycling.

Alternatives

In November 1993 the corridor note/EIA for traffic and transport in the Amsterdam-Utrecht Corridor was published by MVW and NS. The official consultation period was from 15 November 1993 to 20 January 1994.

In the formulation of alternatives, the study took into consideration the accessibility of economically important areas and liveability in the study area in relation to the main transport axes (A2, rail and canal), in order that national policy targets could be met. The study also attempted to provide the foundation for a traffic and transport system which will solve present and future congestion bottlenecks with a minimal effect on the environment (MVW, 1993b, p.8).

The study provided four points which each alternative must meet. Firstly, each alternative would need to indicate the effects on substitution between the different transport modes. Secondly, an alternative will need to consider developments in mobility and the need for infrastructure together. Thirdly, an alternative will need to take into consideration that traffic will be kept within the existing corridor so that no new routes are developed. Fourthly, through traffic on the way to international destinations and regional traffic should be considered separately in each alternative as much as possible. The results from each of the alternatives formulated would need to provide information on the strategic, regional and local level and on how a balance can be achieved between accessibility and liveability targets within the corridor.

To assess the range of alternatives which would be developed for the AUC, the study group developed criteria based on national policy. The VINEX physical planning plan is aimed at ensuring that the Netherlands maintains its accessibility in a climate of international competition. The accessibility of the AUC is considered important for large companies sited within the area, together with the development of Schiphol airport and the economic potential of the 'green heart' (mid-south Holland). Each alternative would be assessed on its direct economic effects, for example, costs for passenger and freight traffic in travel time. Indirect economic effects would also be assessed; these are the effects on the 'production environment' in the northern part of the corridor, which is defined as incentives for the siting of business in a particular location.

The SVV2 illustrated that economic policy goals could only be achieved within a sustainable transport system, a system where the growth of traffic is limited and where less polluting modes are encouraged for freight transport, as well as the development of a transport network which enables mobility policy targets to be achieved. The effect of each alternative on the following variables will be taken into consideration in the final decision: the number of car kilometres and train passengers, chance of congestion, delay of trains, modal split.

Strategic environmental targets would be used to assess the effect of each alternative on liveability. These include improvement of air quality, safety of traffic and of dangerous goods transportation, reduction of noise pollution and reduction of the barrier effect. A number of other variables were also developed which focused mainly on the regional and local effects, such as the effect on landscape and nature, soil, ground and surface water, noise levels in specific areas, residential areas and the risk of transporting dangerous substances (MVW, 1993b, p.4).

In attempting to solve the problem of accessibility along the AUC and taking into consideration the objectives and targets of national policy, the study group formulated a list of alternatives. Alternatives normally consist of the Zero-alternative where no action is taken, a Best Environmental Alternative (BEA), and a range of other alternatives. The study began with ambitious aims to provide alternatives with a package of measures which could be implemented at the regional level. SVV2 (part A) set out a national target for a 50% reduction in the growth in vehicle kilometres by 2010. However, this was reduced in part D of the plan to 35% to ensure targets could be achieved sooner. The SVV2 strengthened the package of measures to be taken on a regional basis. Because of the difficulties encountered, it was decided to eliminate alternatives which were heavily dependent on policy initiatives taken at the regional level. After considering a number of possible alternatives the study group finally reduced the number to five: Zero alternative, Zero-plus alternative, Alternative I, Alternative II and the Best Environmental Alternative. Table 8.10 lists the main SVV2 measures to be included in the Zero-plus alternative, Alternative I and Alternative II.

The alternatives presented within the study did not include any significant development of the Amsterdam-Rhine canal (Table 8.11). The utilisation of the canal by freight could not be achieved solely on a regional level and therefore requires co-operation at the national and European level.

Table 8.10
SVV2 measures included in the alternatives for the AUC

Full SVV2 package of measures (index 2010=135) Zero-plus Alternative and Alternative I	Basic SVV2 Package of measures (index 2010=150) Alternative II
Car pricing policy	
• increase the variable cost of the journey from home to work for journeys of more than 30 kms • raise the real price of fuel by 30% • raise diesel duty (in accordance with NMP)	• increase the variable cost of the journey from home to work for journeys of more than 30 kms • raise the real price of fuel by 30% • raise diesel duty (in accordance with (NMP)
Parking	
• doubling the price of parking tariffs • enlarging the number of pay-parking (in accordance with SVV2 and NMP) • restricting the number of car parking places for A and B locations • for A locations 1 parking space to 10 employees and 1 parking space to 5 employees in B locations	• doubling the price of parking tariffs • enlarging the number of pay-parking (in accordance with SVV2 and NMP) • restricting the number of car parking places for A locations. • for A locations 1 parking space to 5 employees.
Price dependent car journey/trip	
• increase in the variable cost of the car by 50% within the Randstad and 25% outside the Randstad.	• increase in the variable cost of the car by 25% within the Randstad with no increase outside the Randstad.
Price of public transport	
• real cost of public transport should increase by 1.3% per year.	• real cost of public transport should increase by 1.3% per year.

211

The Utrecht curve As part of Rail 21 the railway within the corridor will be doubled from two to four tracks. In 1993 construction was completed on the Southern Link (*Zuidelijke Tak*) connecting south of Diemen with Duivendrecht. Duivendrecht station was redeveloped and now provides transfer points for passengers at three levels. The upper level accommodates stop trains from Amsterdam to Utrecht and the Metro from Gein to Amsterdam Central Station. Trains for the southern link arrive in the middle section, while the bottom level enables the station to be accessible for passengers from Duivendrecht and Venserpolder. It is expected that on average 37,000 passengers each working day will make use of the new link.

At present, passengers travelling from Utrecht Central Station to Schiphol airport need to change trains at Duivendrecht. As part of the rail plans for the corridor Nederlandse Spoorwegen proposed the construction of what they call the Utrecht Curve. This will be an extra link which will begin at Holendrecht metro station and continue parallel to the existing rail track connecting to the southern link. The Utrecht Curve will provide a direct link from Utrecht to Schiphol airport without the need to change at Duivendrecht. This is important if the airport is to be made more easily accessible for passengers by providing a good quality service and reducing road travel. The doubling of the rail and construction of the Utrecht Curve in the corridor will be implemented due to the priority the Dutch Government gives to rail. It therefore formed part of all the alternatives provided in the study.

Zero-alternatives Two Zero-alternatives existed due to the package of measures outlined in SVV2, which would affect the situation within the corridor. The Zero-alternative consists of the existing six-lane highway and two rail tracks. It would act as a reference point and the baseline situation prior to the implementation of the measures contained within the transport structure plan. The Zero-plus alternative consists of the existing six-lane highway and the rail track, which will be doubled from two to four tracks together with the Utrecht Curve. The effect of the measures in SVV2 will be taken into consideration in each alternative. The Zero-plus alternative assumes that SVV2 policy will be implemented, and that there will be a maximum growth in vehicle kilometres of 35% in 2010 compared with 1986.

Alternative I Three alternatives were formulated in addition to the Zero-alternatives. These can be considered as Alternative I, II, and BEA. Alternative I requires the expansion of the A2 from six to eight lanes, the doubling of the rail tracks together with the Utrecht Curve and the application of SVV2 measures. The difference between Alternative I and the Zero-alternative is that, in the former, the section where bottlenecks occur between Holendrecht and Oudenrijn will be enlarged from 2x3 to 2x4 lanes.

212

For Alternative I three variations within the proposed design of the A2 exist. One variant consists of four lanes in each direction (4x4). The second variant consists of a 2-2-2-2 lane system with four main lanes for through traffic and two lanes on each side for local traffic. The third variant consists of a 3-2-3 lane system with two lanes acting as tidal flow lanes. The direction of traffic on these lanes will change according to the peak hour traffic. This system produces optimal use of lanes, provides more capacity than the above two variations and also requires less space.

Alternative II This is based on the assumption that car mobility will increase by 50% by 2010. In this alternative, policy on pricing and parking will be implemented less stringently compared with the Zero-plus alternative and Alternative I. A 50% growth in car mobility is not accepted as national policy. This alternative is therefore not considered to be a feasible option. It serves as an alternative which depicts the worst case conditions.

Two variants have been proposed for the design of the A2 in Alternative II. The first consists of five lanes in each direction (5-5). The second variant consists of a 2-3-3-2 lane system, with six lanes for main through traffic at the junctions of Holendrecht and Oudenrijn.

Best environmental alternative (BEA) The formulation of the best environmental alternative is required under section 41ji3 of the Dutch EIA law which is defined as:

... the alternative in which the best available possibilities for the protection of the environment are applied.

The Best Environmental Alternative should meet the targets and objectives of national policy such as the NMP+, SVV2 and NBP. The main objective in the SVV2 is to find a balance between accessibility and liveability and has therefore been considered in all other alternatives. In the BEA, priority is given to liveability and is based on a comparison of the Zero-plus alternative and Alternative I, which are considered sufficient to meet the SVV2 target of reducing the growth in vehicle kilometres by 35%. The Zero-plus alternative requires no expansion of the road and includes the doubling of the rail and the construction of the Utrecht Curve to provide a sufficient alternative to the car. The rail expansion is included in the BEA to encourage greater use of public transport. No infrastructural changes are suggested for the Amsterdam-Rhine Canal.

Table 8.11
Alternatives for the Amsterdam-Utrecht corridor

	0	0+	Alternative I	Alternative II	BEA
Index	167	135	135	150	135
	Present situation	Zero Plus alternative	Expansion alternative	Worst case scenario	Best Environmental Alternative
Mobility Management Measures		Full SVV2 package	Full SVV2 package	Basic package SVV2	Full SVV2 package
Rail	2 tracks	four tracks + Utrecht Curve	four tracks + Utrecht Curve	four tracks + Utrecht Curve	four tracks + Utrecht Curve
Road	2x3 lanes	2x3 lanes	2x4 lanes	2x4/5 lanes	2x3 lanes
Canal	existing situation	existing situation	existing situation	existing situation	existing situation
VARIANTS					
A2 Road			4+4	5+5	3+3
			2+2+2+2*	3+2+2+3*	
			3+2+3**		
SUBVARIANTS					
Railway		Abcoude:	Abcoude:	Abcoude:	Abcoude:
		(1) viaduct	(1) viaduct	(1) viaduct	(1) viaduct
		(2) above ground level	(2) above ground level	(2) above ground level	(2) above ground level
		(3) ground level	(3) ground level	(3) ground level	(3) ground level
		(4) 4 tracks below ground level	(4) 4 tracks below ground level	(4) 4 tracks below ground level	(4) 4 tracks below ground level
		1 new bridge at Demka	1 new bridge at Demka	1 new bridge at Demka	2 new bridges at Demka
A2					
			Breukelen	Breukelen	
			1 viaduct	1 viaduct	
			2 lanes below ground level	2 lanes below ground level	
			Utrecht West	Utrecht West	
			1 lane at ground level	1 lane at ground level	
			2 lanes below ground level	2 lanes below ground level	

*main road/parallel lane system **main road/tidal flow system

The BEA includes further mitigation measures in addition to those applied generally to all the alternatives, to ensure a positive effect on liveability. The A2 will maintain its six lanes, but the maximum speed limit will be reduced to 80 kph and an ecological tunnel for migrating wildlife will be constructed near the locality of Vinkeveen. Compensation will be made for the loss of meadow bird areas, either by establishing a reserve or by the provision of alternative areas in the agricultural sector. The rail will be doubled to four tracks, including the construction of the Utrecht Curve. Rail bridges over the ARC where the rail curves at Demka will be constructed with noise absorbing ballast beds, although further investigation and cost benefit analysis are needed. The rail near Abcoude will be constructed at a lower level to reduce noise and visual impacts on local residents. An investigation into the hydro-ecological effects of constructing new rail tracks is proposed within this alternative. The canal will continue with existing use but electronic speed controls will be implemented at accident blackspots, especially when docking (MVW, 1993b, p.94).

In Alternatives I and II discussed above, subvariants for the A2 include a lowering of the level of the road at Breukelen and at Utrecht-West. Four subvariants have been examined for the rail track near Abcoude based on the notion of limiting the barrier effect of infrastructural expansion.

Environmental impacts

From the range of alternatives proposed, Alternative II was not included due to the negative effects which this alternative has on mobility and liveability, which do not meet SVV2 policy. The main alternatives considered include the Zero-plus alternative, Alternative I and the Best Environmental Alternative. Table 8.12 below provides an overview of the effects of the alternatives on the accessibility of the road, with the Zero-plus alternative taken as the reference alternative. An improvement compared with the Zero-plus alternative is indicated by 0/+, +, ++ depending on a small, medium or large improvement respectively. A deterioration is indicated by 0/-, - and -- depending on a small, medium or large deterioration respectively, where 0 means that there is no change in relation to the reference alternative. Alternative I has the best score on accessibility, with widening of the A2 having a positive effect on the 'Production Environment' on the northern side of the corridor and on the level of congestion. Alternative I scores better than the BEA, with regard to the effect on other economic activities such as functioning of business traffic and flexibility of the labour market.

Table 8.12
Summary of the effect of each alternative on accessibility by road

Factor	Zero-plus Alternative	Alternative I	Best Environmental Alternative
Congestion costs (car)	ref.	+	0
Congestion costs (lorry)	ref.	+	0
Production environment	ref.	++	0
Indirect economic effect	ref.	+	0
Mobility (car)	ref.	0	0
Mobility (lorry)	ref.	0	0
Congestion chance	ref.	++	0
Transport choice (persons)	ref.	0/-	0
Transport choice (goods)	ref.	0	0
Accessibility by road	ref.	+	0

Source: MVW, 1993b, p.100)

Table 8.13 below summarises the effect of each alternative on accessibility by rail. The doubling of the rail track and the construction of the Utrecht Curve will have a number of positive effects on accessibility by rail when compared with the Zero-alternative.

Table 8.13
Summary of the effect of each alternative on accessibility by rail

Factor	Zero Alternative	Zero-plus Alternative	Alternative I	Alternative II
Travel time costs (persons)	ref.	+	+	+
Travel time costs (goods)	ref.	0/+	0/+	0/+
Production environment	ref.	++	++	++
Indirect economic effects	ref.	++	++	++
Mobility of persons	ref.	++	++	++
Chance of delay	ref.	++	++	++
Transport choice (persons)	ref.	++	+/++	++
Transport choice (goods)	ref.	++	++	++
Accessibility of rail	ref.	++	++	++

Source: MVW, 1993b, p.100

216

Table 8.14 shows the effect of each road alternative on liveability. The BEA alternative has a positive effect on the different aspects of liveability followed by the Zero-plus Alternative and Alternative I. The BEA is considered better due to the extra mitigation and compensation measures, especially with regard to nature, landscape and the living environment.

Table 8.14
Summary of the effect of each road alternative on liveability

Factor	Zero-plus Alternative	Alternative I	Best Environmental Alternative
Nature and landscape			
physical space	ref.	-	0
disturbance of meadow birds	ref.	0/-	++
barrier effect	ref.	++	+
Soil			
soil structure and soil quality	ref.	-	0
Water			
ground and surface water	ref.	-	0
Air emissions			
nitrogen oxides	ref.	0	+
hydrocarbons	ref.	0/-	0/+
carbon dioxide	ref.	-	0/+
Noise			
troubled people	ref.	--	+
acoustic physical space	ref.	--	++
Living environment			
Social security	ref.	0	+
Subjective traffic safety accessibility, barrier effect, visual impact, social integration			
Traffic safety			
Casualties, deaths and injured	ref.	0	0
External risk			
Transport of dangerous goods Individual and group risk	ref.	0	0
Total effect of road on			
liveability	ref.	0/-	0/+

Source: MVW, 1993b, p.100

All three rail alternatives are predicted to have a similar negative effect on liveability. For the factor noise, the BEA scores better than Zero-plus

Alternative and Alternative I, although this is not shown in Table 8.15, because the effect of noise absorbing ballast beds on the Demka curve could not be calculated. Alternative I has a large negative effect on noise and a light positive effect on the living environment (which covers traffic safety and accessibility) in comparison to the Zero alternative.

Table 8.15
Summary of the effect of rail on liveability

Factor	Zero-Alternative	Zero-plus Alternative	Alternative I	Best Environmental Alternative
Nature and landscape	ref.		-	
Soil	ref.		-	
Water	ref.		-	
Noise	ref.		--	
Living environment	ref.		0/+	
Total effect of rail on liveability	ref.		-	

Source: MVW, 1993b, p.101

National policy targets

Table 8.16 compares the three alternatives with national targets for transport which were set out in the SVV2 and the NMP+. The Zero-plus alternative, Alternative I and the Best Environmental Alternative will meet the SVV2 target of limiting traffic growth to 35%. The SVV2 target for a maximum growth of 42% in tonne kilometres by light lorries will be exceeded in all of the alternatives. The target for the chance of congestion will only be met in Alternative I. The BEA and Zero-plus alternative will result in a 17% chance of congestion - much higher than the 2% norm set out in SVV2. The maximum speed of 80 kilometres per hour which was outlined in the BEA would have some effect on the chance of congestion but this could not be measured within the study (MVW, 1993b, p.2). The BEA will therefore have a slightly higher benefit than the Zero-plus Alternative. A change in transport choice from road to rail will occur with the Zero-plus alternative and the BEA. None of the alternatives will affect the transportation of freight. Alternative I will be the most beneficial for more accessibility on the A2. The Zero-plus alternative and Alternative I will not meet the congestion level on the A2.

However, they do succeed in reaching other strategic targets of the SVV2. The alternatives for rail are sufficient for strategic targets of the SVV2 to be met. The rail alternatives will have a positive effect on the mobility of passengers and will meet the target of a 15-20% growth in rail passenger kilometres by 2010 compared with 1986. The congestion norm of 2% is achieved in all the alternatives, these are compared in Table 8.17.

Table 8.16
A comparison of each alternative with national policy targets for accessibility by road

Target goal	Unit	0+	I	BEA	Target	0+	I	BEA
Mobility								
Personal cars	index	131	131	131	135	0/+	0/+	0/+
Lorries	index	145	145	145	142	0/-	0/-	0/-
Congestion chance	%	17	1	17	2	--	0/+	--
Transport choice								
Personal transport	car/train	1	1.1	1		0/+	0	0/+
Freight transport	road/ rail + water	0.7	0.7	0.7		0	0	0
Accessibility by road	++/-					0/-	0/+	0/-

Source: MVW, 1993b, p.102

Table 8.17
A comparison of each alternative with national policy
targets for accessibility by rail

Target goal	Unit	0+	I	BEA	Target	0+	I	BEA
Mobility								
Passengers	index	244	246	244	150-200	+	+	+
Congestion chance	%	<2	<2	<2	2	0/+	0/+	0/+
Transport choice								
Passengers	car/train	1	1.1	1	-	0/+	0	0/+
Freight transport	road/rail + water	0.7	0.7	0.7	-	0	0	0
Accessibility by rail	++/-					0/+	0/+	0/+

0 - target goal has been achieved
The following scores are given when a level higher than the target goal is achieved:
+/0 a little higher, + much higher, ++ very higher
0/- slightly below the target, - below target, -- much below the target
Where there is no target:
0 same level, ++ large increase, -- large decrease

Source: MVW, 1993b, p.102)

The road alternatives were also compared with the strategic targets for liveability (see Table 8.18). The alternatives were not only compared with targets of SVV2 but also with essential environmental targets from other national policies. The target for NO_x and CxHy will not be reached in any of the alternatives. The target goal for CO_2 will be almost reached by the BEA, which achieves a 9% reduction rather than 10% reduction. The target goal for noise, to reduce the number of people affected by 2,776 persons by 2010, will be reached in the BEA and will be almost reached in the Zero-plus alternative.

The individual risk limit is the chance of death of an individual caused by the transport of dangerous goods. The same definition applies to group risk where a group of people are at risk of death caused by the transportation of dangerous goods. The target goal for the safety of transportation of dangerous goods requires the risk limits to be maintained at 1986 levels by 2010. The individual risk limit will be maintained at 1986 levels in each of the alternatives. Alternative I has the most favourable effect on reducing the ecological barrier of the A2. This is due to the construction of three ecological tunnels for

220

migrating wildlife. The BEA will be less effective as it will have only one large ecological tunnel. The Zero-plus alternative will have no benefit at all. None of the alternatives will reach the target goal for traffic safety, which requires the number of injuries and the number of deaths to decrease by 40% and 50% respectively. The indices were calculated on the availability of Dutch Ken (*Kengetallen*) numbers which represent traffic accidents on major roads in the Netherlands and are measured in unit kilometres. The average 'Ken' number for roads is 67 (1987-1990). The A2 has a Ken number of 54 (1987-1990), which indicates that it is a reasonably safe road. In the calculation of the Ken numbers in the EIS, policy measures of the SVV2 were not taken into consideration. The results are therefore higher than would be expected. There is no difference between the alternatives. The calculation of the Ken numbers is based on the present maximum speed of 100-120 kph. In the BEA there will be a maximum speed of 80 kph and the road should therefore be a little safer for all the traffic.

The strategic targets for liveability are principally drawn up for road traffic. When the results of the assessment for the railway are compared with the rail target goals, the study concludes that none of the target goals is achieved (MVW, 1993b, p.13). The inability of the rail options to meet liveability targets was not discussed further in the study. This was due to the overall benefits derived from rail compared with road and the need for the implementation of Rail 21.

The total investment and maintenance costs for each alternative are shown in Table 8.19. Alternative I with the second variant of a 2+2+2+2 lane system has the highest cost for investment and maintenance.

Table 8.18
A comparison of road alternatives against strategic liveability targets

Impact	Unit	0+	I	BEA	Target	0+	I	BEA
Air pollution								
NO_x emissions	%	-49	-50	-58	-75	--	--	-
C_xH_y emissions	%	-68	-64	-69	-75	-	-	-
CO_2 emissions	%	-7	-5	-9	-10	-	-	0/+
Noise pollution								
Serious trouble	person	-2,618	-1,800	-3,614	-2,776	-	--	+
Moderate trouble	person	446	4,949	-4,963	0	-	--	++
Agricultural areas	hectare	339	1,744	-1,023	0	-	--	++
External safety								
Individual risk limit	unit km	0	0	0	0	0	0	0
Individual risk	unit km	5	5	5	0	-	-	-
Group risk limit	unit km	2	2	2	0	-	-	-
Group risk	unit km	1	1	1	0	-	-	-
Traffic safety (1987=100)								
Deaths	%	+10	+10	+10	-50	--	--	--
Injured	%	+10	+10	+10	-40	--	--	--
Ecology								
Decrease barrier function	++/--	no eco-tunnel	3 eco-tunnels	1 large eco-tunnel	++	--	0	0/-
Judgement	++/--	+	+/--			--	--	0/-

Source: MVW, 1993b, p.103

The final assessment for the three alternatives and their effects on accessibility, liveability and cost are presented in Table 8.20. The alternative which succeeds in reaching the target goal is given '3', '2' and '1'. Alternative I scores the best for the liveability factor (3) and cost (3) while BEA scores the best on accessibility (2). The Zero-plus alternative scores 2 for both accessibility and liveability. Therefore, neither of the alternatives scores well on either accessibility nor liveability factors, while the highest cost is for Alternative I, followed by the BEA and Zero-plus alternative.

Table 8.19
Total cost of each alternative

Cost			Million guilders			
	0	0+	I variant 1	I variant 2	I variant 3	BEA
Investment	5	1,258	2,382	2,508	2,474	1,628
Maintenance*	6.1	9.6	9.4	10.2	9.8	9.6

* per year

Source: MVW, 1993b, p.106

Table 8.20
The effect of all road and rail alternatives on accessibility and liveability factors within the AUC

Factor	0+	I	BEA
Accessibility	2	1	2
Liveability	2	3	1
Cost	1	3	2

Source: MVW, 1993b, p.13

Assessment of uncertainty within the study

The aim of implementing the measures contained in the SVV2 is to achieve a sustainable transport system, one which does not move environmental problems to future generations and which minimises the conflict between accessibility and liveability objectives. Measures contained in the SVV2 for the alternatives, include the complete implementation of Rail 21. The policy package is based on a large number of targets and assumptions concerning the effectiveness of measures. It was therefore necessary within the AUC to concentrate on two kinds of uncertainty within the SVV2 framework:

1. Uncertainties regarding the national and regional, political and social acceptance of the measures proposed.
2. Uncertainties concerning the effectiveness of these measures.

(Dekker et al., 1992, p.14).

Due to uncertainties within the existing SVV2, the AUC study also had to make a number of assumptions in the formulation of different alternatives, traffic forecasts and prediction of impacts.

The uncertainties about the feasibility of the SVV2 cannot be completely removed and will exist until the final infrastructural development has been decided. The available financial resources for implementing the SVV2 policy and infrastructure projects and the implementation of SVV2 in transport regions are considered to be more expensive than when the SVV2 was prepared. The AUC, however, is considered an important strategic route between the Randstad and its hinterland. It therefore needs to be given a high priority (Dekker et al., 1992, p.14).

Decision on the Amsterdam-Utrecht corridor study

After the EIS was published in November 1993 it was sent to the EIA Commission, which accepted the contents. The Commission considered the EIS suitable for a decision to be made. The Utrecht Curve was included within the EIS, although the proponents stated that another route was under consideration due to a request from the Municipality of Amsterdam (MVW, 1994b, p.71). The Municipality requested that the technical feasibility of an alternative route which begins from Bijlmer station rather than Holendrecht metro station should be investigated. The area of influence in this alternative is considered to be much smaller than the original proposal and would cause less disturbance to allotments located within the area. If the Bijlmer alternative is chosen as the best route, this will be assessed under the Routing Act, which allows the proposed routing to be moved by a maximum of 100 metres horizontally and 2 metres vertically. If the alternative exceeds these limits, an addition to the EIS will be necessary, although it is expected that any new alternative will remain within the above limits of the new Routing Act (Personal Communication, Odijk, 1995).

After the EIS had been accepted by the Commission and advice had been given to the competent authority, the City of Utrecht proposed a housing development under the physical planning plan (VINEX). A master plan was published to a create a new residential development of 31,000 houses which will be called *Leidsche Rijn* and will be located west of the A2 between Maarssen and Oudenrijn. The plan requires the motorway to be moved to create space for transport connections between the development and the city, and to assist landscaping. A decision is will be taken in 1996 on how the A2 and the proposed housing development can be integrated into the landscape (Personal Communication, Odijk, 1995).

The decision on the Amsterdam-Utrecht corridor study was published in a letter from the Minster of Transport, Public Works and Water Management on 25 April 1995 to the Second Chamber of the Dutch Parliament. The Minister of Transport, Public Works and Water Management, in collaboration with the Minister of Environment, took the decision to accept Alternative I to be implemented in the Amsterdam-Utrecht corridor. This includes widening the A2 from 2x3 to 2x4 lanes from Holendrecht to Oudenrijn and the doubling of the railway track from Duivendrecht to Utrecht Central Station and the construction of the Utrecht Curve. No major changes were recommended for the Amsterdam-Rhine Canal. The total investment in the road and rail improvements is about 2.2 billion guilders of which 1.3 billion is allocated for the rail and 960 million for the road.

The decision to improve the infrastructure within the AUC was taken because of the need to ensure accessibility to Schiphol airport and the Amsterdam North Sea channel and its hinterland (MVW, 28 April 1995). The infrastructure will be improved in the AUC with an emphasis on achieving a shift of passenger and freight transport from road to rail and to a lesser extent to waterway. In order to achieve this shift, the expansion of the rail will be improved before the widening of the A2. In the meantime, measures will be taken to optimise the road capacity of the A2. A range of measures is being studied, which include such things as temporary 'half' junctions where only entry or exit is allowed to and from the A2, traffic lights at junctions to allow traffic only to enter on the A2 when there is available capacity, measures to reduce the delays in bus traffic, and the use of changing information panels.

Analysis of the Corridor Approach

Dutch policy on transport and the environment is based on specific objectives and the setting of targets for different aspects of policy at the national level. The translation of objectives from the macro-level to the micro-level is important if policy is to be effective. The implementation of objectives into

225

practice can be achieved by a number of measures. Some can be implemented at the regional or local level, for example, restriction of car parking and provision of public transport via structure and local plans. Some objectives, however, are more effective if implemented at the national level, such as taxes on car drivers, due to the presence of a better administrative structure.

The objectives of transport and environmental policies provided a framework in which the alternatives considered in the AUC could be assessed, for example, policies to reduce the growth in vehicle kilometres by 35% by 2010. National objectives have had a number of environmental benefits within the AUC study for they provided a basis on which the alternatives have been formulated. The SVV2 has provided a package of measures to be implemented within the corridor to achieve targets such as a reduction in mobility. The success of these measures is important if traffic flow within the corridor is to be reduced. Due to the SVV2 and NMP, environmental considerations have played an important role in examining the solutions to congestion within the AUC. Transport modes, other than the motor vehicle, have been studied rather than the study being directly concerned with provision of extra road capacity.

The benefits of having a more objective-led style of planning will be determined by the results which are achieved in practice. Within the AUC the success of implementing a package of measures will need to be assessed in the long-term. Only then will the true advantages of setting specific objectives and targets be revealed. It is, however, possible to conclude that the setting of objectives at the national level enables a strategy to be developed to solve different aspects of the transport problem. The setting of objectives and targets ultimately leads to the need to devise measures to implement them. The advantage of setting specific targets is that it will be clear when they are not being achieved. This enables progress to be re-assessed and further action to be taken in order to meet the targets set.

A number of conclusions can be drawn with regard to the implementation of the corridor approach, with its three components of open planning, substitution and integrated approach. Firstly, the rigid terms of reference outlined in SVV2 (part D) together with the strategic approval of Rail 21, while ensuring that all modes were considered, to some extent restricted the freedom of presenting a broad range of alternatives.

Substitution from road to canal will not undergo any major change within the final alternative chosen. Within the AUC study, a shift from road to waterway could not be achieved at the corridor level. A transport corridor can vary in both size and importance depending on its geographical scale, whether it be at the international, national, regional or local level. The Amsterdam-Utrecht corridor forms part of a European route and the study considered only a small section of this route. A shift from road to water is not possible over a short distance. The nature of water transport and the position of the

Netherlands on the continent means that initiatives are required to be undertaken at the national and European level, if the Amsterdam-Rhine Canal is to be utilised more by freight traffic. The Amsterdam-Rhine Canal needs to be examined within a wider European context to enable potential improvements to be identified and implemented. This could be achieved at the European Union level with the possibility of developing a master plan for the greater utilisation of the European inland waterway system for the movement of freight. The same idea can be applied to rail to identify main routes for the movement of freight. The exclusion of water, however, as a viable mode in the study, to some extent detracted from the usefulness of a corridor study which aims to examine the possibility of splitting travel across all modes of transport rather than one or two.

The second component of the corridor approach is open planning. The process of wide consultation and participation of different groups in the decision-making process is not unique in the Netherlands, but is well developed partly due to the political culture which is corporatist and encourages greater participation from the majority. Within the Press Release of 28 April 1995 the Minister stated that the AUC is the first study in which the surrounding areas to the corridor have been consulted and all three modes of transport considered together. The open planning process enabled a large input from different groups and on the basis of this process, it was decided to undertake rail improvement first and minor improvements to road capacity to fulfil the demand within the corridor.

The component which is considered the most valuable and unique to the corridor study is its integrated approach. This allows greater co-ordination of infrastructure development, with Rijkswaterstaat and Nederlandse Spoorwegen working together to provide a solution to deal with different transport modes and collaborating to solve transport problems on a specific corridor. The level of co-ordination enables different alternatives to be considered and environmental issues to be addressed. The Rail 21 plan has meant a doubling of rail track which has been a main feature in each of the alternatives from the beginning of the study, due to the plan being accepted by national government in its entirety. Collaboration between Nederlandse Spoorwegen and Rijkswaterstaat has not really made a significant difference in the formulation of alternatives. If the Rail 21 plan did not exist, the collaboration would have had greater importance, for any decision regarding the expansion of the rail would have been based solely on the results of the AUC study. The collaboration, however, has focused more on the technicalities of doubling the rail track. The final decision to expand the road from 6 to 8 lanes has been a decision based on the economic importance of the corridor to the surrounding area. The Minister stated the need to ensure the accessibility of the regions of Amsterdam and Schiphol. A package of measures will be implemented by the transport regions and the rail will be expanded before the road. It was, however, not possible for the A2 to remain unchanged due to the importance of the corridor for accessibility to Schiphol airport and for the Dutch economy.

The use of policy measures on the A2 to prevent the overspill of traffic to roads through surrounding villages, was not considered sufficient to deal with traffic congestion. In the final analysis, the economic importance of the country and this particular corridor played an important role in the final decision, despite the concern given in the corridor study to an integrated examination of all modes together with policy measures. In reality, the Netherlands' main priority is to maintain its economic position within a Single European Market. The importance of this objective was discussed in Chapter 5 and briefly above. Extra road capacity is therefore considered important in the short-term to relieve congestion and to safeguard the Dutch economy. The package of measures to reduce mobility will in some way halt the growth in vehicle kilometres and provide alternative modes of transport, but this is considered a long-term process.

The concept of a corridor study does have a number of beneficial components for developing a more integrated and environment-based transport planning approach within the context of a sustainable transport policy. The value of a corridor style approach will, however, be dependent on the final decision to deal with the traffic congestion problem within a corridor without causing a significant impact on the environment. The expansion of the A2 will not meet some national targets for air pollution and safety. Despite this, the expansion has been seen as a short-term measure to meet immediate demand with rail expansion considered to be more long-term. The extent to which the alternative will meet national targets in practice will be dependent on the success of policy measures and the accuracy of traffic growth predictions. SACTRA (1994) showed that an expansion of a road may not necessarily solve the traffic problems which it was supposed to solve. One advantage of the decision on the AUC is that rail expansion will be undertaken before the road, which will allow time to achieve a modal shift.

The corridor study concluded that it is difficult to develop a solution which deals with both liveability and accessibility. One solution proposed by the study which may accommodate both factors is based on speed limits. A reduction of speed to 80 kph will be beneficial for both liveability such as air and noise pollution and accessibility (MVW, 1993b) However, the study suggests that such a measure needs to be taken on a national or European level because the corridor plays an important role within the economic functioning of the Netherlands.

A Corridor approach for Britain?

The main difference between Britain and the Netherlands is that the Dutch have a co-ordinated transport policy with set objectives and targets. This has enabled a strategy to be developed to solve the problem of transport and reduce its impact on the environment.

In contrast, Britain has no real transport policy *per se*. There are three main objectives and no targets exist to reduce the environmental impact of transport, except the reduction in carbon dioxide emissions which are not specifically in the transport sector. Problems of road congestion are examined case by case with no real framework to guide the decisions on expanding or building roads. Public transport alternatives are not normally considered as real alternatives in the examination of transport problems along main transport corridors. The benefits of having explicitly stated objectives have been demonstrated within the Amsterdam-Utrecht corridor study, in that they provide a level of co-ordination in transport policy and ensure that consideration is given to a wide range of alternatives.

The application of the corridor approach to transport planning in Britain would have a number of benefits, although an 'open planning process', which enables greater consultation and participation, may be considered by some as a means for objectors to delay the implementation of specific transport projects. At the same time, by having greater public participation and involvement of representative bodies, a more acceptable solution to the transport problem may be found. The substitution effect, which implies a shift in the modal split from road to rail and waterway, has a number of environmental benefits. Britain, however, will face the same problems as the Netherlands in attempting to resolve this at the corridor level, especially with regard to inland transport by water. Efforts to achieve any shift to inland waterway need to be implemented at the national level if any change is to occur at the corridor level.

Corridors on the continent cross a number of national boundaries and are therefore important in the development of greater cohesion and trade within the European Union. In contrast, many of Britain's corridors are of more national importance and provide links to sea ports which give access to mainland Europe. A corridor may vary in its national and European importance.

With regard to an 'integrated approach' the privatisation of British Rail may mean that the level of co-ordination to implement such a study may be more difficult to achieve with the privatised rail company and the Department of Transport. The notion of the Dutch corridor approach provides a planning approach which ensures consideration is given to the environment and a number of modes are considered together.

It therefore has a role to play within the context of a sustainable objective-led transport policy in ensuring that the rhetoric of policy is achieved in practice. It also provides an approach to transport planning on which European transport policy could be based in the development of Trans-European networks, rather than considering road, rail and waterway separately which is currently the case with policy on the High Speed Train and Trans-European Road Networks. A more multi-modal approach could be taken to deal with congestion on main European transport corridors with a greater integration of modes and participation of Member States.

9 Objective-led transport planning

This book began with a discussion of sustainable development and the need to deal with the problem of transport in order to achieve a more sustainable society. Traditional approaches to transport planning have been based on the notion of 'predict and provide', i.e. meeting the demand of transport by providing extra infrastructural capacity. A mono-modal approach has been a main characteristic of the traditional transport process, giving priority to the motor vehicle. Transport has also been traditionally associated with delivering economic benefits by enabling industries to be more accessible and thus more competitive. With the continuing growth in traffic and the increased awareness of the impact of transport on the environment, these basic tenets on which the traditional transport planning approach has been founded are now being challenged. New principles of sustainability are being applied to transport, with some countries beginning to make progress towards implementing policies for a multi-modal sustainable transport system.

An increase in environmental awareness and the adoption of the concept of sustainable development have highlighted the issue of transport as an important environmental problem. A wider consideration is being given to the environmental impacts of transport, to include the use of land, noise and air pollution. The effects of urban pollution such as the Los Angeles smog and the 1991 winter smog episode in London, which have been followed by the recurrence of summer smog alerts, have caused concern about the impact of traffic on human health. Links are being established between air pollution from motor vehicles and respiratory conditions such as asthma or general ill health. In many metropolises of the world the limits set by the World Health Organisation are being exceeded. The issue of transport has now taken on a global dimension, with the recognition that transport contributes to global atmospheric problems such as climate change and acid rain. Growing prosperity has become increasingly equated with greater mobility and demand to travel over longer distances. Developing countries are following the same path as the developed world, with greater urbanisation and increasing car use, which poses problems for the future.

It is now clear that simply meeting the demand to travel will not solve the transport problem, and in some cases actually exacerbates the problem which it was intended to resolve. Concern over increasing traffic as a future problem was expressed in the 1963 Buchanan Report. Yet past approaches to transport have continually failed to deal with the problem of transport adequately. There has now been a new realisation that these approaches have failed, with, for example, the 1994 SACTRA report providing evidence to suggest that trip generation is a phenomenon which actually occurs and which should be taken seriously. Developments in environmental awareness, together with the continued failure to meet the insatiable demand for transport, have resulted in new more strategic approaches being developed to deal with the transport problem.

A reactive approach has often been characteristic of British transport planning. This approach is exemplified by a three-stage development: examination of existing traffic problems, predicting future growth and developing a strategy to meet or deal with this growth. The analysis of the case study on the Trans-Pennine corridor has illustrated how the absence of a strategic transport policy led to the consideration of only one mode without the uses of policy measures to reduce demand. The result has been a failure to deal with increasing traffic growth in the long-term on Trans-Pennine routes by encouraging a shift in the modal split or reducing the demand to travel. The lack of a coherent transport policy has encouraged an over-dependence on road, and the under-utilisation of other modes such as rail. In the case of the Trans-Pennine corridor studies, there was a need for a consortium of local authorities, together with the Peak District National Park, to initiate a rail study to ensure that rail options were considered.

To achieve a sustainable transport system, a transport planning process which ensures a minimal impact on the environment, both in the short and long-term, needs to be adopted. A sustainable transport system will need to reduce the demand to travel, while at the same time promoting the use of less polluting modes of transport for passenger and freight transport. Strategic planning is important in order to ensure that transport problems are dealt with adequately and that a whole range of alternatives are considered before a decision is made. Strategic planning plays an important role in the implementation and realisation of sustainable development. The notion of strategic environmental assessment has emerged as an issue in response to the

232

inadequacies and piecemeal approach of the present EIA system. In order to assess the environmental impact of policies, plans and programmes, policy needs to state objectives and outline the results which it hopes to achieve. Clear objectives may take the form of quantitative targets or qualitative statements for a wide range of transport alternatives. SEA can provide a mechanism to ensure that the full and wider-ranging impacts of transport are taken into consideration before a policy, plan or programme is approved and implemented. This enables the possibility of a wide range of alternatives to be considered early in the planning process. If transport plans and programmes preceding a transport project have been subject to an SEA, then criteria and thresholds for the assessment of the transport project will have been established. This would enable the application of EIA at the project level to be more clearly defined. The advantages of adopting a strategic planning approach have been illustrated in Chapter 8 on the Amsterdam-Utrecht corridor, with national targets playing an important role in the determination of the alternatives considered.

Transport policy in Britain has tended to be dominated by the 'predict and provide' approach, with the widening of existing roads and the provision of completely new roads incrementally. The approach taken towards the M62, which is considered a main route linking North Lancashire with West Yorkshire and beyond, has been to widen different sections of the road. Generally, there has been a lack of a strategic approach to deal with transport problems and a *ad hoc* approach has been adopted. The importance of the M62 goes beyond the standard link between Lancashire and Yorkshire and the major cities of Manchester, Leeds and Bradford. The M62 is a main corridor for trips which have been initiated further afield from the major conurbations within the corridor. It will continue to play an important role in the plans to develop a Euro-Pennine corridor from the west to the east of England to the Continent. The Department of Transport adopted a mono-modal approach to deal with congestion on the Trans-Pennine corridor with overemphasis on road expansion, while rail transport was considered largely irrelevant for Trans-Pennine traffic growth. It is important to acknowledge, however, that the rail study did provide a strategy for rail within the context of the Trans-Pennine study with some funding from the DOT, which would not have been the case in the past. Consideration of rail, albeit tokenistic, illustrates how the British government is slowly awakening to the need to consider transport in a multi-modal way.

The past four years have seen changes in thinking taking shape in the form of the Planning Policy Guidance on Transport (PPG13), and the report, *Reducing Transport Emissions through Planning* (1993) which have been augmented by the SACTRA reports (1992 and 1994) and the Royal

Commission's Report on Transport and Environment (1994). However, further steps need to be taken in order to ensure that results are achieved in practice.

In contrast, the Dutch have provided strategic policy plans on transport and the environment with clear objectives and targets. These have provided a framework for decisions to be taken on transport schemes at the project level. National Policy on transport, environment and physical planning restricted the range of alternatives to be considered and required a number of policy measures and mitigation measures to be taken, to ensure that targets for factors such as noise, air, traffic growth, accidents and modal split are achieved in practice. A more objective-led planning approach enables priority to be given to environmental targets, which was often not the case in the traditional approach of trying to meet traffic growth. However, the final choice will be determined by the economic importance given to transport over environmental considerations.

Both case studies used within this book have been based on strategic transport corridors in Britain and the Netherlands. The European Commission considers greater social and economic integration of importance for a Single Europe, especially for Southern European countries. Strategic European corridors will gain greater importance in linking major European capitals with greater European integration and the development of a Single European Market. The approaches taken to deal with transport on the two corridors discussed within this book have differed according to national policy on transport and the environment. The lack of national policy on transport and the absence of any strategic policy targets resulted in road being given priority in the case of the Trans-Pennine study. In the case of the Amsterdam-Utrecht corridor the Dutch plans on transport, environment, and physical planning ensured that a wide range of modes and policy measures were considered. However, the final decision on the Amsterdam-Utrecht corridor study to expand the road from four to six lanes was determined by the economic importance of the corridor and the need to maintain accessibility to Schiphol airport and the Amsterdam North Sea Channel and its hinterland.

The concept of the Dutch corridor study is a multi-modal approach used to examine transport corridors in their totality within the context of a national strategic transport policy. As illustrated within the Amsterdam-Utrecht corridor study, national policy targets played an important role in determining alternatives. Dutch Transport Regions provide the administrative structures to implement measures to control demand and encourage the use of other less polluting modes via regional transport plans.

The main range of measures considered include parking charges and the number of parking spaces available for the different types of locations, and the price of transport. Other fiscal measures are required to be implemented at the national level, such as the increase in the variable cost of the home to work journey and the price of fuel.

The three components of the corridor approach - the open planning process, substitution and an integrated approach - can be deemed useful in the consideration of planning for transport within a corridor. The three components, which are not necessarily unique to Dutch transport planning, can serve as useful points to be included within the British transport planning process. The component of an integrated approach is considered important to deliver benefits in the consideration of the different modes of road, rail and canal. This approach could be adopted in Britain with Department of Transport, Railtrack and the privatised rail companies working together to provide the necessary infrastructural development within the corridor. Such an approach may need to be based on necessary legislation equivalent to the Dutch Routing Act, to ensure that these components become part of the transport planning process.

A corridor approach can provide an alternative planning approach to deal with growth in the demand for transport, particularly on main strategic routes. A corridor approach, however, may not be useful for every type of transport project. The combination of strategic environmental assessment and the corridor approach can provide a means of moving towards a more sustainable transport planning process. Strategic environmental assessment enables an appraisal of policies, plans and programmes before they are actually implemented in practice (see Figure 9.1). This would act as a first step in assessing the environmental implications of PPPs and would provide a framework in which a corridor approach could implement policy into practice at the project level. SEA would ensure that environmental targets are taken into consideration and that all modes are examined in an integrated way.

Taking into consideration strategic environment assessment and the Dutch approach to transport policy and the concept of corridor studies, a more objective-led and environment-based approach to transport planning can be outlined. Figure 9.2 outlines the main structure of an environment-based approach to transport planning together with the notion of corridors. An environment-based approach consists of ten main steps:

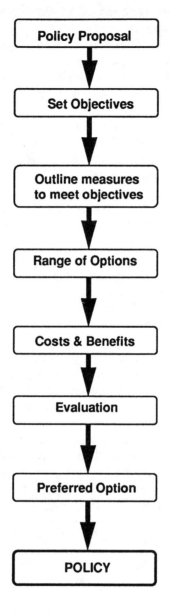

Figure 9.1 The strategic environmental assessment process

1. Outlining the objectives of a national transport, environment and physical policy based on sustainable development.
2. Setting of quantitative and qualitative environmental targets for different components, outlining measures to achieve objectives and undertaking an SEA to determine preferred policy option.
3. Identification of corridor and main existing infrastructure.
4. Outlining a range of different infrastructure options divided between passenger and freight and covering the modes such as bicycle, road, rail and waterway.
5. Devising a set of policy measures to achieve the environmental targets set.
6. Mix of alternative combinations of policy measures and infrastructural options.
7. Environmental assessment of main options.
8. Option selection to determine the best environmental alternative.
9. Implementation of preferred option.
10. Monitoring and post-auditing once the preferred option has been implemented to ensure that targets are met in practice.

As discussed in Chapter 3, a number of contradictions exist in European policy on transport and the environment. Despite the EC espousing concerns over achieving sustainable mobility, its policy on liberalisation, based on the free movement of goods, people and capital services and the priority given to the Single European Market, has the effect of increasing mobility. Plans for greater road construction via the development of the Trans-European road network attempts to achieve greater integration in Europe to reduce 'missing links' and the development of the High Speed Train Network encourages greater mobility. The EC Task Force estimated that the SEM would increase transfrontier lorry movements by 30-50%, resulting in greater levels of polluting emissions (CEC, 1990a).

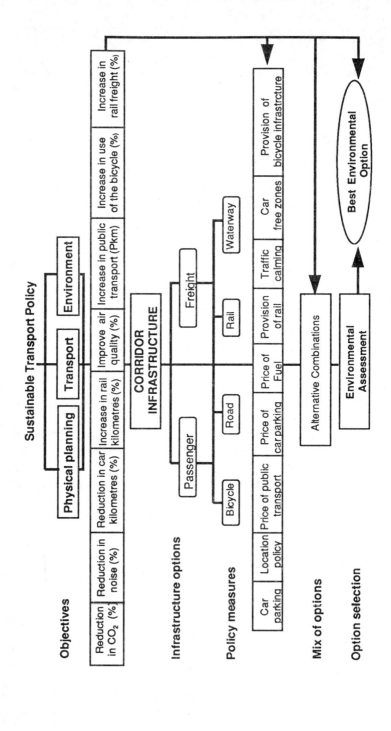

Figure 9.2 An environment-based approach to transport planning

238

Although EC policy is making progress in identifying the problem of transport and attempting to put the necessary policy instruments in place to achieve a more sustainable policy, it still has a long way to go. The Commission can learn from the approaches taken by the EU Member Sates in directing its transport policy. It is in a position to initiate a wide range of measures at the European level to halt the growth in transport, such as a carbon tax and other fiscal measures to reduce the demand to travel and encourage greater use of public transport. More sustainable environmental practices will, however, eventually be achieved at the local level where it matters the most. The Fifth European Environmental Action Programme outlined a number of initiatives to be taken within the transport sector covering cleaner cars and fuels, rationalisation of infrastructure and improved driver behaviour. It set a number of targets for air pollutants and CO_2 emissions. The Commission can learn from the Netherlands by providing more wide-ranging targets for transport, such as increasing rail kilometres and reducing the number of vehicle kilometres travelled. The strategic environmental assessment of transport policy was advocated in paragraph 383 of the Common Transport Policy to be used in the decision-making process of policies, plans and programmes for transport infrastructure, although the draft SEA Directive is still under discussion. The use of the corridor studies to identify main European corridors of importance can be useful in achieving greater cohesion, at the same time ensuring that both road and rail are considered together. This would enable the Trans-European network of main road and rail corridors to be more defined.

This book has analysed how the concept of sustainability has been addressed and integrated into policy at the European, national and local level. It has highlighted the conflicts and contradictions which continue to exist in European and British policy on transport and environment. It has provided an examination of the rhetoric of Dutch policy and the extent to which environmental objectives and targets are being implemented in practice. A comparative study of Britain and the Netherlands and the use of case studies of transport projects in practice has illustrated how different approaches to transport influence the final decision taken at the project level. An integrated transport policy which is objective-led and which has set targets can provide better guidance on decisions taken on transport projects, ensuring that all modal alternatives are taken into consideration. In contrast, policy which has lacked integration with other modes and which has few specific objectives and targets has been more reactive and has dealt with transport problems in a piecemeal fashion.

In conclusion, a more strategic transport planning approach is necessary to deal with the increasing growth in mobility and traffic, with some countries having made progress towards implementing strategic transport policies based on sustainable development. The approach of the Netherlands to transport and the environment has a number of benefits, with the evaluation of policy showing that some targets can be achieved. The lessons learnt from the differing approaches of Britain and the Netherlands and the associated advantages and disadvantages are important in order to achieve a 'Best Practice' for transport planning which can be implemented at the European, national and corridor level. Strategic environmental assessment and the Dutch corridor approach are two concepts which could improve and enhance the transport planning process to achieve a more environmentally sustainable form of transport planning.

Transport will continue to be an important environmental problem into the twenty-first century and the implementation of objective-led transport planning based on concepts such as strategic environment assessment and corridor studies will become increasingly necessary in order to deal with the future growth in transport and to achieve a more sustainable transport system.

Bibliography

Alcomo, J, Amann, M, Hettelingh, J, Holmberg, M, Hordijk, L, Kamari, J, Kauppi (1987), Acidification in Europe: A Simulation Mode for Evaluating Control Strategies, *Ambio* Vol. 16, No.5, pp. 232-245.

Advisory Committee for Trunk Road Assessment (ACTRA) (1977), *Report of the Advisory Committee on Trunk Road Assessment,* HMSO, London.

Ahmad, Y J & Sammy, G K (1985), *Guidelines for Environmental Impact Assessment in Developing Countries*, Hodder & Stoughton, London.

Association for County Councils (1991), *Towards A Sustainable Transport Policy,* ACA, London.

Bainbridge, C (1992), The Blueprint Wayout of Traffic Congestion in Whitelegg, J (ed.), *Traffic Congestion: Is There A Way Out?,* Leading Edge, North Yorkshire, pp. 71-106.

Bannister, D (1991), UK Policy on Transport and the Environment, Paper presented at *ERSC/SERC Conference on Transport & Environment,* Pembroke College, Oxford, 12-13 September 1991.

Barde, J P & Button K (eds.) (1990), *Transportation Policy and the Environment: Six Case-Studies,* Earthscan, London.

Bayliss, B (1979), Transport in the European Communities, *Journal of Transport Economics and Policy,* 13, 1, pp. 28-43.

Bell, P & Cloke, P (eds.) (1990), *Deregulation and Transport: Market Forces in The Modern World,* Fulton, London.

Birol, F & Guerer, N (1993), Modelling the Transport Sector Fuel Demand for Developing Economies, *Energy Policy,* December 1993, pp. 1163-1172.

241

Buchan, K (1992), Enhancing the Quality of Life in Roberts, J, Cleary, J, Hamilton, K and Hanna, J (eds.), *Travel Sickness*, Lawerence & Wishart, London, pp. 7-34.

Callery, M F (1991), *A European Policy for Transport Infrastructure*, Lancashire County Council, Preston.

Carson, R (1962), *Silent Spring*, Penguin, London.

Central Region Council (1993), *All Change!: The Transport Challenge for Central Region*, Central Region Council.

Centre for the Exploitation of Science and Technology CEST (1993), *Road Transport and the Environment: The Future Agenda in the UK*, HMSO, London.

Chartered Institute of Transport (1993), *Trans-Pennine Study: Strategy Report -Response of a Working Group of the Chartered Institute of Transport*, CIT, London.

Clark, B D (1981), Environmental Impact Assessment in the UK: Its current status in light of the proposed EEC Directive, Paper presented at *The Clean Air Conference*, Brighton, 6-8 October 1981.

Commission of the European Communities (1973), Common Transport Policy: Objectives and Programme, *Official Bulletin of the European Communities*, Supplement 16/73.

Commission of the European Communities (1983), *Progress Towards A Common Transport Policy - Inland Transport*, COM(83)58, CEC, Brussels, February 1983.

Commission of the European Communities (1985), Council Directive 85/337/EEC of 27 June 1985 on the assessment of the effects of certain public and private projects on the environment, *Official Journal of the European Communities*, No. L175/40, July 1985.

Commission of the European Communities (1988), Proposal for a Council Regulation for an Action Programme in the Field of Transport Infrastructure with a View to the Completion of an Integrated Transport Market in 1992, *Official Journal of the European Communities*, No. C 270/6, 19 October 1988.

Commission of the European Communities (1989a), *Draft Council Resolution on Trans-European Networks*, COM(89) 643 final, Brussels, 18 December 1989.

Commission of the European Communities (1989c), Communication from the Commission regarding a Transport Policy Infrastructure Policy, COM(89) 238 final, Brussels, 5 June 1989.

Commission of the European Communities (1990a), *1992, the Environmental Dimension Task Force Report on the Environment and the Internal Market*, CEC, Brussels.

242

Commission of the European Communities (1990b), *Towards Trans-European Networks for a Community Action Programme,* COM(90) 585 final, Brussels, 10 December 1990.

Commission of the European Communities (1990c), Council Resolution concerning Trans-European Networks, *Official Journal of the European Communities,* No C 27/8, 4 February 1990.

Commission of the European Communities (1990d), *Green Paper on the Urban Environment,* COM(90) 218 final, Brussels, 27 June 1990.

Commission of the European Communities (1992a), *Towards Sustainability: A European Community Programme of Policy and Action in Relation to Environment and Sustainable Development,* COM(92) 23 final Vol. II, Brussels, 27 March 1992.

Commission of the European Communities (1992b), *The Future Development of the Common Transport Policy,* COM (92) 494, CEC, Brussels, 2 December 1992.

Commission of the European Communities (1992c), *Report of the Commission of the European Communities to the United Nations Conference on Environment and Development,* EC, Brussels.

Commission of the European Communities (1992d), *Green Paper on Transport and the Environment,* COM (92) 46 final, 20 February 1992.

Commission of the European Communities (1993a), *Trans-European Networks: Towards a Master Plan for Road Network and Road Traffic,* Luxembourg.

Commission of the European Communities (1993b), *Implementation of Directive 85/337/EEC,* COM (93) 28 Final - Vol. 12, 2 April 1993.

Confederation of British Industry (1989), *Transport in London: The Capital at Risk,* CBI, London.

Council for the Protection of Rural England (1991), *The Environmental Assessment Directive - Five Years On,* CPRE, London.

Council for the Protection of Rural England (1992a), *Transport and the Environment,* CPRE, London.

Council for the Protection of Rural England (1992b), *Where Motor Car is Master: How the Department of Transport became bewitched by roads,* CPRE, London.

Council for the Protection of Rural England (1992c), *Concrete and Tyres: The Development Effects of Major Roads: A Case Study of the M40,* CPRE, London.

Council for the Protection of Rural England (1995), *Transport and Land take,* CPRE, London.

Cox, A & o'Sullivan, N (eds.) (1988), *The Corporate State: Corporatism and the State Tradition in Western Europe,* Edward Elgar, Aldershot, UK.

243

Dekker, J A J, Houtman, J W, Altena, P J (1992), *The Benefits of the Corridor Approach: Theory and Practice,* Ministerie van Verkeer en Waterstaat, Directie-General Rijkswaterstaat, Directie Utrecht, Utrecht, the Netherlands.

Department of the Environment (1988), Circular 15/88, 26 January 1988, DOE, London.

Department of the Environment (1989), *Sustaining Our Common Future,* HMSO, London.

Department of the Environment (1990), *This Common Inheritance - Britain's Environmental Strategy,* HMSO, London.

Department of the Environment (1991a), *The Potential Effects of Climate Change in the United Kingdom,* HMSO, London.

Department of the Environment (1991b), *Policy Appraisal and the Environment,* HMSO, London.

Department of the Environment (1992a), *Digest of Environmental Protection and Water Statistics,* HMSO, London.

Department of the Environment (1992b), *Planning Policy Guidance: Development Plans and Regional Planning (PPG12),* HMSO, London.

Department of the Environment & Department of Transport (1993), *Reducing Transport Emissions Through Planning,* HMSO, London.

Department of the Environment (1994a), *Environmental Appraisal in Government Departments,* HMSO, London.

Department of the Environment & Department of Transport (1994b), *Planning Policy Guidance: Transport (PPG13),* HMSO, London.

Department of the Environment (1994c), *Sustainable Development: The UK Strategy,* HMSO, London.

Department of the Environment (1994d), *Climatic Change: The UK Strategy,* HMSO, London.

Department of Transport (n.d.), *M62 Relief Road - Further Information,* DOT, Manchester.

Department of Transport (1963), *Traffic in Towns,* HMSO, London.

Department of Transport (1983), *Manual for Environmental Appraisal,* HMSO, London.

Department of Transport (1989a), *Roads for Prosperity* (Cmnd. 693), HMSO, London.

Department of Transport (1989b), *Departmental Standard HD 18/88,* DOT, London.

Department of Transport (1989c), *Section 56 Grant for Public Transport,* Circular 3/89, DOT, London.

Department of Transport (1991), *Paying for Local Roads in England: A Brief Guide,* December, DOT.

244

Department of Transport (1992a), *The Role of Investment Appraisal in Road and Rail Transport,* DOT, London.

Department of Transport (1993a), *Transport Statistics - Great Britain 1993,* HMSO, London.

Department of Transport (1993b), *The Government's Expenditure Plans for Transport 1993-94 to 1995-96,* HMSO, London.

Department of Transport (1993c), *Press Notice on Trans-Pennine Study - 30 November 1993,* DOT, London.

Department of Transport (1994a), *Trunk Roads in England: 1994 Review,* HMSO, London.

Department of Transport (1994b), *Letter from Minister of Roads and Traffic to Peak District National Park,* DOT, London.

Department of Transport (1995), *Secretary of State for Transport: Speech on Transport and the Environment,* 27 February 1995, DOT, London.

Despicht, N (1969), *The Transport Policy of the European Communities,* European Series, No. 12 (PEP), Chartham House, London.

Dimitriou, H (1990), *Transport Planning for Third World Cities,* Routledge, London.

Drupsteen, T & Gilhuis, P (1989), The Netherlands in Smith, T T (ed.), *Understanding US and European Environmental Policy - A Practitioner's Guide,* Graham & Trutman, USA.

English Nature (1992), *Strategic Planning and Sustainable Development,* English Nature, London.

Environmental Data Services (1993), UK makes a slow start towards sustainable development in *ENDS Report,* 222, pp. 22-24.

Environmental Data Services (1995), Brussels draft revised rules on strategic environmental assessment, *ENDS Report,* 248, pp. 37-38.

Erdmenger, J (1983), *The European Community Transport Policy,* Gower, Aldershot.

European Documentation (1989), *Europe without Frontiers - Completing the Internal Market,* ED, Luxembourg.

European Research Associates (1992), *Europe in the 90s: From Maastricht to European Union,* ERA, Brussels.

Fleming, D (1993), Special Supplement: The Fifth EC Environmental Action Programme, *European Environment,* February 1993.

Friends of the Earth (n.d.), *Trans-Pennine Study: Response from Friends of the Earth,* FoE, London.

Godlee, F (1992), Transport: a public health issue, *British Medical Journal,* 304, pp. 48-50.

Gorham, E (1989), Scientific understanding of ecosystem acidification: A historical review, *Ambio,* Vol. 18, No.3, pp. 150-153.

Gossop, C (1990), Choose it or Lose it - Lessons from the Netherlands NEPP, *Town and Country Planning*, pp. 179-181.

Goldsmith, G, Allen, R, Allaby, M, Davoll, J, Lawerence, S (1972), A Blueprint for Survival, *The Ecologist*, Vol. 2, No. 1.

Gwilliam, K M (1980), Realism and the Common Transport Policy of the EEC in Polak J B & Van der Kamp, J B (eds.), *Changes in the field of Transport Studies,* Martinus Nijhoff, The Hague.

Gwilliam, K M & Gommers, M J P F (1992), Transport Project Appraisal in the Netherlands, *Project Appraisal,* Vol. 7, No. 4, pp. 237-248.

Haigh, N (1991), *EEC Environmental Policy and Britain,* Second Edition, Longman, Essex.

Hameed, S & Dignon, J (1992), Global Emissions of Nitrogen and Sulfur oxides in Fossil Fuel Combustion 1970-1986, *Journal of Air and Waste Management Association,* Vol.42, pp. 159-163.

Haq, G (1991), *The Emergence and Development of Environmental Auditing within Local Government,* Unpublished MSc Dissertation, University College of Wales, Aberystwyth.

Hartman, J (1990), The Delft Bicycle Network in Tolley, R (ed.), *The Greening of Urban Transport,* Belhaven Press, London, pp. 193-200.

Hasselar, H (1993), The Quality of Life in the City of Groningen, Paper presented at *'Velocity '93'* conference, Nottingham, England, 6 September 1993.

Henshaw, D (1991), *The Great Railway Conspiracy,* Leading Edge, North Yorkshire.

Her Majesty's Stationery Office (1977), *Transport Policy - A Consultation Document,* Volume I, HMSO, London.

Her Majesty's Stationery Office (1980), *Lorries, People and the Environment,* HMSO, London.

Herson, A I & Bogden, K M (1991), Cumulative Impact Analysis under NEPA, *The Environmental Professional,* pp. 100-6.

Hilbers, H D & Verroen, E J (1992), Mobility Profiles and Accessibility Profiles, elaborated for a land use policy to reduce car use, Paper presented at the *PTRC, Summer Annual Meeting XXth,* University of Manchester (UMIST), UK.

Holmberg, J, Thomson, K, Timberlake, L (1993), *Facing The Future: Beyond The Earth Summit,* Earthscan, London.

Hoyle, B S & Knowles, R D (1992), *Modern Transport Geography,* Belhaven Press, London.

Institution of Highways & Transportation and Department of Transport (IHT) (1987), *Roads and Traffic in Urban Areas,* IHT, London.

International Road Federation (1990), *Aimse, The Motorway Project for the Europe of Tomorrow,* Geneva.

IUCN, UNEP, WWF (1991), *Caring For The Earth: A Strategy For Sustainable Living,* Earthscan, London.

Knowles, R D (1992), Light Rail Transport in Whitelegg, J (ed.), *Traffic Congestion: Is There a Wayout?,* Leading Edge, North Yorkshire, pp. 107-103.

Lander, R & Mass, R (1990), The Economics of Sustainability, *Town and Country Planning,* pp. 182-185.

Lee, N (1983), Environmental Impact Assessment: A Review, *Applied Geography,* Vol. 3, pp 5-27.

Lee, N & Colley, R (1990), *Reviewing Environmental Statements,* Occasional Paper No. 24, EIA Centre, University of Manchester.

Lee, N & Walsh, F (1992), Strategic Environmental Assessment: An Overview, *Project Appraisal,* Vol. 7:3, pp. 126-36.

Lee, N & Hughes, J (1995), Strategic Environmental Assessment: Legislation and Procedures in the Community, EIA Centre, University of Manchester, UK.

Leeds (1990), *Transport Leeds: To the 21st Century,* Leeds City Council.

Lemmers, L (1993), *Amsterdam to Cut Back Cars in Centre,* Physical Planning Department, City of Amsterdam, the Netherlands.

Lemmers, L (1994), Traffic Reform in Amsterdam, Paper presented at the conference of *'Car Free Cities',* 24-25 March 1994, Amsterdam, the Netherlands.

Local Transport Today (1992), *EC Plans Stronger Environmental Impact Assessment of Transport Strategies,* 12 November 1992, p.11

Local Transport Today (1993), *Switch to the Package Approach Changes the Face of TPPs,* 13 May 1993, pp. 12-13.

Lothian Region (n.d.), *Joint Authorities Transportation and Environmental Study,* Lothian Regional council.

Manchester Area Pollution Advisory Council (1993), *A Breathing Space: Vehicle-Related Air Pollution in North-West England,* MAPAC, Manchester.

McKay D H & Cox A W (1979), *The Politics of Urban Change,* Croom Helm, London.

MacKenzie, J J & Walsh, M P (1990), *DRIVING FORCES: Motor vehicle Trends and their Implications for Global Warming, Energy Strategies, and Transportation Planning,* World Resources Institute, USA.

Meadows D H, Meadows, D L, Randers, J and Behrens, W (1972), *The Limits to Growth: a Report for the Club of Rome's Project on the Predicament of Mankind,* Universe, New York.

MER Commission (1990), *Advies voor Richtlijnen voor het milieu-effectrapport bij de Corridorstudie Amsterdam-Utrecht,* MER Commission, Utrecht, the Netherlands.

Ministry of Housing, Physical Planning and Environment (VROM) (n.d.),
Environmental Impact Assessment: The Netherlands - fit for future life,
The Hague, the Netherlands.

Ministry of Housing, Physical Planning and Environment (VROM) (1987),
The Right Business in the Right Place, The Hague, the Netherlands.

Ministry of Housing, Physical Planning and Environment (VROM) (1988), *On
the Road to 2015:Comprehensive Summary of the Fourth Report on
Physical Planning in the Netherlands (Policy Intentions),* The Hague, the
Netherlands.

Ministry of Housing, Physical Planning and Environment (VROM) (1989a),
National Environmental Policy Plan: To Choose or Lose, The Hague, the
Netherlands.

Ministry of Housing, Physical Planning and Environment (VROM) (1989b),
Comprehensive Summary of the Four Report Extra, The Hague, the
Netherlands.

Ministry of Housing, Physical Planning and Environment (VROM) (1990),
National Environmental Policy Plan Plus, The Hague, the Netherlands.

Ministry of Housing, Physical Planning and Environment (VROM) (1994),
National Environmental Policy Plan 2 (Summary), The Hague, the
Netherlands.

Ministry of Transport, Public Works and Water Management (MVW) (1987),
Evaluation of the Delft Bicycle Network Plan, The Hague, The
Netherlands.

Ministry of Transport, Public Works and Water Management (MVW) (1988),
The Second Transport Structure Plan (Part A - Government Intentions),
The Hague, The Netherlands.

Ministry of Transport, Public Works and Water Management (MVW) (1990),
The Second Transport Structure Plan (Part D - Government Decisions),
The Hague, The Netherlands.

Ministry of Transport, Public Works and Water Management (MVW) (1992a),
Bicycles First: The Bicycle Master Plan, The Hague, The Netherlands.

Ministerie van Verkeer en Waterstaat, Directie-General Rijkswaterstaat,
Directie Utrecht (March 1992b), *Lichte Evalutie Corridorstudie
Amsterdam-Utrecht,* Rijkswaterstaat, Utrecht, the Netherlands.

Ministerie van Verkeer en Waterstaat (MVW) (1993a), *Beleidseffectmeting
Verkeer en Vervoer:Beleidseffectrapportage 1992,* The Hague, The
Netherlands.

Ministerie van Verkeer en Waterstaat (MVW), Directie-General
Rijkswaterstaat, Directie Utrecht (November 1993b), *Corridorstudie
Amsterdam-Utrecht -Nota: Corridornota/MER Verkeer en vervoer in de
corridor Amsterdam-Utrecht (Hoofnota),* Rijkswaterstaat, Utrecht, the
Netherlands.

Ministerie van Verkeer en Waterstaat (MVW) (1994), *Beleidseffectmeting Verkeer en Vervoer:Beleidseffectrapportage 1993,* The Hague, The Netherlands.

Ministerie van Verkeer en Waterstaat (MVW) (1995), *Beleidseffectmeting Verkeer en Vervoer:Beleidseffectrapportage 1994,* The Hague, The Netherlands.

Ministerie van Verkeer en Waterstaat (MVW) (28 April 1995), Meer Capaciteit voor Spoorwegen Wegennet tussen Amsterdam en Utrecht, the Hague, the Netherlands.

Munn, R E (1979), *Environmental Impact Assessment,* Scope Report 5, Second Edition, Wiley, Chichester.

Nederlandse Spoorwegen (1991), *The Train Heading for the 21st Century: From Planning to Implementation,* Nederlandse Spoorwegen, Utrecht, the Netherlands.

Odèn, S (1968), The Acidification of Air and Precipitation and its Consequences in the Natural Environment, *Ecology Committee Bulletin* No. 1, Swedish National Research Council, Stockholm, Sweden.

Odijk, M *Personal Communication* (1995), MER Commission, the Netherlands, 7 February 1995.

Organisation for Economic Cooperation and Development (OECD) (1988), *Transport and the Environment,* OECD, Paris.

Organisation for Economic Cooperation and Development (OECD) (1994), *Environmental Impact Assessment of Roads,* OECD, Paris.

O' Riordan, T & Sewell, W R D (1981), *Project Appraisal and Policy Review,* Wiley, Chichester.

Oscar Faber TPA (1995), *South Pennines Transport Needs Study: Final Report - Executive Summary,* TPA, Cheshire.

Peak District National Park (1993), *Peak National Park Structure Plan,* PDNP, Derbyshire.

Pearce, D, Markandya, A, Babier, B (1989), *Blueprint for a Green Economy,* Earthscan, London.

Pearce, D & Turner, R (1990), *Economics of Natural Resources and the Environment,* Harvester Wheatsheaf, Hemel Hampstead.

Pearce, D (ed.) (1991), *Blueprint 2: Greening The World Economy,* Earthscan, London.

Pearce D (1993), *Blueprint 3: Measuring Sustainable Development,* Earthscan, London.

Polestra, H (1993), *Step by Step Reducing Traffic in the City of Amsterdam,* City of Amsterdam, the Netherlands.

Replogle, M (1988), *Sustainable Transportation Strategies for Third World Development,* Conference Paper, Institute for Transportation and Development Policy, Washington DC, USA.

Rijksinstituut Voor Volksgezondheid en Milieuhygiëne (RIVM)   (1988), *Concern for Tomorrow - A National Environmental Survey 1985-2010,* RIVM, Bilthoven, the Netherlands.

Rodhe, H (1989), Acidification in a Global Perspective, *Ambio,* Vol. 18, No. 3, pp. 155-160

Royal Commission on Environmental Pollution (1994), *Transport and the Environment - Eighteenth Report,* HMSO, London.

Sandbach, F (1980), *Environment, Ideology and Policy,* Blackwell, Oxford.

Serageldin, I (1993), Environmentally Sustainable Urban Transport: Defining a Global Policy, *Public Transport International* Vol.2, pp.17-24.

Sheate, W R (1995), Amending the EC Directive (85/337/EEC) on Environmental Impact Assessment, *European Environmental Law Review,* March 1995, pp. 77-82.

Smorenburg, K (1992), *An Integrated Town Planning and Traffic Policy,* City of Groningen, the Netherlands.

Southampton (1992), *Southampton: Transportation Strategy,* Hampshire County Council.

Standing Advisory Committee on Trunk Road Assessment (1986), *Urban Road Appraisal,* HMSO, London.

Standing Advisory Committee on Trunk Road Assessment (1992), *Assessing the Environmental Impact of Road Schemes,* HMSO, London.

Standing Advisory Committee on Trunk Road Assessment (1994), *Trunk Roads and the Generation of Traffic,* HMSO, London.

Starkie, D (1982), *The Motorway Age: Road and Traffic Policies in Post-War Britain,* Pergamon Press, Oxford.

Swedish Environmental Protection Agency (1992), Lake acidification still a major problem in Sweden, *enviro - Magazine of Transboundary Air pollution,* No. 13, May.

T & E - European Federation for Transport and Environment (1992), *The EC White Paper on Transport: A Guide For the Environmental Campaigner (Provisional Version),* T&E, Brussels.

Therivel, R (1993), Systems of Strategic Environmental Assessment, *Environmental Impact Assessment Review,* Vol. 13, pp. 45-168.

Therivel, R, Wilson, E, Thompson, S, Heaney, D, Pritchard, D (1992), *Strategic Environmental Assessment,* Earthscan, London.

Tellegen, E (1989), The Dutch National Environmental Policy Plan, *The Netherlands Journal of Housing and Environmental Resources,* Vol. 4, pp. 337-345.

Ten Grotenhuis, D H (1988), The Delft Cycle Plan - Characteristics of the Concept, in CROW Proceedings of *Velocity '87* International Congress on *Planning for the Urban Cyclist*, Martinhol Centre, Groningen, 22-26 September 1987, CROW, the Netherlands.

TEST (1991), *Wrong Side of the Tracks?*, TEST, London.

Teufel, D (1991), *Ökologische und Soziale Kosten der Umweltbelastung in der BRD 1989*, UPI-Bericht 20, Germany.

Tolba, M, El-Kholy, O A, El-Hinnawi, E, Holdgate, M W, McMichael, D F & Munn, R E (1992), *The World Environment 1972-1992*, Chapman & Hall, London.

Tolley, R (ed.) (1990), *The Greening of Urban Transport*, Belhaven Press, London.

Transnet (1990), *Energy, Transport and Environment*, Transnet, London Transportation Planning Associates (1991), *Trans-Pennine Study: Survey Report*, TPA, Warrington.

Transport Planning Associates (1992a), *Trans-Pennine Study: Strategy Report*, TPA, Warrington.

Transport Planning Associates (1992b), *Trans-Pennine Rail Strategy: Study Report*, TPA, Warrington.

Transport 2000 & Institute for Public Policy Research (1992), *All Change: A New Transport Policy for Britain*, Transport 2000 & IPPR, London.

Truelove, P (1992), *Decision-making in Transport Planning*, Longman, London.

Turton, B (1992), Inter-urban Transport in Hoyle, B S & Knowles, R D (eds.), *Modern Transport Geography*, Belhaven Press, London, pp. 91-124.

United Nations Conference on Environment and Development (1992), *Earth Summit 92*, Rio de Janeiro, Brazil

United National Economic Commission For Europe (1991), *Policies and Systems of Environmental Impact Assessment*, UNECE, Geneva.

United Nations Economic Commission for Europe (1992), *International Transport in Europe: An Analysis of Major Traffic Flows in Corridors*, UNECE, Geneva.

United Nations Environment Programme- Industry and Environment (1993a), *Industry and Environment (special issue on Transport and the Environment)*, Volume 16, No. 1-2, January-June.

United Nations Environment Programme (1993b), *Environmental Data Report 1993-94*, Blackwell, Oxford.

United Nations Environment Programme & World Health Organisation (1992), *Urban Air Pollution in Megacities of the World*, Blackwell, Oxford.

Vandermeersch, D (1987), The Single European Act and the environmental policy of the European Economic Community, *European Law Review*, 12/06, pp. 407-429.

Verheem, R (1992), Environmental Assessment at the Strategic Level in the Netherlands, *Policy Appraisal* Vol. 7 No. 3, pp. 150-156.

Verroen, E J & Jansen, G R M (1991), *Location Planning for Companies and Public Facilities, A Promising Policy to Reduce Car Use,* TNO, Delft, the Netherlands.

Vleugel, J, van Gent, H & Nijkamp, P (1990), The Netherlands in Barde, J P & Button, K (eds.) (1990), *Transportation Policy and the Environment: Six Case Studies,* Earthscan Publishers Ltd, London.

Wellemen, A G (1992), National Bicycle Policy and the Role of the Bicycle in the Urban Transport System in CROW (1992) *Still More Bikes than Dikes* CROW, the Netherlands.

Wandsworth (1989), *Wandsworth's Alternative* Wandsworth City Council.

Wathern, P (ed.) (1988), *Environmental Impact Assessment - Theory and Practice,* Unwin Hyman, London.

Whitelegg, J (1979), The Common Transport Policy: A Case of Lost Direction? *Transportation Science*, Vol. 13, No. 4, November 1979.

Whitelegg, J (1988), *Transport Policy in the EEC,* Routledge, London.

Whitelegg, J (1992), *Traffic Congestion: Is There a Way Out?,* Leading Edge, North Yorkshire.

Whitelegg, J (1993), *Transport for A Sustainable Future: The Case For Europe,* Belhaven Press, London.

Whitelegg, J, Gatrell, A, Naumann, P (1993), *Traffic and Health,* Department of Geography, Lancaster University.

Wood, C (1988), EIA in Plan Making in Wathern, P (ed.) (1988), *Environmental Impact Assessment - Theory and Practice,* Unwin Hyman, London, pp. 98-114.

Wood, C and Jones, C E (1991), *Monitoring Environmental Assessment and Planning,* HMSO, London.

Wood, C & McDonic, G (1989), Environmental Assessment: Challenge and Opportunity, *The Planner,* July: 75, pp. 12-18.

Wood, C & Dejeddour, M (1992), Strategic Environmental Assessment: EA of Policies, Plans and Programmes, *Impact Assessment Bulletin,* Vol. 10, No.1, pp. 3-22.

World Commission on Environment and Development (1987), *Our Common Future,* Oxford University Press, Oxford.

World Health Organisation (1992), *Our Planet, our health: Report of the WHO Commission on Health and Environment,* WHO, Geneva.

World Resources Institute (1992), *World Resources 1992-93,* Oxford University Press, Oxford.